Jenny has written a book that confronts the patterns you inherited and offers you a path forward. This is not theory or inspiration alone. It is a road map for breaking what has held your family captive and establishing a legacy of freedom that will outlast you by generations.

Mike Signorelli
Lead Pastor, V1 Church

Jenny carries a joy that's impossible to fake. Her life puts the goodness of the Lord on full display. Her story doesn't just inspire—it builds hope and strengthens faith. When you hear what Jesus brought her out of, you're reminded that He can deliver anyone from anything.

Raven Hartwell
Prophetic Voice, Media Personality
@raventhomashartwell

Jenny courageously invites readers into her journey from deep darkness to light and freedom that only Christ can bring. Her vulnerability shines a spotlight on conversations the Church urgently needs to have—mental illness, trauma, healing, and lasting freedom. Through her honest storytelling and compassion, she creates a safe space where readers can learn from her experiences and discover hope, restoration, and the tools necessary for their own breakthrough.

Tailah Scroggins
Author of *Breaking Demonic Chains*

Jenny Joy is a burning torch in this generation—one of the most powerful voices I've ever encountered when it comes to exposing darkness and pointing people toward the freedom found only in Jesus Christ. I had the honor of interviewing her on my podcast, *Faith and Friction*, and I was undone by her testimony. Her story of being rescued out of witchcraft, deception, torment, and demonic oppression—and then being radically set on fire for Jesus—is one of the clearest pictures of the Gospel's power at work today.

The Witch and the Lamb is raw, bold, and anointed. Jenny doesn't sensationalize darkness; she exposes it. She doesn't elevate the demonic; she magnifies the Deliverer. Every chapter is soaked in truth, courage, and the relentless love of the One who chased her down. As someone who also came out of the New Age and survived spiritual counterfeits firsthand, I felt seen, strengthened, and stirred as I read her words.

If you've ever wondered whether Jesus still sets captives free… read this book. If you've ever questioned whether deliverance is real… read this book. And if you're hungry for the kind of revival that begins in the hidden places of the heart—this is it. Jenny's story will wake you up, shake you awake, and remind you that no one is too far gone for the Lamb who breaks every chain.

I wholeheartedly recommend *The Witch and the Lamb*. It is more than a testimony—it's a weapon of freedom.

Tracy Onyekanne
Emmy Award–winning Television Host
Host of the *Faith & Friction* Podcast

THE WITCH AND THE LAMB

THE WITCH *AND* THE LAMB

30 EXORCISMS LATER

DISCERN OCCULT DECEPTION, EXPOSE WITCHCRAFT AND FIND HEALING FROM TRAUMA, MENTAL ILLNESS AND DEMONIC OPPRESSION

JENNY JOY

© Copyright 2026– Jenny Joy

All rights reserved. This book is protected by the copyright laws of the United States of America. This book may not be copied or reprinted for commercial gain or profit. The use of short quotations or occasional page copying for personal or group study is permitted and encouraged. Permission will be granted upon request. Scripture quotations marked NKJV are taken from the New King James Version. Copyright © 1982 by Thomas Nelson, Inc. Used by permission. All rights reserved. Scripture quotations marked ESV are taken from The Holy Bible, English Standard Version® (ESV®), copyright © 2001 by Crossway, a publishing ministry of Good News Publishers. Used by permission. All rights reserved. Scripture quotations marked KJV are taken from the King James Version. Scripture quotations marked NASB are taken from the NEW AMERICAN STANDARD BIBLE®, Copyright © 1960, 1962, 1963, 1968, 1971, 1972, 1973, 1975, 1977, 1995, 2020 by The Lockman Foundation. Used by permission. Scripture quotations marked NASB are taken from the NEW AMERICAN STANDARD BIBLE®, Copyright © 1960, 1962, 1963, 1968, 1971, 1972, 1973, 1975, 1977, 1995 by The Lockman Foundation. Used by permission. Scripture quotations marked NIV are taken from the HOLY BIBLE, NEW INTERNATIONAL VERSION®, Copyright © 1973, 1978, 1984, 2011 International Bible Society. Used by permission of Zondervan. All rights reserved. All emphasis within Scripture quotations is the author's own. Take note that the name satan and related names are not capitalized. We choose not to acknowledge him, even to the point of violating grammatical rules.

DESTINY IMAGE® PUBLISHERS, INC.
P.O. Box 310, Shippensburg, PA 17257-0310
"Publishing cutting-edge prophetic resources to supernaturally empower the body of Christ"

This book and all other Destiny Image and Destiny Image Fiction books are available at Christian bookstores and distributors worldwide.

For more information on foreign distributors, call 717-532-3040.
Reach us on the Internet: www.destinyimage.com.

ISBN 13 TP: 979-8-8815-0765-7
ISBN 13 eBook: 979-8-8815-0766-4

For Worldwide Distribution, Printed in the U.S.A.
1 2 3 4 5 6 7 8 / 30 29 28 27 26

Dedicated to the tormented.

May your hearts be mended and your minds restored.

This is not your life sentence—I love you.

ACKNOWLEDGMENTS

To my Grandmother Evie, your selflessness has been a lifeboat for me. I don't think I would have survived my childhood without you. Your merciful heart has been medicine for many. My BFF, I love you and I miss you and your cheese sandwiches. You were a place of rest for my soul.

To Ashley Anderson, you sowed innumerable seeds of faith during my days of witchcraft and torment. Not one seed burned up and perished. They were all worth it.

To Sean, I am so thankful for your support as a therapist for so many years. Your prayers and encouragement catapulted me into freedom.

To Marcia, my trauma therapist, you gently tended to my wounds. You were sent by God, and I am forever grateful. I could not have gotten this far without you!

To my friend Taylor (my bridge!) You were my bridge to sobriety, a bridge to facing my trauma, and my bridge to Hawaii, where Jesus met me. You, friend, are a bridge for many.

To my friend Amanda, you showed me the *real* love and acceptance of Christ when others could not. You truly lead with love leading up to my salvation.

To Julie, you baptized me and shared the truth despite my offense. Your wisdom has been a lamp to my feet, and your prayers have changed lives.

To Sue, you spent countless hours delivering me from hundreds of demons and even more hours on the phone, walking me through life and my final exit out of abuse. There truly is no one like you: my greatest teacher and my biggest cheerleader. There are many treasures in Heaven for you!

To Mavis, my mentor and friend. You have filled a part of my heart that many couldn't access. Thank you for always being my safe place.

To Stuart and Cathy Greer, your life mission of exposing the demonic and evicting them has changed so many lives. Your fearlessness and diligence completely changed mine. The Lord has many treasures in Heaven for you both!

To my best friend Maura, you have never let me do life alone. A listening ear, a hug, a rant, or a cry, you have always been a cushion for me to lay my heart on. Your gentleness, humility, and willingness to change and grow, produces flowers in your life that others get to pick from. You are altogether lovely! I'm beyond blessed to have you.

To Aryn and Garner, who became a life raft for my son and me when we needed it most. We love you so much.

To my parents, you supported me when it was hard, cut me off when it was neccesary and showed up for me in a season of great loss. Thank you and I love you.

To my editors, who tirelessly worked on refining this book with me. Your late hours, and many phone calls are so appreciated. Thank you, thank you, thank you.

To all the teachers, coaches, therapists, and mentors who have gotten me to this point: Your words, wisdom, and guidance have placed shoes on my once bare feet. I have never walked through a rocky terrain alone. My freedom is, of course, because of Jesus, but it is also because of *you*. Thank you forever. I love you.

They overcame him by the blood of the Lamb and the word of their testimony....

—Revelation 12:11 NKJV

CONTENTS

FOREWORD

I've seen revival up close. I've seen demons flee and miracles in the water of baptisms, but what grips me most about this story is not the spectacle; it's the intimacy. It's the way Jesus sits down beside a broken woman and calls her *daughter*. It's the way He redeems years that the enemy devoured and restores beauty to what was utterly destroyed. Jenny isn't just another Christian voice among the crowds; she is the Mary Magdalene of our generation.

> *Mary, called Magdalene, from whom seven demons had gone out.*
>
> — Luke 8:2 (ESV)

Like Mary, Jenny moves from torment to tenderness, from bondage to belonging. Once held captive by darkness, she now walks in the light, proclaiming what only the truly redeemed can say: "I have seen the Lord."

When I read *The Witch and the Lamb*, my heart burned with expectation. Jenny's testimony is not a polished Christian fairy tale. It's raw. It's gritty. It's drenched in mercy, and I honor her for not sugarcoating it. You can feel the war between darkness and light in every line, and yet what overcomes it all is love. Real love, not ritual and routine. The relentless love of the Lamb.

This book isn't for the faint of heart. The blood of Jesus—His death and resurrection—was for you to live free from death and be made fully alive in Christ. I have had the privilege of both watching Jenny go through costly surrender and now pastoring Jenny in our church. I have witnessed firsthand the transformation… her life in witchcraft and darkness to a life of joy, freedom, and humility.

I believe that we are entering into an era of both experiential, real deliverance and lifelong discipleship as we do the deep work of following Jesus and renewing our minds. I believe this book by Jenny is an invitation to both, and it will confront head-on any lingering demonic thoughts that are trying to convince you that you can't live 100% free.

It's for the hungry—for those who know there must be more than just church attendance and status-quo religion. It's for those who have been tormented and, like the man who was delivered of the legion of demons, want to live free from every torment.

In every generation, Jesus is still finding His Marys. Perhaps, after reading this book, that will be you—those whom the world has written off but Heaven has chosen. This book is living proof that no chain is too thick, no past too dark, and no heart too far gone for the Lamb who still sets people free.

Jenny's courage to tell the truth—to expose the darkness to the light—is what makes this book so important right now. We are living in an hour when counterfeit spirituality is everywhere and the demonic is disguised as enlightenment. But the same power that raised Jesus from the dead is still setting captives free. Her life is evidence.

As you turn these pages, don't rush. Let the Holy Spirit speak. You may find parts of your own story woven through hers—the ache, the shame, the searching—and you'll discover what Jenny discovered: no one is too far gone, and no amount of darkness can resist the light of Christ.

May you encounter that same love as you read.

With love,
Jessi Green
Author of *Wildfires* and *Saturate*
Leader of Saturate Global and Salt Church

PROLOGUE

This poem reflects how Jesus found and saved me and how He wants to do the same for you.

Once upon a time there was a young witch. She had long golden locks that she braided, where hints of pink, purple, and blue wove in and out through them. Feathers hung from her ears, rings decorated her fingers, crystals clung to her neck, and freckles adorned her face. Although fair on the outside, a deep storm waged within. The witch would dance and chant, she would basket herbs, and converse with the dead. The spirits she conjured eventually moved in and created a home within her.

As the seasons changed outside of her quarters, winter remained the state of her heart, where rainfall and snow were no strangers and a lake of ice became her foundation. The witch lived in a cottage in the woods, far away, and alone. A fence surrounded her home, keeping her inside, and everyone else out.

One spring day, a Lamb came to the fence. He would graze just outside of it, and then lie down to rest at her gate. He did this for quite some time, wanting to befriend the witch. The young witch was so consumed in herself that she paid no mind. Each day the Lamb would come back and nudge at the witch's gate, hoping that she would notice Him. On Monday he nudged, on Tuesday he nudged, on Wednesday he nudged, and Thursday through Sunday, he nudged at the gate.

All summer long, all autumn long, all winter long, and throughout the springtime, He nudged. No matter what storm or season surrounded her home, the Lamb was there, rain, shine, sleet, or snow.

One summer day, the Lamb nudged the gate with His nose again. This time, it opened. The witch noticed the movement through her kitchen window but continued with her magic. The following week the Lamb did the same thing. He did this weekly and then daily, pushing open the gate with his nose. Once the witch noticed the Lamb, she studied Him from afar. Still, she toiled inside. As the seasons passed, the witch's house began to deteriorate. The paint was chipping. A step on her porch broke. Half of the windows wouldn't latch, and where there used to be an abundance of flowers in her garden, weeds took over and choked out many of the blossoms.

One afternoon, before the Lamb got to her gate, the witch decided to open it all the way. When the Lamb grazed his way along her fence, He stopped at the open gate. He still did not step inside, for He had not been invited in. As He looked up, His eyes locked with those of the witch. Her countenance was forlorn and exhausted, eyes dry and vacant with dark circles beneath them. She was so thin. Still, she smiled through her embitterment.

The Lamb's soft eyes seemed to radiate gentleness and love, something the witch was not familiar with, and quite frankly, made her uncomfortable. Her eyes welled with tears, and she turned away quickly, back to the task at hand inside the home she never left. The witch's heart had been without rest for a very long time. The Lamb laid down at the gate that night and slept there until dawn, something He didn't typically do.

He was waiting.

When the sun rose in the east, like a golden balloon in the sky, the witch stepped out onto her porch. The Lamb lifted His head in acknowledgment and then bowed His head to her, as if humbly saying, "Everything will be fine; you can come to Me." The witch stayed on her porch, but she was no longer in oblivion. She was afraid that her harshness might deter the Lamb. So, she didn't step out. The Lamb, however, did not leave her gate. He was there when the sun rose and each evening when the sun set.

One afternoon, the witch stepped off her porch and into her garden. Her bare feet pressed down patches of soft grass, leaving footprints behind her as she carefully approached the Lamb. The Lamb patiently waited at the witch's gate. Still, He made no move to come inside. As the witch approached the Lamb, a flood of tears consumed her, and she fell to her knees in exhaustion and shame. She placed her hands in front of her as if offering something up. *I have nothing to give,* she thought. Her hands were empty, but she was desperate.

Just then, the Lamb stepped inside the gate and moved swiftly over to her, nuzzling His face against hers and lying down next to her as she wept. Her frost-covered heart began to melt. And with it went ice caps of wickedness and glaciers of pain. She shrieked in agony and despair as years of torment left her in the presence of the Lamb.

Love and gentleness will always melt a hardened heart. As the sky turned dark, the moon rose and stars glittered in the sky, while the witch fell asleep next to the Lamb. She slept from Monday through Tuesday through Wednesday through Thursday through Friday and Saturday—yet the Lamb did not move a hair. The witch could *finally* rest. On Sunday morning, the rays of the sun tapped her on the shoulder and she woke up to a new life. She wrapped her arms around the neck of the Lamb and He led her beyond the gate, to the river that rushed by her home.

Although she had not stepped foot from what was familiar within her fence, she put her trust in the Lamb's love. As she approached the riverbed, the Lamb went with her into the waters and she bathed in the river, as if washing away all the remnants of her old life. When she lifted her head from the smooth waters, still wearing her old clothes, a brand-new cloak lay on the rock, white, and warmed by the sun. The Lamb nudged her to put it on, and she did.

Her heart was in her throat, and tears of thankfulness burst from her eyes. She was not the same anymore.

As the witch and Lamb turned back to her home, the Lamb approached the garden. The Lamb chewed through the weeds in her garden, uprooting what was never meant to be there in the first place. The witch swept out her home. Spellbooks, potions, and herbs used for magic were thrown into the fire. Shelves were dusted, dishes were cleaned, and a single daisy that had grown in her garden was plucked and put into a vase on her now clean table.

Together they painted the home a new color, fixed the broken porch, and changed the window latches. As the sun began to sink, and the work was now done, it started to sprinkle rain. Flower buds lifted their heads and began to open, and a faint rainbow embraced the sky above the witch's home. The Lamb and the witch went inside and sat down for a cup of tea. The fire crackled beside them as they nestled in the warmth of each other's presence. Then the Lamb spoke for the first time.

"You are no longer a witch, but a daughter." His words felt like a warm hug. "Welcome home," He said.

And the daughter embraced the Lamb, as they went forth together, never alone, and always in love.

INTRODUCTION

Exorcism: The removal of evil spirits from a person or place by the use of prayer.

You are my hiding place; You preserve me from trouble; You surround me with songs of deliverance.

—Psalm 32:7 NASB1995

One thousand, five hundred demons. That is how many devils were cast out of me over a year and a half. It all happened at random when I was 28 years old. I say at random, but deep within me, I knew something was gravely wrong. This awareness began to emerge in middle school. Not because being a teenager is awkward and uncomfortable in and of itself, but because the experiences I began having in succession, and the fear that accompanied them, demonstrated just that. Things *were* off, and wickedness *was* present.

I did not have the support needed to face the demonic in my life when it truly began. My parents were dealing with their own problems, my friends were immersed in the joys and dramas of middle school, and my world felt lonely and fractured. This was a triple malady of mind, body, and spirit in my case. I was facing spiritual torment, sexual abuse, physical addiction, and emotional disease.

My body, mind, and spirit were exhausted, and I was only 13. I was interested in God to a degree. I knew there was something out there. Sometimes I would go to teen worship nights at the church down the street from my childhood home, mostly because the ninth-grade boys were there—but sometimes, when I would sing along to a worship song in the dimly lit sanctuary, I would cry. I didn't know why that happened, but when it did, it felt like I was allowed to. That was a big deal for me as a teen feeling like I was allowed to have feelings. My grandmother told me it was the Holy Spirit.

Throughout high school, I experienced multiple painful and traumatic events. By the age of 17, my heart had hardened significantly. At 18, I met a witch who gave me direction for my life that I did not have before. You see, the enemy of my soul knew the depth of my shame, loneliness, rejection, and deep feelings of insignificance. He waited for the perfect moment to pounce and thus capitalize on all those things.

> *Be sober, be vigilant; because your adversary the devil walks about like a roaring lion, seeking whom he may devour* (1 Peter 5:8 NKJV).

After feeling invisible for so long, satan threw this witch in my path who would "see me" for the first time. She recognized the power (or giftings) in me immediately, and because of that, I listened to her advice. Thankfully, after years of my descent and immersion into witchcraft, hope came in the form of a Person. His name is Jesus Christ, and with Jesus came exorcisms.

Who knew exorcisms actually worked? I sure didn't. Not really. They freaked me out more than anything, but they still fascinated me. I would see them performed occasionally on some of my favorite paranormal television shows, but they always left me feeling nervous, confused, and somewhat hopeless. I was addicted to the fear. I figured people who had demons in them only existed as paid actors in Hollywood or outright satanists or lived in countries where voodoo was as commonplace as little dogs are in southern California. Go figure, *I* had them.

If you saw me walking down the street, you more than likely would not suspect the severity of my demonic torment. Five feet, five inches tall with blonde hair—sometimes, pink, purple, or blue—fair skin that I bronzed, a somewhat thin build, and light blue eyes with a dark ring around the iris. Tattoos on my body, lots of rings on my hands, and a big personality that blended comedy with intensity and attracted *all* the wrong people.

You either got all of me or none of me; I was either very hot or ice-cold. To the outside world, I looked like just another beach girl who maybe hung out in L.A. on the weekends, but on the inside of me, a dark war was raging over my soul. I was severely tormented, and the closer you were to me the more likely you were to witness the battle or find yourself in it. My skies were always gray; I just made you think they were pink.

I had never really heard much about deliverance from demonic oppression at church. Occasionally I recognized the word in a sermon or Scripture, but it was not explained, and I never witnessed it on a Sunday morning. Another word for *exorcism* is *deliverance,* which means to liberate, rescue, or set free. It is the casting out of demons, evil spirits, and tormentors, whether they are physically inhabiting your body or inhabiting your mind.

Mind you, Christians can have demons too, and many do. We are mind, body, and spirit, and the Holy Spirit resides in our spirit, so many can still be afflicted in mind and body. Deliverance, taking thoughts captive, and turning from sin all help greatly. Matthew 6:22 (NIV) says *"The eye is the lamp of the body. If your eyes are healthy, your whole body will be full of light."*

After going through my own deliverances, I recognized how taboo this subject seemed to be among some churches and church members, *even though* it is listed in the Bible time and time again. We are commanded as believers to cast devils out and lay hands on the sick. It was one-third of Jesus's ministry (Mark 16:16-19). As a result of being obedient to this Scripture, our fellows are freed, and the sick are healed. So why isn't this happening as often as it should be? Why isn't it encouraged by every pastor? Or by Christians in general?

I believe it is because the Church in the United States has been lukewarm and asleep. Therefore, I believe it is my duty as a follower of Christ to shake people awake, to bring freedom back into the Church, and to teach others what deliverance is, how bondage occurs, and how to maintain freedom once the devils have been evicted from your life.

A fire has been set ablaze in my once desolate soul and I cannot rest until the people of America begin to rise up from their slumber. My question for you before we start is this: Are you awake or asleep? And if you've been asleep, do you want to wake up?

The time is now.

This is my story.

1

GOD, IS THAT YOU?

"Freedom." I breathed out. "And 30-plus exorcisms later." Everything had been pretty abstract up until this point. I guess most people would look at my life and still call it unconventional in many ways.

As I reached for my hot tea, my freckled lips met the brim of a mug with a watercolor fox painted on it. I sat back in my seat and surveyed a pile of logs that were pushed up against the fence, a group of optimistic daffodils peeked out from behind the logs. I've been hibernating on the porch of my family's cabin in the woods for a couple of days now; sipping tea, saturating myself in nature, and calling my dogs back to the top deck when they've wandered too far under it. I'm cloaked in a frizzy ombre dad sweater, big faux Chanel sunglasses, leg warmers, boots that I got from a client, and wearing mascara remnants on my lash line from the day before with tea on one side of the table and an ice-cold glass of Gatorade on the other.

I breathed in the fresh, cold air and let the rays of the sun wrap around me like a warm hug, which felt comforting after an argument with my husband. Pine needles swing-danced across the sky as I was cushioned by loud and soft hushes, chirps, squeaks, and caws that encircled me. The howling wind comically reminded me of the 405 freeway that sits just a couple of blocks from my home in urban Orange County, California. The pine soap at my workplace hardly compares to the keen scent of real-life evergreens up here in the mountains.

There is something to be said about how gentle, yet confrontational, nature is. It offends, it threatens, it sings, it responds, it moves when you want it to be still, and it holds position when you're begging it to dance. It isn't a ball of clay in your hands; you are a ball of clay in its hand. It changes you if you have the heart to sit with it long enough—to cry out to the big blue sky, "Is there anyone even up there?"

I remember when I didn't think so. When I thought the things of this world were my end-all and be-all. When my passions rigidly resided in divination and magic, in bottles and syringes, in mental illness and pity, in art and attention, in abuse and in secrets, in vanity and sex, in men and in women, in lies and in self.

I remember when God was just an occasional character who stumbled across the pages of my poetry like a drunkard throughout the years. He was a distant captain who unaffectedly watched me tread water and refused to send out a lifeline; an all-powerful being who demonstrated tenacious disregard, professional distance, and exquisite apathy. A man behind a curtain I could not see. A narcissist. An Oz. I believed God was the director and producer of the world's worst drama—my life.

I made the mistakes, but He got the credit for the crummy outcome. Still, I cried out to Him when I had my arms wrapped around the base of the toilet after a long day of drinking. Although I wallowed in the lie that "God didn't care," I was *very* deceived.

The Lord cares for His children, regardless of circumstance, what the world has told us about ourselves, or how important or unimportant we may feel. He cares.

Even prior to what I used to consider my "burning bush" moments, or my true coming to the Creator, God periodically used nature to confront me. God will use whatever He can to get *your* attention. That said, I am now confident that it wasn't actually nature that moved me or responded to my cries in the rainstorms or my bellowing in the fields or my awakenings in the ocean or my songs from the mountaintops—it was the mastermind of God behind it all, actively listening and responding to me.

The supernatural Artist who has my life and your life premeditated, yet lovingly allows space for free will, allowing *us* to choose. He is the Creator of our laughs and even of our cries. How wild is that to think about? Really, think about the unique quirks you have, your individuality. He did that! He is the Truth. Still, some would rather gloss over "God" as a lie, a cultural belief, a philosophical perspective, an imaginary being, a simple "comfort," or maybe even a genie.

God, with a capital G, seems to be one whom many refuse to acknowledge, know, or truly even live for, if they do, in fact, believe. Admittedly, I was one of them for a long period of time.

I come from an age when everyone has their own version of truth and believe that we must surround everyone's emotions with a love bubble. Don't misunderstand me, truth should *always* be doused in love, and if it's not, then it won't be received. But too often in recent generations it is politically incorrect, expecting everyone to have to tailor each word that falls from our lips in hopes of not offending a person or group of people. We are walking on societal eggshells.

There is a nonverbal expectancy in today's world that we should *never* offend by telling the truth, and we must gauge our boldness when it is deemed appropriate. But the truth is, just as nature is confrontational, so is God and so is the Gospel. Confrontation doesn't always translate to "harsh" either, and anything that may feel harsh, forced, or controlling is not the Spirit of God. In the same breath, love exposes evil and delights in good. You can lovingly accept a person without being permissive.

Despite all this, coming to the truth, can, and often does, feel uncomfortable, as it was for me. I could only take a teaspoon at a time due to the nature of my distance from God. I was "spiritual" by the world's standards, but I was far from the Person named Truth. The Bible unyieldingly threatened the so-called comfort that I lived in when I was running the show for myself.

God's Word offended me when I lived in disagreement with it. It disinterested me. I didn't want to give it any of my attention, because on a subconscious level, I feared that it would dismantle me and the sin I so desperately clung to. I believed the Holy Bible set me apart in the worst way. I either felt undeniably unholy, or better than. I ignored it because I did not want to listen, nor did I have the capacity to do so. I thought it was all wrong, that it proved my beliefs wrong, was unimportant, mean, and rejecting.

That was my experience when I encountered the Gospel from wounded or religious people.

Truly though, the Bible is not a list of guidelines to follow partnered with empty rituals. At its core, it is a love letter, covered in blood, edified with the most selfless act of all time.

Theologians even agree that Christ crucified was just that: entirely selfless. When you look into the details of Jesus's life, you cannot deny this. The Bible is gold bound together in book form, warm honey in the morning, and a cozy blanket at night. It is rich and comforting. People lose their lives to see what's inside this book, as well as share it.

Paradoxically, it is a double-edged sword, sharp and active, breaking all chains, exposing every lie, and dismembering and destroying any demon. I know this to be true because my entire life was infested with them. The demonic ruled me!

Literally. The infestation kept me at a distance from God, but the devil's army could not prevent the Father's love from entering my life and reminding me that freedom was possible, over and over again. I was impious but I sure was resilient. God's faithfulness, combined with His Word and deliverance, inched hell out of my heart. Jesus was actually, and will always be, my one-step program to peace!

Although my life was very far from peace, I strove for it ever so contumaciously. I honestly tried everything in this world I could find that brought me temporary tranquility. Starting with destructive habits and coping patterns, then eventually graduating into recovery-based skillful living.

Upon my first exorcism, I had been through a total of ten years of counseling, ten years of talk therapy, three years of intensive trauma therapy, couple's counseling (we saw eight therapists), weekend intensives, multiple detoxes, one psych ward, life groups, behavioral modification through medication, three baptisms, EMDR (Eye Movement Desensitization and Reprocessing), jail, somatic experiencing, self-development seminars, outpatient treatment for mental illness, outpatient treatment for addiction, inpatient treatment for substance abuse and trauma, another inpatient trauma center, service work in and out of a nonprofit, Bible studies, restorative yoga and physical therapy, burn ceremonies, chakra-healing and cleansing during my New Age years, multiple witchcraft ceremonies, a public declaration at a Christian internship to sever all ties from witchcraft and the destruction of those tools, art therapy, float therapy, equine therapy, and 12-step programs for drugs and alcohol, sex and love addiction, self-harm, dysfunctional family systems, and codependency.

I had five years of sobriety from substances and almost two years of recovery from self-injury when I found myself walking into a healing prayer session at some megachurch in Irvine, California. That prayer session, which is known as the "Well Intake," was the beginning of the end for me. Well, the end of my demons, and the true beginning of who I was meant to be in Christ.

Through the discovery of building a relationship with a "God of my own understanding," as it is frequently referenced in 12-step rooms, I became diligent in seeking, persistent in praying, and motivated in meditating. I was obsessed with encountering this being called God, this being that I knew existed. *How close could I get?* I wondered. I began to have brief moments of serenity and a newfound, irresistible pull toward the God of the universe.

This "God as I understood Him" evolved into forming an intimate relationship with Jesus Christ. Twelve-step programs were my launching pad for wrangling back my sanity and catapulting myself—as dark and broken as I was—into the heart of God. I had been fighting a supernatural battle alone my entire life; and for the past ten years, I felt like I was moving as quickly as I could, backward and knee-deep in wet cement.

One morning I was in my quiet place with God when I got an abstract vision. The vision was of me, hunched over an assembly line of people, praying for each of them. Black and red ink filled this image. In the snapshot I was in agonizing pain, my spine and neck highlighted where the pain was centered. After a certain amount of people passed by me on this conveyor belt that I was praying over, I stood up in elation and freedom. The pain in my body had vanished.

The colors in the vision had changed and I stood tall with a bright yellow and white light that shone from my heart and glowed all around me. *Could I be healed if I follow this vision's direction,* I thought? With 16 years of incurable pain in my back and neck, I wondered. Immediately, I went into prayer, asking Jesus for a verse to verify that this was, in fact, from Him. Then a Scripture from Acts was quickly impressed upon my heart:

> *Whom they set before the apostles: and when they had prayed, they laid their hands on them* (Acts 6:6 KJV).

I had never read this book of the Bible and wasn't even sure it was a book of the Bible then. It continues about how Stephen performed many signs and wonders by the grace of God. At that moment, the Holy Spirit was firm in His fathering: "Join the prayer team, Jenny." This excited me and also intimidated me greatly because I tried joining a prayer team once before: six years earlier when I was a witch. (Don't worry, I tell that story later.) At this point, I had entirely stopped my practices, but still felt like a counterfeit Christian.

Regardless of my feelings, I went for it. At five years sober, when I received this vision, I responded rapidly by searching the internet for a prayer team application at one of the churches I had been regularly attending at the time, one Thursday afternoon. The prayer team's orientation was two days later on that upcoming Saturday.

God, is that You?

2

THE WELL AND MULTIPLE PERSONALITIES

It was an overcast Friday morning in June. Gray skies met the man-made babbling brook outside the chapel. The gurgling creek was the background music to my feet dragging across the courtyard, up the steps, and into the tinted double doors of the ministry building at the church. I thought I might cry, so I didn't wear mascara. I had just hung up on my boyfriend. "What the heck was that argument even about?" I muttered to myself. We had lots of those—arguments about nothing that always led nowhere. The toxicity in our relationship was often at a level ten.

Upon entering the second floor, I was greeted by Destiny, a tiny woman wearing black flats with hair to her hips and a hard pink blush on the apples of her cheeks. She took me down the hall and to the left.

"How are you doing this morning?" she asked meekly.

"I don't know, okay. Nervous. Kinda tired." Honestly, I was shaking in my Nikes.

"That's normal," she responded.

I walked into a large group room with windows all around me. Banquet tables arranged in the shape of a rectangle in the center of the room.

"You can take a seat over here, Jenny." She pointed to a close group of four chairs off to the side. "We're glad you're here."

I smiled through my discomfort. Why was I this nervous about prayer? I prayed with my friends often. Plus, I had been on the prayer team for one month at that time, praying for whoever came forward at the end of the service. Still, because of my history of trying to join a Christian prayer team when I was active in New Age and witchcraft, I felt paranoid about being part of a team now that I was saved. I always felt like I had so much to hide. I hated that feeling. Having hands laid on me in prayer also struck a seriously uncomfortable chord, as it does for many.

Although I had not participated in occult practices for years and my heart was in a different place, I still felt like I was living in lies and guilt. The demonic had used my body as their home for decades, so naturally fear cloaked me when I entered the room. My demons knew their time was up before I did. Satan and the demonic are show-offs. They *will try* to put on a show. They will rage, wreak havoc, wickedly entertain, instill fear, torment, manipulate, allure, distract, and deceive, and sometimes even perform miracles, but always at a cost.

Likewise, magicians performed many miraculous signs before Pharaoh (Exodus 7–8). They were able to duplicate the works of Moses on three occasions. After that, their powers stopped, and they could not replicate any of the plagues. That is because demonic power can only go so far. In fact, demons and satan himself are terrified of Jesus. They must submit to the blood of Christ and the name of Jesus when spoken with authority. Nothing scares a devil more than a Christian who confidently knows who they are in Christ. When the Lord is truly on the throne of your heart, you are dangerous to the kingdom of darkness! It's not just about accepting Jesus, it's about making Him Lord of your *life!*

The demonic hate God, and they hate God's creations, meaning you and me. However, as written, *"Every knee shall bow, every tongue will confess that Jesus Christ is Lord"* (see Philippians 2:10-11 and Romans 14:11). This includes all of hell and its workers. Demons *have* to submit to the authority of God. A person on fire for the Lord is the devil's worst nightmare; and my resilience, combined with my deliverance, was about to set me ablaze for the right Kingdom. Nonetheless, I felt petrified walking into that prayer room. I had not been in a setting quite like this one before. At least not for a very long time.

Because I was already on the team, I managed to book a private prayer session fairly fast. I was always somewhat hopeful that I would be healed of my grueling, chronic neck and back pain. For years I had approached prayer team members at the end of services to pray for my back. Healing never happened. I had even driven ten hours north of my home to Bethel, a church *known* for healing—and nothing. I also received prayer support in the middle of a cobblestone road from three people in Birmingham, England, in the United Kingdom.

Yet, still no relief. I had people pray over my back, my offset hips, my neck, and my migraines over and over again in Hawaii, and nothing. Before all of this, I sought energy healing, information and help through occult practices like reiki, energetic myofascial release, chakra alignment, past-life regressions, crystal healing, various forms of divination, and charm bags to minimize my pain. Still, nothing was effective.

When I lived in Hawaii, my friend's ankle was healed right in front of me at the Surfers Church. I had witnessed healing before, so I knew it was possible; I just didn't think it was accessible for me. Nonetheless, I still yearned for it. I had that mustard seed of faith. I mean, seriously, have you seen a mustard seed? They are tiny! Despite my minimal faith, I still had hope; I wouldn't accept my circumstances.

Many Christians don't believe that healing is for today, that God only has a certain amount of healing He can offer. Some even think only Jesus and His disciples were given the authority to heal, but that is not what Scripture tells us. Jesus says, *"Very truly I tell you, whoever believes in me will do the works I have been doing, and they will do even greater things than these...*" (John 14:12 NIV). Jesus spoke directly, saying we as Christians would do what He did and more. Paul was given authority and the spiritual gift of healing and that was after Christ was crucified. Paul never met Jesus when He physically walked this earth.

I thought because I had lived a life of sin that God might not be open to healing me. Just that word *sin* alone brought a lot of discomfort to the surface. I hated the word and felt condemned by it for a long time. In my mind, I assumed God only healed those He truly loved or those who deserved it. I didn't think I was lovable, nor did I truly believe I deserved much. My lack of self-worth is extremely evident throughout my story. Fortunately, what I believed was not the truth, it was a lie from hell. The Lord heals, regardless! He heals because He is loving, and He heals because He is good—not because we are. Healing is a gift, not a reward.

So, I was at the point in my spiritual walk where I wanted to completely live my life for Jesus. Still, I just could not stop certain behaviors no matter how much I prayed about them, how much therapy I did, how often I read the Bible, or how much work in 12-step programs I was doing. I had not participated in witchcraft for some time, and I ached for freedom. I wondered if I was always going to be miserable, challenged, and tormented. Still, a sliver of hope existed within me.

The Lord's guidance for me to join the prayer team was more of a gateway into freedom as opposed to a way of being of service to others at first. Although the service aspect is what initially drew me to join the team, the end result was the devil's hand being lifted from my life, one finger at a time. God Himself was orchestrating my deliverance. When I sat down for my session at the church, chaos filled the space. Each person on the team seemed tired, distracted, and winded.

"Whew!" An older woman named Sue said as she sat in one of the four seats. "Hi, honey, how are you?" She leaned in like she already knew me, her Midwestern accent faint but unmistakable.

"I'm okay, tired. I'm a little nervous." My hands were trembling, but I kept them pressed to my knees.

"Yes, a lot has gone on this morning! Destiny got sick in the middle of the night; she almost couldn't make it and I had trouble sleeping. Has anything gone on with you?" she asked.

"Yeah, I just got in a fight with my boyfriend over nothing." I said, shaking my head and rolling my eyes.

"Oh yeah," she said nonchalantly. "That's normal. This is going to be good! We find that when we experience warfare prior to a Well Session, there will be freedom! So, let's just soak in some worship music and calm our hearts before we pray, okay honey?" she said, smiling at me.

I gulped, nodded, and closed my eyes. One song felt like an entire album. *Maybe I should just leave*, I thought.

Once the song ended, Sue leaned over and began sharing what the Holy Spirit had given her as she prayed for me throughout the week. Destiny shared next and then,

Deanna. I was overwhelmed. I was instantly confronted with how much unforgiveness I was holding on to. I began to sob. Just then Sue reached over and put one hand on my knee and one on my shoulder and began to pray. She could hardly get a few words in before I went into what I have known as an "alter."

With years of compounded sexual abuse in addition to other disturbing encounters in childhood and adulthood, I sadly, was an open vessel for the demonic.

My trauma was the initial gateway. Unfortunately, trauma acts as a legal right for the demonic, meaning it gives demons access to you. There are multiple gateways that the demonic can enter, which I will discuss later. I had been originally diagnosed with Bipolar 1 disorder nine years prior and battled all the symptoms of this diagnosis including the severe depression and mania that define this disorder, and then I was dual-diagnosed and then misdiagnosed, and then re-diagnosed years later with C-PTSD (complex post-traumatic stress disorder) and DID (dissociative identity disorder), or in layman's terms: multiple personalities, resulting from severe trauma.

Dissociative Identity Disorder (DID) is considered a complex disorder where psychologists believe splits or alters in personality happen and new identities with their own histories, memories, and preferences come forth due to disturbing, violent, distressing, or traumatic events that cause individuals to dissociate from their original identity.

Two or more of these identities can take control of a person's conduct when they feel threatened at any given time. Dissociative Identity Disorder (DID), once called multiple personality disorder, is defined as having two or more distinct personality states that affect one's behavior, memory, and sense of self. These identities vary in how visible they are. People with DID often struggle with memory gaps, or blackouts, which can even affect daily life far beyond normal forgetting. The symptoms cause significant distress or problems in day to day life and aren't explained by cultural practices, childhood imagination, substance abuse, or medical conditions. In some cultures DID is described as an experience of possession. For more information, consult the DSM-5.

Many victims will subconsciously create a new identity to cope as their bodies and minds cannot handle the present trauma. Psychologists call this a defense mechanism, the brain protecting itself.

From a psychological standpoint, this is a pretty incredible phenomenon. Humans can only endure so much before the mind chooses to block out memories (sometimes months or even years) if it is too much to bear. Many people who have faced trauma of this severity will have memories of out-of-body experiences (OBE) while the traumatic event was occurring, myself included. People will see themselves next to and sometimes above their situation as I did.

Because the experience is so painful, the human spirit literally exits the body. Wonderful, because it is a survival tactic, but terrible for the fact that when the human spirit leaves the body something else must inhabit the human cavity. This began for me at three years old (and what my therapist and I concluded could have actually been earlier) and persisted many times afterward.

In addition to the OBE, agreements to lies or false beliefs in the mind also occur. Some examples of lies include: "I will never be safe"; "Someone is always going to abuse me"; "Nobody cares about me"; "It's all my fault"; "I should have done something different"; "I am alone." These are natural responses and thoughts during a traumatic experience or event.

However, if an individual hangs on to lies and difficult emotions like these and continues to make agreements with them long-term, it allows the demonic to have legal access to a person's life. So not only can demons enter or stay through the initial trauma, but they also are granted access by the perpetual inhibiting thoughts or emotions that come afterward.

I do want to say, though, that there is no shame if you currently have regular thoughts like these. I want to encourage you to identify what regular lies you find circulating in your mind and release them to God. Write down the lie, and then find the truth in Scripture and write that down and declare it. *"Faith comes by hearing, and hearing by the word of God"* (Romans 10:17 NKJV). Speaking the truth of the word *out loud* has tremendous power!

Part of healing is blocking your thoughts that are not God-centered and do not serve you. Combatting these lies from the enemy with Scripture will completely change your life. The truth is not your experience (and I am not invalidating your experience!) but the Truth is, and always will be, the Word of God.

When we take the truth to the lie, those flaming arrows (negative thoughts and demonic attacks) fall to the ground and burn out. It can take practice, though, so be patient with yourself. If you identify with this right now, please stop reading and take some time to pray on this. It is entirely possible to get free from these thoughts and agreements!

As I endured years of my DID diagnosis to the point that it actually became crippling, I sensed a present evil. I had gotten sober and gained some control over my life, only to have horrific memories surface and debilitate me again. What was happening? Why did I feel like I was always being held down?

This diagnosis is without a doubt demonic, and I know this because I am now free from it. The person who has it is not a demon, though, and I want to be sensitive to that. I was not a demon. Bad things happened to me that allowed the demonic into my life, and then I made choices based on that trauma that took me deeper into addictions and other evils.

God's loving-kindness set me free from this, but I had to do my part and seek help.

"Parts" or "alters" can vary from acute to severe in their behaviors and personalities. Some are outright noticeable by everyone around the victim while other "alters" may be less obvious at first. For years I had been aware of what I called my "three-year-old part." This "part" had few words and was typically activated when being intimate with a boyfriend, in addition to a few other triggers. What's fascinating is that once I became intimate with a partner who was a sexual predator (which I clearly did not know at first), the alters (or the demons) would manifest more!

That is because on a complex level we are mind (which is the soul), body, and spirit. On a psychological or mind level, the person was not safe. There was also a spiritual exchange happening through sin (me having sex before marriage) and it caused these things to be exposed! The demonic will transfer through sex if you are doing it sinfully, meaning outside of the covenant of marriage. Again, I know from experience and biblical text (Hebrews 13:4, 1 Corinthians 6:18-20, Matthew 5:28). Cheating, pornography, masturbation, sex outside of marriage, same-sex relations, sexual abuse, fetishes, etc., are all sexual avenues for the demonic to trot into your life. I personally, had all of these paths open and available for demons before deliverance happened to me.

Growing up, I always had intense fear around anything sexual, yet addictively pursued it and immersed myself in a sexually explicit and provocative lifestyle. When I would switch to the three-year-old "alter," I would go into awful flashbacks and regress into this "part," causing me to think my partner was my abuser. It was like I knew deep down, though, that some of the men I was with were predators.

In these situations, I would cry, convulse, and mutter. I always covered my face, suddenly terrified of the man I was with, thinking I was getting raped when I willfully made the choice to be intimate. Not only was it re-traumatizing for me, but it was also difficult for past partners who were close enough to experience me this way. I typically could only remember pieces of what occurred. Because I was also demonized with a large number of sexual spirits that surfaced and were cast out during my deliverances, I could *not* stop having sex.

So often I would become intimate with a partner, go into a flashback, regress, come out of it, and then have sex the same day; and often, it would occur again. I would retraumatize myself and had to be put in cold showers, have ice put on my hands or neck, or have a pet placed near me to pull me out of the dissociation and back into the present moment. It was so awful.

It was a wicked game of Russian Roulette, and I was holding the gun to myself. This was a habitual and extremely painful cycle for which I saw no end. I was not only living in sin, but I had no control over the sin that flooded my life. This was sin living in me (Romans 7:15-20).

When Sue started to pray for me, I immediately regressed into this three-year-old part and began pushing her off me and pulling away. I was screaming, "No! No! No!" I covered my head and began to shake it violently. "No, no, no!" I repeated again and again and again. Louder and louder. All the women jumped to their feet and began casting devils out of me. Their hands burned my back and my head. They were speaking in tongues, and it was making me angry. My head shot back, and my arms went rigid. My fingers curled inward toward my palms like a cat. Nonhuman shrieks and wails escaped my mouth over and over again.

At first the spirits howled in anger and then in desperation. They sounded scared. I had no control over my body or my voice and went in and out of consciousness for about three hours. I physically saw multiple demons in the room that day. The other women and I saw these things physically leaving my body. It was very intense. Periodically, I would regain control, consumed in tears. I was spiritually, emotionally, and physically exhausted.

Sue and Deanna asked if there was anyone I needed to forgive and encouraged me to say who I forgive and what I needed to forgive them for. I listed all of my abusers, my parents, ex-boyfriends, my current boyfriend, and anyone else I could think of. I had tried to forgive them for years but still felt stuck. Sue asked, "Is there anything you need to forgive yourself for?" The room grew painfully still. Embarrassment washed over me.

"About four years ago," I stammered, "When I *really* began struggling with my sexuality because of my trauma, I, um..."

"Yes, honey?" Sue said.

"I summoned sex demons to enter me."

I had done this out of mere hopelessness. I had thought the trade-off was a good idea and would keep me in full sexual functioning, maybe even enhance it. Sometimes it seemed to work to my advantage, but after a short time, I became a slave to those sexual spirits. This may sound bizarre or frightening for you to read this. It is. But with my background in witchcraft, I had encountered the spirit realm so much that I had become desensitized to it and also accustomed to it.

Sadly, this occurred after a very impactful baptism I encountered in Hawaii, but I was lost after coming home. I felt I could not forgive myself. Drugs and alcohol had coated my past for so long that when I finally sobered up after more than a year, all the molestations and assaults rose to the surface, my "alters" were exposed, and my sexuality suffered. I suffered. I was searching for my identity in sex at that time, not in Jesus Christ, and I paid for that.

* * * * *

I want to pause for a moment and say if this is you, I want you to know that there is grace for you. What is grace? It is an unmerited favor. Jesus forgives you. God is not angry with you. God does not hate you if you are struggling with your sexuality. He doesn't even hate you if you do whatever you want, not caring how it affects you or others. However, if you are seeking out sex in an addictive and sinful way, there is peace available, and that peace is not found in another person or body. It is found in your heavenly Father who loves you more than you can comprehend.

If you are broken and traumatized by the pain of life, that is not your life sentence. You are seen, heard, worthy, and loved. Ask the Holy Spirit to correct the wrong things in your life and be patient with yourself as you heal. Jesus died on the Cross with His arms open, not closed. It's not about going to Him in perfect shape; it's just about going to Him. My heart is with you.

* * * * *

After I shared with these women that I had summoned demons into me, they heard me, and without judgment encouraged me to forgive myself. They prayed for me and walked me through *repentance.* I had heard this term before, and just like the word *sin,* it also rubbed me the wrong way. I had been a Christian for years but didn't understand the basics. It was explained that repentance is turning away from something that harms myself, others, and my relationship with God. When you repent from stealing, you are making a life choice to turn away from that behavior despite future temptations. These women spoke in a way I could understand, and I repented from many things I truthfully wanted to walk away from.

"I forgive myself," I said with hot tears running down my red face.

They laid hands on me again, and more demonic manifestations occurred. Witchcraft spirits were called out of me. My body shook, and my arms went stiff. At one point I remember sitting in the chair, hands gripping the sides of it, drenched in sweat. My head tilted upward, and a chilling nonhuman shriek escaped me. In the physical, I saw a large, clear-green, wavy-like spirit exit my mouth, about six feet in length. I had never seen anything like this before. It felt huge. Then, immense relief!

Do you remember losing your teeth as a child? Sometimes teeth came out painlessly and effortlessly, other times they hung on by a thread that felt terrifying to sever. Sometimes they would come out in a sandwich and other times you would maneuver food and drink around it in hopes of avoiding the necessary removal of it. Maybe a parent or even a sibling assisted in taking it out. That is what this extraction reminded me of in the spirit. A useless thing (demon) that caused pain (chaos), that needed to be removed for new and necessary things to take place (a closer relationship with God). I had been trying on my own for years, but apparently I needed assistance!

After that massive demon departed from my body, I fell forward and wept. I was not crying because I was scared or because I felt sad; it was like an aftershock effect. The type of crying that comes with relief. With freedom! And then, an influx of God's love consumed me. I was being filled with the Holy Spirit.

The women handed me tissues and encouraged me as my first exorcism came to a close. Suddenly I felt a new and radical conviction. How could I move forward and still have sex with my boyfriend? This reality shifted my entire world. I knew I couldn't return to that.

"One more thing..."

"Yes?" Sue's blue eyes looked through me.

"Um, I don't know. I have a question."

Suddenly I felt ashamed to ask if this was okay because I knew in my heart of hearts it was not.

"Is it okay to be sexual with my boyfriend? I mean we've been trying not to have sex since we are both in a sex and love addiction program and I'm not sure if it's okay to do other things. I don't know."

I want you as the reader to know, I didn't speak up because it was a church and I felt judged or because I thought these people wanted me to abstain. I wasn't seeking approval, either. This was a personal conviction not inspired by anyone but God. Apart from popular belief about the Church, conviction is not condemnation, and many do not know the difference.

Conviction is an inner knowing that some behavior or habit is not truly self-serving or God-serving even if it feels that way in the body. Condemnation is deep ridicule and intense criticism. Let it be made clear that conviction is from God; condemnation is not. A harsh line separates the two.

Unfortunately, many churchgoers who do not have a deep and true relationship with the living God will react and respond from a hyper-religious and judgmental standpoint. This religious superiority often turns most people away. So if you have experienced this type of spiritual damage, I encourage you to forgive the person who has misrepresented Christianity and give Jesus another try. Though He was direct and truthful, He was *never* cruel. Hence, the Church should not be either.

The conviction I felt at this moment was God-inspired. Deanna smiled and Destiny took a breath. I looked over at Sue. There was something so different about Sue, something so honest about her. I had not experienced a person quite like her before. She was humble yet somehow nonverbally demanded respect. She walked in the true authority of Jesus Christ.

Sue inhaled. "I think for you," she said, "since you have had such a difficult past involving a lot of sexual trauma and sexual perversion, it would be best to abstain from anything sexual. I believe this to be a breeding ground for the demonic in your life. It would be in your best interest to not be intimate in that way."

"Okay," I said relieved.

In that moment the Lord gave me a vision of a cleaning rag I had back at home. It had been so used that its edges were mostly frayed and there were holes all through it. Some parts of the towel were still intact while other parts were extremely thin. God told me this was my spiritual condition—that the holes represented access points the demonic had in my life and if I truly wanted the demons gone for good, I best not keep these holes (spiritual doors) open.

After a deliverance like that, it was a very easy decision for me. I have since framed this towel.

The three women and I closed the session in prayer and some small talk. It was almost noon. I stood up, hiked the hips of my leggings upward, pulled the bottom of my shirt down, and thanked them for spending so much time and energy to help me. I felt euphoric and calm. I felt like I had been walking around for years with a mouthful of loose teeth and somebody finally pulled them out for me. The amount of relief I felt is truly indescribable and probably difficult to relate to unless you have experienced something similar.

I waved and smiled goodbye, and as I exited the room, I heard a familiar voice I thought was God. "Jenny," and then there was a pause. "All of your friends, all of your family, and all of Jay's family will be saved and delivered. You are not a sex and love addict, and you are to marry Jay (not his real name) in ninety days."

"Whoa." My eyes widened. "That's crazy." I knew I would have to really pray about the last one. I yawned, wiped my face, and pushed the door open to my new life.

Was this actual freedom?

3

REHAB AND REBIRTH

Before deliverance, I experienced little bouts of feeling free. My road to recovery placed me in a position to receive a new life. When I used to think of "new life," I imagined babies coming into the world and flowers blooming in dewy fields. I envisioned the predictable "new life" phenomena like caterpillars transforming into butterflies and tadpoles changing into frogs.

I never really considered the middle stages when it came to growth, or the not-so-pretty parts. For instance, caterpillars actually liquify themselves in their cocoon before they emerge as butterflies, and then essentially hatch into a flying piece of art. This transition phase looks awkward and even ugly, but I believe this is by design. How could it not be? God is a poet, and nature is one of His many books. Even destruction can be beautiful, but rarely do people think of devastation, destruction, and decomposition when hearing the words "new life."

Yet, it has to happen to some extent for new life to occur. It is part of the cycle.

For example, when a seed is subjected to darkness—covered in soil and beginning to germinate—it *looks* like it is exploding and falling apart when it's actually growing roots that can reach greater depths. A flower has to blossom and then wither to drop new seeds into that soil. A plant even pushes off the seed's shell underground before the smallest sprout breaches the soil's surface.

Believe it or not, fires are a natural part of nature, too. Fires can be all-consuming, and leave nothing behind, yet many ecosystems benefit from periodic fires. There is an ecological benefit to this type of "destruction." God is literally in everything.

Things can look uncomfortable and even backward in nature when transformation is occurring. When plants die off in the winter, their leaves, which eventually turn brown and ugly, act as a natural fertilizer for the following spring! There is truly purpose in everything. Getting sober was a painful transition for me.

CREATING A NEW LIFE IN SOBRIETY

When I got sober in 2013, I didn't have a plan. Most addicts don't when approaching recovery. I'd be impressed if I met an addict who did! I just knew it was time to get sober and stay sober. I was not hopeful in the slightest and, understandably, very afraid of what my life would look like without substances ruling it. I did not imagine myself spinning around in a sundress on the island of Molokai or dancing across 15 feet of burning coals, getting delivered from a thousand demons, or having a son (yet I did all of these in sobriety). I just knew that I was getting closer to death and those around me were growing more and more concerned—many of whom began disappearing as I deteriorated into my addictive abyss.

Addiction is a fascinating phenomenon, from a psychological perspective and also from a spiritual point of view. It took me a bit to eventually become a more productive member of society. This normalization period took a lot of therapy, a lot of recovery-based support, the 12-steps, and a lot of *time* before my heart was ripe enough to be transformed by Jesus.

Many Christians will argue that all someone in that position needs *is* Jesus. While this is true, for people like me, the process can be quite lengthy. I was so demonized and so consumed in myself as well as the desires of this world, that I was not ready or willing to give Jesus my life until I had fought for a very, very long while to do things my way.

Approaching absolute surrender was a journey. I now surrender daily. As I stated previously, the 12 steps were a launching pad for me. It was like a spiritual kindergarten. I needed help; someone who knew how to maintain sobriety and demonstrated trust in a "higher power." And then, I met Liz.

Liz had long sandy hair, round cheeks that looked like pink blooming roses, and a huge smile. I had multiple sponsors before her, had been hospitalized a few times, and received a scholarship through a dual-diagnosis, thirty-day program in Tennessee. After treatment I returned to California with fresh eyes. I needed a different experience. In 12-step programs, it is encouraged to find a sponsor who has what you want, whatever that is.

All I knew about Liz was that I had seen her around for a while and she was always smiling, and I mean *always*. I didn't get it, basically because I was so depressed, angry, and chaotic. I didn't want to be that way anymore, so naturally, I asked Liz to sponsor me. She complied and mentored me through the first three years of my sobriety. I loved her so much and I wanted to do right by her. She did not push God on me; she did not criticize or judge the way I thought or acted as a newly sober person. She mothered me, corrected me, and introduced me to a new way of living—which was exactly what I needed.

Change sometimes happens quickly and other times slowly. She made sure to tell me on my one year of sobriety date that it was "slower" for me. We laughed because it was true! There was no judgment, just the reality. And I could accept it.

Prior to going through treatment in Memphis, I had done quite a bit of research as an addict and alcoholic. What I mean by that is that I would get sober for a short amount of time, leave the meeting rooms for a while, and experiment more with substances. I was "researching" just how bad it could really get, all the while trying to convince myself I was not a true alcoholic. I always came back to my recovery family in worse condition—physically, mentally, and, of course, spiritually.

I originally found myself in this 12-step program through a court order. I was not convinced I was an alcoholic at that time; I figured I had just had a rough go of it. The spirit of addiction would often whisper to me that I was, in fact, an exception and I could go out and drink like men, which was honestly never the case. Drinking led to drugs and drugs led to insanity every time.

Although most of my nonrecovery friends were hard drinkers, they did not have the same consequences I had when I drank, and they did not like to use drugs the way I did either. I was always searching for people who used substances the way I did, and I so desperately wanted to drink like other people could.

However, they weren't ending up in the drunk tank; I was. They didn't have the police regularly show up at their residence; I did. They weren't getting hospitalized for alcohol poisoning, drug overdoses, or suicide attempts; I was. They weren't self-harming when loaded; I was. They weren't blacking out while driving on a regular basis; I was. They weren't being admitted to psych wards, losing jobs, failing classes, or liquifying cocaine and streamlining it so they could get higher quicker; I was.

I tried as many things as I could to control my drinking and using. At one point I even "hired" a friend to follow me around to bars and parties who would put a stop to my drinking after I had had three drinks. Needless to say, that didn't last. God bless her for trying though!

I'm reminded of the catalyst that led me into recovery, and that was my trip to the psych ward in 2012. I was admitted to the emergency room for an overdose of Nyquil and Adderall of all things. If an overdose was ever considered "cool," this was not it. After taking some Adderall the night before college finals, a friend suggested I take a shot of Nyquil to get to sleep—but an alcoholic never takes one shot of anything.

I found myself drinking bottle after bottle of cold medicine, driving to get more at three in the morning, and hallucinating the entire time. While driving, I saw herds of black shadowy figures racing next to my car. Hallucinations were not uncommon for me when I was loaded; they actually accompanied the majority of my drug use. This was because I was creating a massive doorway for demons to come into my life, and I could see that. Whether you can see into the spirit realm or not, I promise you, there are spirits involved if you are in addiction.

Toward the end of my addiction, my benders seemed to escalate and always involved self-mutilation. I had a history of cutting and even burning myself at times, which started in middle school. I had a notebook between myself and two other girls then, where we would write notes to one another fantasizing about all the ways we wanted to commit suicide and just how much we wanted to die. I sadly was a regular in suicide chat rooms online by the age of 13. It seemed like it was the only thing that brought me peace at that age.

I believe that a solid Christian home, with emotionally regulated, nonjudgmental, and respectful adults could be a total life game changer for so many teens. Homes that create an atmosphere for the Holy Spirit to dwell in provide a sense of well-being and safety, which many do not have growing up.

There was a very large part of me that didn't have the endurance to live early on. So that winter night in college, I sat in the orange bedroom of my small apartment and thought, *Maybe if I keep drinking this cold medicine, I will eventually fall asleep forever. That would be just fine.*

This suicide attempt was messy. It was not deliberately planned or thought out but instead very impulsive, and it failed. I stormed into my roommate's room hallucinating. She helped me contact my therapist that morning, who called my mom. She immediately showed up at my apartment and drove me to the hospital. She was angry. Not a great vibe when you've been tripping for 12 hours straight.

At the emergency room, I was placed in a wheelchair due to my instability and my mother sat with me that morning as I traveled in and out of reality. What I felt was a normally distant and cold parent, there sat a disheveled and heartbroken woman, melting into her hospital chair. I had put my poor mother through so much.

"What were you trying to do, Jen?" she asked, clearly upset.

The incoherent me shrugged.

"You realize you could have died, right?" she asked.

"Yeah," my eyelids were heavy.

She looked at me, and for the first time in my life, I felt like I could see real emotion in my mom. Her heart was breaking as hot tears ran down her blotched and freckled skin. For years she had been terrified that I was going to die, either through substances, by the hands of someone else, or by my own accord. In my experience, she hadn't vulnerably expressed that fear until that moment when it couldn't be hidden any longer.

"Do you even care?" She choked on her words.

My dazed eyes scanned the ceiling corners and in a matter-of-fact way, I responded, "Nope."

She stared at me, astonished and tearful.

My heart had turned so hard toward my mother. Feeling distant from her my whole life and feeling like I was never heard. The pain of the affair I caught her in as a teen destroyed me and acted as my final push into addiction. At 17 I stopped caring, and here I was at 21, dead inside.

This is just one small glimpse into the selfishness of addiction. Addiction is out for itself. Addiction does not have time to care about your true feelings, your family's, friends, or colleagues' feelings.

Addiction is entirely unnatural, and the opposite of self-preservation. It does not care about your job, your hopes, your dreams, or your physical and mental well-being. It does not care if you are rich, broke, or middle class. Addiction does not discriminate, and it wants one thing—to get you alone so it can kill you. If it cannot do this, it will torment you and those around you.

Addiction will do whatever it takes to fulfill this goal, unless or until it is stopped and replaced with a spiritual way of living.

That morning in the ER I was evaluated by multiple nurses and then placed on a 72-hour hold at a different hospital and admitted into the psych unit. I was then re-evaluated there. I saw horses in the hospital rooms and bugs popping out of stains on the carpet or discolorations on the wall. My time in the psych ward was spotty. I was detoxing, still actively suicidal, and highly medicated, so I only remember pieces.

The mirrors were made of plastic, and they took my shoelaces and Q-tips because people try to kill themselves by hanging or bleeding their ears. I was put in a room with four other beds and shared the space with a Bipolar 1 patient with psychotic features. In her case, psychotic features meant she was hearing voices. A man in her head would tell her when to self-harm and he wouldn't get quiet until she did it, sometimes screaming at her until it was done.

She had been admitted multiple times and the staff knew her. I now know this to be a demon and this poor woman just needed deliverance. Still, she talked to me about Jesus and how she was a Christian; although totally tormented, I could feel the love of Jesus emanating from her. I can't recall her name, but I think of her from time to time. Even Jesus is in the psych wards.

At lunch hour the next day I sat at a table with patients who shared their war stories and the reasons why they were in there. A young Korean woman named Peach would sit down at the piano in the lunchroom and play. She didn't talk. She also hardly slept. She read books from sunset to sunrise. My lunchtime tablemates spoke of overdoses, psychosis, self-harm, suicide attempts, manic episodes, severe depressive episodes, and the list goes on.

We talked about our diagnoses. We showed each other our scars. One man was entirely defaced by them. His arms, legs, hands, feet, neck, some of his face, and even his abdomen told of his painful and obsessive journey with self-harm. I finally felt a strange sense of peace and community. I wouldn't say that it was the peace of God that fell on me quite yet, it was more of a peace that comes with being seen.

The first process group I was admitted into was on the topic of grief. I had been secretly grieving for a very long time. The clinician who led the group opened by saying, "Many of us have gone through grief. Maybe we have lost a loved one, a mom or a dad, a lover, or a pet. Maybe some of us feel like we have lost our mental health and are grieving that."

I sat in the back of the room and cried the entire hour. Two years prior, I had been diagnosed with Bipolar 1 disorder and I was just coming to terms with the fact that I might be an alcoholic and drug addict too. Everything had been so high and so low for years, it was exhausting, and it was even exhausting for the people in my life to watch. I grieved for myself. I grieved for my family. I grieved for an empty future. I grieved and believed that I would never be restored to sanity and that this was my life sentence. How could this be?

I had so much more to offer the world. *I was better than this,* I kept telling myself. I was so creative, people liked me. Why was this my lot in life? Shame clung to my body like wet clothes. I was so unbearably sad. I walked out of the room and down the long white hall toward the smoking area when another patient ran up to me and placed her hand on my shoulder. She leaned in and said, "You know, sometimes it's better if you talk about it. I just wanted to tell you that." She was young and encouraging. I nodded through my tears and didn't say much. I never got her name, but we sat outside smoking for a while. She encouraged me as I fearfully began my recovery journey.

During my stay in the psych unit, I was put on multiple new medications. Mood management by the use of medication was necessary for a time in my life. Many Christians go back and forth on this topic or have very black-and-white ideologies connected to it. Some completely shy away from the topic due to a lack of biblical knowledge, minimal mental health education, or out of fear of being offensive.

I believe many rely too heavily on psychology and remain bound to their diagnosis without faith in God's ability to heal. Controversial, I know. But what does the Bible say? Since it *is* the standard for truth, it tells us to be transformed by renewing our minds (Romans 12:2). Meaning, we should renew our minds with the Word of God and its Truth.

When you take an old piece of furniture, refinish it, reupholster it, etc., it can often be sold for more than the original price when it was first on the market. It has been renewed with creative expression; it is valuable. Similarly, we are valuable to God. Yet our minds become affected by our circumstances. They can become worn out, much like furniture that has been used for long periods of time and treated poorly. But when we renew our mind with God's Word, we reupholster it. God is making it new.

After being on Lithium for a total of ten years, the Lord told me to get off medication after my first deliverance. It was liberating. I encourage you to ask Him what He says about your situation if you are currently taking medication for your mental health. The truth is that the Lord promises us a sound mind through the Bible. Keyword: *promise*. However, sometimes (such as cases like mine) there can be a long detour before arriving at a mentally stable destination to fully receive what God has. I wasn't ready for a long time.

> *For God has not given us a spirit of fear, but of power and of love and of a sound mind* (2 Timothy 1:7 NKJV).

> *You will keep him in perfect peace, whose mind stays on You, because he trusts in You* (Isaiah 26:3 NKJV).

Verses like this meant nothing to me until I went through multiple exorcisms and began to experience the true freedom of the Holy Spirit many years later. Through my deliverance process, I learned how to take thoughts captive (2 Corinthians 10:5). I would read through verses like this online. I would hear them at church or from Christians trying to encourage me.

Unfortunately, there was always a disconnect. I wondered, *If God promised a sound mind, why doesn't He just give it to me right now? Do I have to work for it?* I didn't get it. Why couldn't I snap my fingers and be healed? How many times did I have to get on my knees in a bathroom and weep, begging God to help me, to rid me of my torment, to give me a better life? How many times did I have to say the Serenity Prayer before it started working? Did I not have enough faith? How could I have any hope when it felt like hope was a waste of my time?

How could I ever get free from mental illness when doctors told me I was dealing with a progressive disorder that I would have for the rest of my life? How could I trust this being I could not see or even hear? Didn't doctors know everything? Shouldn't I put all my trust in someone who has studied the brain? At that time, I did. I put my trust in a student of the brain instead of the Creator of the brain.

I didn't know how to trust this God guy. I had so many questions that remained unanswered. Partly because I don't think I was truly ready or willing to be entirely set free just yet. There were parts of me I did not want to give up or change.

My sin kept me separated from Him. Some cannot surrender their pride or "knowledge of the brain and medication" so they stay on medication for a long time, sometimes even a lifetime.

This makes me think of the paralytic man Jesus encountered in the Gospel of John. He was at the pagan pool of Bethesda when Jesus approached him on the Sabbath. This man had been at this pool for 38 years hoping an angel would come and swirl the water and he would be the first one in the water to be healed. Because he was paralyzed from the waist down, he never made it into the water; as the years passed, he became more bitter and self-pitying. When Jesus approached he asked the man, *"Do you* ***want*** *to be healed?"* (John 5:6 ESV).

Why do you think He asked him that? Wasn't it obvious the man was at a place that offered healing? When I read between the lines of this story, an important theme of people in pain was uncovered. Some are so comfortable in their suffering that they would rather grumble than accept help or change. I was once there. Have you ever been there? So embedded into the sorrow of your life that it just seems easier to stay there? Maybe your misery is comfortable, and you think it is because of a person or situation in your life.

Jesus told the man, *"Get up, take up your bed, and walk"* (John 5:8 ESV). The man met the Savior of the world that day and was healed and filled with joy. Then, he stood and stopped feeling sorry for himself. I know the first part of changing is a desire for it. Pride never wants change, but it's always best to bury your pride before your pride buries you!

Misery and pride can feel safe, and many prefer pity or being "right" over the challenges that can come during the process of true change and repentance. The Father knows our hearts. That means He knows and deeply understands our individual reasonings, our doubts, our bitterness, our despair, our anger, and all our complexities.

God has mercy and takes it all into account. He also understands our family systems, our traumatic experiences, and that things happen outside of our control that directly affect us and inhibit us. He knows our harmful reactions or stress responses that can take place when we are in our flesh or don't fully know Him. He knows that doors can be opened in the spiritual realm as a result of our sin (or damage) or someone else's sin that has influenced our lives. He understands that people make mistakes—He hates sin, yet loves the sinner.

He has oceans of compassion, and each person is judged different from how we may judge them based on what we personally know about them. He knows when we are surrendered and when and how to answer our life's questions. He is the God of correction who is also filled to the heavens and beyond with grace, mercy, and understanding. Think of the most accepting, loving, and understanding person you know, and then amplify their tender qualities by a billion. That's God. I cannot stress enough to people how kind God truly is—and it's His kindness that brings us to repentance, that willingness to *actually* change.

With that, eventually, my millions of questions about my own mental health did get answered. Yet, it was over a long course of time that felt treacherous during the majority of it. He still speaks today and His ways are infinite.

When we cannot hear Him or struggle to, it's not that He isn't speaking, it's typically because we are not listening. Is there a lot of noise in your life? Figure out what that noise is and shut it off. Get quiet and listen to the Lord. How desperate are you for God, really? How desperate are you for change, healing, or restoration? Your to-do list isn't going to go with you to Heaven. When I was in my early days of seeking, no one could force me into a spiritual experience.

The Father was very strategic about who He placed in my life, when and why He placed them there. I could safely bet He is doing the same for you. The love of Christ is what healed me and continues to heal me. The Lord is extremely detailed, and my journey from darkness to light has His fingerprints all over it. My life is glittered with His hope! I am praying that if you feel lost and hopeless, know that the best is yet to come. If you're not dead, God's not done!

After my term in the psych ward, a couple more destructive experiences, and rehab, I was finally ready to begin to look at my life and untangle it one knot at a time. I participated in an intensive outpatient program for the first six months of my sobriety. I worked part-time and attended treatment part-time. I regularly went to meetings and followed my sponsor's direction as best I could. I had a hard time following directions, but my imperfections did not disqualify me from receiving this new life.

In the recovery community, many people share about what they got back in their first year of sobriety. However, this was not my story. I lost a lot. I came back from residential treatment and lost my apartment, all my plants, and my cat. I lost friends, I lost my boyfriend, and I almost lost my grandma (my life's biggest cheerleader) to multiple strokes. I also lost the ability to suppress my excruciating emotional pain and the denial of my traumatic childhood. I did, however, manage to keep my 15-hour-a-week job and my beat-up old car; which I honestly was really grateful for.

I often had $25 or less in my bank account and remained on food stamps for the next four years. This wasn't the glamour I envisioned after getting a little bit of sober time under my belt. I assumed I would instantly "come up" once I was clean, but my first year of sobriety was chaotic, to say the least.

I still attended bars regularly, hung out in trap houses and strip clubs, got runner-up for a pole-dancing competition in Vegas (not an accomplishment), visited psychic mediums bi-weekly, went on drug runs dead sober, did explicit modeling, hung around gang members, self-harmed, restricted my food intake, pursued witchcraft with even more fervor, got into bar fights with men and only men, visited my boyfriend at the community jail every Friday, Saturday, and Sunday morning whenever he was locked up, and stayed with that violent and heroin-addicted boyfriend until that relationship came to an abrupt halt. The list goes on, but I'll spare you.

I didn't know how to make peace my priority. Sanity was not my strong suit. I had very few healthy coping tools. Yet regardless of my circumstances, I maintained my physical sobriety, which was a pretty big deal. For that, I was proud.

September 20, 2014, marked an entire year free of substances for me. In the 12-step rooms, this is considered a sober birthday and I was acknowledged by the group for my hard work. On your birthday you get to share with the group just how you managed to stay sober for X amount of time. These speeches are designed to give hope to the new person in recovery: "If I can do it, so can you" type of thing.

That evening, after taking my chip and leaving the meeting I got into my car, put my hands on the wheel, and heard this voice in my head. "Go to Greg's house (not his real name). You are not going to like what you find but go anyway." I rarely actually heard or comprehended God's voice in my life with such clarity, but this was one of those moments. I drove over to our apartment in Huntington Beach, shaking.

I had moved out a little over a month or so before due to the abuse and the extremity of his heroin habit. I had moved all my things out in the middle of the night while he was working a graveyard shift and I finally told my parents what the heck was going on. I was inching my way toward escaping this abusive relationship.

That night, I discovered that he had been cheating on me. This was a shock yet also not surprising. I unintentionally broke a window by throwing my keys at it. Some girl he was cheating on me with, and her baby, were kicked out of the apartment, and the Huntington Beach police were called. Greg and I had been together for a little over two years. He shot me up with drugs for the first time, introduced me to the gang life and mentality (which I really tried to distance myself from), took me to punk rock shows, stole my things and sold them for drug money, cheated on me regularly, and abused me in all ways.

Still, the physical attraction was so addictive and my obsession to rescue was so deeply embedded in me that I stayed. We were enmeshed in the chaos. I had always been fiery and aggressive, especially toward men. A deep-seated resentment toward previous abusers had created a self-protective counterfeit version of myself. The subsurface me was typically terrified, but a hard, humorous, and hypersexual facade masked that. In my relationship with Greg, the aggressor in me was snuffed out quickly. Right away I learned who was boss, what to say or not to say, what to do or not to do, and what to hide and how to hide it from him, those close to me, and myself.

Those stuck in abusive relationships are typically so gaslighted by the abuser that they even begin to deceive themselves of the reality of their situation. I pray the Lord frees anyone who is dealing with a manipulative person or manipulative tendencies in their own life now in Jesus's name! Sadly, this wasn't the last of my abusive relationships.

I mostly looked at the ground when I was with Greg in public, I didn't smile at other men because I would get in trouble, and after one time of hitting him back, I learned to *never* do that again. That was the first time someone spit in my face. The cycle of abuse is an interesting occurrence. It is like a merry-go-round. The longer you stay in the cycle, the faster it goes, and the harder it is to get off. This is the nature of a trauma bond and a soul-tie. Abusive cycles suck the life out of you when you are in them.

The cycle of abuse consists of four stages. The first is the calm phase; the second is the phase where tension builds due to life stressors or conflict (often this phase gives the feeling of "walking on eggshells"); the third phase is the abusive incident or the explosion; followed by the fourth phase, the ever-enchanting and self-deceiving honeymoon phase. Most men or women stay in these cycles because the honeymoon stage can be so euphoric. In addition to that, they have likely been trauma-bonded to one another as this cycle perpetuates. The longer the cycle continues, the more deeply trauma-bonded the individuals are to one another.

Usually over time though, the honeymoon phase becomes shorter and less appealing, often increasing the desire in the victim to leave. Just like drug addiction, the feeling of the first high (the honeymoon phase) becomes the goal. This is unattainable, but narcissists who are almost always abusers, have their victims relish in this delusion. Drug addicts literally die clinging to this obsession with the first high.

The same goes for the cycle of abuse. The clinging despite the painful reality of the relationship is often a characteristic of sex and love addiction and early childhood trauma. Men and women alike dig their claws into the "nirvana," only to realize it will never be what they thought it initially was. That is, unless they seek help. People can die as a result of clinging to this obsession, either by accident in a brawl with one another, or at the rage or fear of the other person. Addiction is addiction is addiction! No matter what the "substance" being used is. All addictions are destructive, and addiction is a wicked demon. Remember, its goal is to isolate and kill (John 10:10). And when we zoom out, addiction is without a doubt idolatry.

Unfortunately, when abuse has played a large role in someone's childhood, the pandemonium feels plush. The highs and lows are familiar, and the chaos is familiar. Survivors of childhood abuse often develop a subconscious addiction to the stress hormone cortisol and seek people who embody the same feelings that their abuser did—partially because they subconsciously want to find a solution to the problem.

Cortisol and adrenal levels spike in fight or flight mode. Abusers and victims alike usually experience the internal flooding of this hormone to a degree. When chaos has been a person's baseline his or her entire life, abusive relationships, fear, and high risk-taking feel normal, among many other unhealthy behaviors. Although some childhoods seem to set up many for disaster in adulthood, healing is always possible, and may just take extra work for some.

It is very rare that abusive people recover; however, everything is possible with Jesus and a truly repentant heart. Some people become a product of their environment, repeating the same cycles without the tools or knowledge to change. As someone who comes out of multiple 12-step programs, rehabilitations centers and trauma programs, I have heard stories and met people who were taught how to abuse others by their caregiver.

Can you believe that? How heart-wrenching and corrupt is that? When you hear stories like this, you aren't surprised if a man grows up to be a serial rapist, or a woman grows up to be a prostitute when they were literally taught and exploited in their developmental years to be this way. And of course, this isn't *always* the case. Some people are just so hungry for power and control, that they let evil into their hearts and allow sin full rein in their lives. All that to say, trauma is not always our fault, but it is *always* our responsibility to deal with it and allow the Holy Spirit to heal us.

Both Greg and I had been subjected to early childhood abuse and found ourselves in one dismantling relationship after another prior to meeting. He was also narcissistic, and I was very empathetic and codependent. A common and deadly duo. Our fights consisted of the destruction of one another's properties, cut-throat verbal abuse on both ends, and me always trying to leave yet never being able to.

Toward the end of our drug-addicted, sex-addicted, and abuse-addicted relationship, I found myself on the ground holding my throbbing head that had just been slammed into our bedroom wall. This followed his multiple attempts to strangle me and gouge out my eyes. I remember him putting all his weight into his thumbs that were in my eye sockets. At that moment I remember thinking, *This is really weird.* Rarely in high-intensity abusive situations did I have thoughts other than "cover your face" or "run away," which were more like reflexes.

The small part of me that had experienced some recovery by being part of the 12 steps recognized that this *was* "weird." This was not normal and even though I hadn't taken a drink or drug for some time, this made me feel like I was getting loaded. I felt emotionally unstable and obviously unsafe. After this incident, I told my family what had been going on and they helped me book a trip to San Francisco for two weeks to stay with some close friends. They were convinced he was going to kill me.

He had told me on multiple occasions that he was going to kill me and bury my body in the desert. These "jokes" were always followed by his charming smile and childish laugh. And me being the codependent placater, I brushed it off. Codependency is not dependency, by the way, for those who don't fully understand the term. Codependency is an act of regular self-sacrifice to one's own detriment. People who are enablers are codependent. You see this in addiction, mental illness, and all forms of abuse. Helping someone to the point that you are no longer caring for yourself or your own boundaries is a perfect example.

Again, this is typical of people who endured abuse growing up or were raised in a family where this behavior was normalized. Essentially, it's a lack of boundaries and a compulsion to fix someone else's problems.

Protective of my sick relationship with Greg, I usually disregarded his statements—a longtime habit of mine. Though with Gang Unit steadily on his tracks, reality demonstrated otherwise. He had a background in satanism, a tattoo that read "**** the cops" on his forehead, and a massive racist symbol on the back of his head. I tried to tell myself he wasn't as threatening as he seemed. Clearly, I was drowning in an ocean of denial that kept me with him.

Three months after returning from San Francisco and finding him cheating on me (because yep, I went back), I decided to press charges and put a restraining order on him. The last night I saw him he had put a knife to his stomach and threatened to kill himself in the bathroom. My foot slipped through the door just in time and I talked him off the ledge, once again.

This was usually a manipulative tactic of his and can be characteristic of narcissistic personality disorder sufferers and sociopaths alike. He cried, came out of the bathroom, cooked up his heroin in a spoon, slid a belt around his bicep, and shot up. I had been around this so much that I wasn't even fazed by it anymore. I was, however, over it. The black tar hit his bloodstream, he shifted back onto the bed and put his head against the wall.

I stared at him and thought, *This is the last time I will ever see you*—and it was. One month later I got a call from the Newport Beach Police Department. Greg had been arrested again. For once, I missed the call and made the healthy decision to not pick up his calls from jail moving forward for the next year. I had to pay for the calls anyway. My restraining order and charges against him did not look good in court and his recent arrest was his third charge as a violent criminal. It turned out that Greg was being convicted of murder and sentenced to 15 years to life in prison.

Truthfully, I was beside myself when I learned of his sentencing. My therapist convinced me this was "God working in my favor." I wasn't sure about that, but I did feel a sense of relief muddled with confusion and guilt. Just because someone is broken does *not* mean we need to fix them. I had a pretty ridiculous savior complex if I'm being honest. That was a hard pill for me to swallow. I wanted to *fix* everyone, but it wasn't my job. I was *not* God.

Not every broken person on the face of this earth is my assignment. This is where I cannot stress enough the importance of spending intimate time with the Lord. The closer you get to God, the louder and clearer His voice becomes. There are some people in my life to whom the Lord has directed me. I was to stand by and help (when I honestly have not wanted to), while others He has directed me to walk away from. Some for a time, and some indefinitely. Helping everyone excessively can create a savior complex and codependency that is detrimental for the "helper" as well as the afflicted person!

I am finally, actually, out, I thought after learning of Greg's incarceration.

There weren't going to be any more jail visits or putting money on his books. The relationship was over. My therapist, Sean, suggested I spend some time outside of Orange County. He recommended a yoga retreat, which I didn't have the money for, and then he recommended missions work.

"Missions work, huh?" I said in our session.

"Yeah. It's like being of service, like the twelfth step says to do," Sean responded.

"Okay, that might be a good idea." My wheels were turning.

That night, I went to my sober home group at seven p.m. I told a friend of mine about what my therapist said.

"Yeah, he said I could do mission work or something. He says it's a way to be of service, which might actually be really good for me right now," I said.

"Dude, Jenny!" my friend Taylor responded excitedly.

"What?" I laughed.

"I did mission work in Hawaii for six years!"

"You did?" I vaguely remember him mentioning that.

"Yeah, dude, I can help you get in there! It's a nonprofit on Oahu. You would love it."

"Does it cost money, though?"

"Yeah, but you fundraise. It'll be totally easy. I'll help you."

"Okay." I smiled.

A light at the end of what felt like my endless and ever-dimming tunnel. Maybe this would be like a little vacation, I shrugged to myself. To my surprise, it actually wasn't. It was a rebirth, and it was intense. God clearly had a plan for my life, and it *didn't* look like mine. Also, the island would be my stepping stone into just that—a rebirth.

4

HELL ON PARADISE ISLAND

I landed in Honolulu, Hawaii, just three months later. I packed up all my itty-bitty clothes, my colorful collection of bikinis, my self-tanner, oracle cards, sage, purple hair dye, most of my crystals, my carnelian pendulum I had charged in the full moon, and at the last minute, a Bible.

My grandma had gifted me this Bible when I was 12 years old. It was caked in dust, but somehow it grew legs and walked its way into my duffel bag. I nonchalantly threw it in there, wondering if I would even use it. That was the Holy Spirit!

I was picked up from the airport and driven to Wahiawa, Oahu. Wahiawa is a town near the middle of the island, not far from the North Shore. The crime rate was high there, and the organization I had raised all this money to go to was smack dab in the center of it. Had I known I was about to be encapsulated in a Jesus bubble, I probably would not have gone. I honestly felt safer around criminals than I did around kumbaya-singing, Jesus-obsessed surfers. My friend Taylor had filled out most of my application for me, blindsiding me that this was, in fact, a Christian-based 90-day internship at a nonprofit organization called Surfing the Nations. I was officially trapped.

"Oh, yeah, all different types of people go there to help out," Taylor assured me prior to my leaving California. "You don't have to be a Christian. They might ask you about Jesus, but it'll be so chill, Jenny. You'll love it."

Taylor was a Christian at the time, and I was, well, a practicing witch. I convinced myself I was partaking in ceremonial healing rituals and expanding my spirituality, but it was witchcraft. This was before New Age practices made their trendy debut on social media and before goddesses and divine feminine energy were as mainstream as they are now. I did favor Jesus as one of my many deities, but I definitely wasn't expecting to embark on a three-month-long Bible camp.

Naturally, Hawaii quickly became hell in paradise for me. For the unhealed, sick version of me, it was the exact medicine I needed. A week or so in, I was told that I could not wear the majority of the clothes I had brought with me, I couldn't date, drink, do drugs, smoke, swear, or practice witchcraft. This was the ultimate detox, and I was angry. And no, it wasn't a cult.

I called my sponsor, crying, "This is worse than rehab, Liz!"

"Jenny..."

"No! Seriously, this is hell. If you can fly me home, I promise I will pay you back. I promise."

"Absolutely not." Her voice cut my ego. "You had a lot of people raise money for you to do this internship. The least you can do is stick it out."

Shortly thereafter, I was approached by one of the two owners asking that I not post any more provocative photos on my social media pages during this internship. The founder, Tom, told me that if I continued doing so, I would be asked to leave. I was so offended that I couldn't understand what they were asking of me, which made perfect sense. I was a volunteer who was representing their nonprofit; therefore, I had to climb into what *I thought* was a tiny Christian box, and I hated that. Boy, did I hate that.

I couldn't stand anyone telling me to be a certain way, and I especially hated someone telling me not to be who I was and what I strongly identified with—which was my overbearing sexuality.

They were simply asking me to stay within their boundaries while I participated in the internship, but boundaries don't make any sense to a boundary-less person, and that's who I was then.

"This is what is wrong with Christians and religious people. They never let anyone be themselves!" I practically stomped my feet over to the Walgreens next door, sat down, and chain-smoked at their expense. Sabotaging myself was a common response when I felt rejected.

A pack of cigarettes and 50 F-bombs later, I slowly began to surrender.

I lived with ten girls in a small two-bedroom, one-bathroom, dorm-like apartment with a micro-kitchen. Most of my roommates came from Christian families and had some money in their bank accounts.

We had to make our beds every morning because this activated integrity. "I'm sorry, but I didn't know I was signing up for a Bible camp and the military all in one." I was constantly diffusing sarcasm. I've always been a very orderly person, but still did not fully understand what starting the day off with an act of integrity had to do with anything at the time, or how making my bed translated as such. My small, twin-size bunker felt like a jail.

Honestly, anything that tried to halt my witchcraft or sexuality felt like bondage to me, even though both of those things, specifically, were why most bondage in my life had occurred. I found my place on the bottom bunk, where I added blue twinkly lights from a donation box, a shelf with my crystals on it, and a small fleece blanket from the movie *Frozen*.

We were subject to Bible teachings a few mornings out of the week, typically followed by community prayer or service work during the second half of the day, which I enjoyed. One Tuesday, I spent hours washing a wall between dorms. It was like a Christian ashram (a spiritual or religious retreat), I kept telling myself, *Eat, pray, love vibes, right?*

Since I had been apprenticing with a psychic medium the last year of my sobriety and had been in an ascension school for psychics, clairvoyants, energy healers, and the like, I figured I knew way more than these people did. My arrogance told me I saw things that they did not or could not, which was so ridiculous because when you are dealing with Christians who truly know their authority and walk in their spiritual giftings, they are way more powerful than any witch. I didn't know that then, though.

As interns, we had to spend the first hour of our mornings in "quiet time."

I laughed. "What is quiet time?" reminiscing about napping on a mat in preschool.

"Quiet time is how you spend the first hour of the day with God. How do you connect with Jesus daily?" one of the leaders, named Julie, asked me.

"I don't know, meditation. Kundalini."

Julie was kind, but she didn't put up with anybody's bad attitude. If someone was going to tell you like it was, it would be Julie. A little intimidating, yet I was very fond of her. She told me, "You can read the Word, pray, journal, worship, and hear from God. Personally, sometimes I run and pray. Think about how you connect with Him."

This was a little different from the 12-step way of connecting to my "higher power." Mostly because it was required the first hour of the morning, which I wasn't necessarily accustomed to, although I did like the idea. I was spiritually open and had tried connecting to the "source" in a multitude of ways, so I was willing to try something different. I did like "different," after all.

The staff also encouraged us to have our noses in our Bibles daily. I figured I would start with the last book of the Bible, the book of Revelation. I knew this book was all prophecy and that it freaked out what I considered boring Christians. So of course, that seemed like the *perfect* place for someone like *me*—a real-life rebel—to start.

Because of the divination practices I had immersed myself in for years, I had a huge passion for symbolism and patterns. In fact, I still do, but now God uses it in different ways. I believe the Lord created me this way, but the enemy will warp any good thing to advance the kingdom of darkness. I felt I had a spiritual advantage in decoding the book of Revelation because two of my favorite things was to analyze and interpret.

To my surprise, I had no idea what the heck any of that book meant. I completed Revelation and moved on to what I learned was the Gospels. I always thought the Gospel was just another name for the Holy Bible, but I was wrong. The Gospels are the first four books of the New Testament—Matthew Mark, Luke, John—essentially the four books that reveal the birth, life, death, and resurrection of Jesus Christ.

Hmm. I'll start with Mark out of these four books. I had known a Mark, so I figured this was a good place to start. *This better not be boring,* I thought to myself.

Part of me was deeply intrigued by the life of Jesus, but I didn't know much about the 33 years He spent on earth. I knew some things about Him from my grandma and some Sunday school I attended as a child. I knew from my New Age community that He represented pure love and was the only "ascended master" who called Himself the "Son of God." I had been part of church things here and there, but didn't know much about it.

People I knew who practiced Reiki would often try to "channel" Jesus as a healer. Oh how easily deceived we can be by the world when we don't intimately know Him! I was hesitant to read about Jesus from the *actual* Bible (isn't that interesting?), but there was such a supernatural draw. That draw was the Holy Spirit!

I read from the book of Mark each morning until I was finished. I was captivated! Jesus healed and exorcized demons out of people regularly! The following are just a few of my favorite verses from the book of Mark confirming this about Him (I encourage you to read each chapter):

> *And He healed many who were ill with various diseases, and cast out many demons; and He was not permitting the demons to speak, because they knew who He was* (Mark 1:34 NASB1995).

> *And He went into their synagogues throughout all Galilee, preaching and casting out the demons* (Mark 1:39 NASB1995).

> *For He had been saying to him, "Come out of the man, you unclean spirit!"* (Mark 5:8 NASB1995).

> *When Jesus saw that a crowd was rapidly gathering, He rebuked the unclean spirit, saying to it, "You deaf and mute spirit, I command you, come out of him and do not enter him again"* (Mark 9:25 NASB1995).

> *Now the woman was a Gentile, of the Syrophoenician race. And she kept asking Him to cast the demon out of her daughter* (Mark 7:26 NASB1995).

> *These signs will accompany those who have believed: in My name they will cast out demons, they will speak with new tongues; they will pick up serpents, and if they drink any deadly poison, it will not harm them; they will lay hands on the sick, and they will recover* (Mark 16:17-18 NASB).

The casting out of devils always resulted in freedom—and Jesus actually set the captives free on a regular basis! (See Luke 4:18.) This blew my mind. Additionally, it blew my mind even more that we as Christians are supposed to be doing the same things! Not just pastors or priests, or experts or exorcists, or seers or intercessors, or the most qualified. Casting out devils is one of the first true signs of a believer.

Reading the book of Mark was unexpectedly comforting to me. I had experienced the demonic since I was a little girl, and never had I ever been educated about the multiple demons mentioned in the Bible, and Jesus and His followers had the authority to cast them out and banish them—and that we (Christians) are called to do the same, without fear!

Fear had me for so long. Fear was all-consuming when it decided to crawl out of the pit of my stomach and make its debilitating debut in my life, time and again. On my path to freedom, I learned that this fear is an actual spirit! Because it was familiar, I came into agreement with it repeatedly, and it came back multiple times. You can always spot a spirit of fear because it will plague your mind with negative "What if?" questions. Renewing my mind and being transformed by God's Word felt like heavy lifting at times.

As I embarked on my new journey through the Bible, my perspectives didn't shift right away. Yet, as I read through the book of Mark, it was like something inside me was beginning to change. I went from disinterested to captivated. I went from resistant to soft, and from rebellious to willing. Don't get me wrong, I still had my rough edges. Though, the Word of God was changing my heart. I didn't know that right away. What I did know, though, was that I was beginning to tap into a peace I had never known or felt before; I was entering a holy space by reading the Word of God, and I could feel it.

My bunkmate at Surfing the Nations told me toward the end of our internship that she had been afraid of me for the first month of her stay. I was aggressive and intense and insisted on doing things my way. Once my heart began to tenderize and I stopped calling my sponsor to pay for my flight to leave, I started to surrender—one millimeter at a time.

Once that started to happen, it became much easier to get close to the other interns.

Each morning, my alarm would sound at six o'clock. I would make my bed and then go outside or across the street to McDonald's. Sometimes, I would buy a small orange juice, but most days, I walked in through the side door and sat in a booth to the back left. I would read my Bible or write in my journal. I soon found that prayer journaling was soothing and emotionally and spiritually beneficial.

I would pray for myself, my family, friends, exes, and people I knew and didn't know, and then I started praying for those typically rejected and hated by society. I prayed for the homeless, drug addicts, prostitutes, and the abused and their abusers. I didn't know it then, but I was being called to intercession. *What a strange concept,* I thought, *to pray for abusive people, yet my prayers keep turning down that road.* I prayed for murderers, rapists, and child molesters. I began praying for their freedom, for their hearts to be changed, and for help to be offered to them, because I imagined what a lonely, cold, and tormenting place some of them had to be in to be capable of horrific acts such as these.

This was a new lane for me to operate in—love without judgment. My heart wept for the lost, for those who needed to be reconciled to God. I didn't know that God was preparing my heart for something that would come up and shatter me months later. I just prayed as I felt led.

As my heart began to shed its old skin, my desire to release past pains and habits surfaced even more. *Up and out,* I thought. One evening, there was a staff and intern worship night. We could sit wherever we wanted in Surfer's Church and soak in the healing music. The floor, walls, and ceiling were all paneled with wood, and little wooden chairs were set up throughout the building. Some people prayed for those in need, others stood, sang, and danced, the rest sat in their chairs or knelt on the ground.

I sat in my seat, eyes closed for a while. I had such a heaviness in my heart that never seemed to go away. Despite medications, therapy, sobriety, and so on, it was always there. As I quietly began to weep, I suddenly felt a powerful presence of love consume me—it was all around me. Love without limits or judgment or expectation or condemnation. Boundless, radical love. Tender yet profound and fierce.

I had unique spiritual experiences through kundalini and transcendental meditation practices, with fleeting moments of God in them (I believe God can meet anyone, anywhere, at any time, even when they are sinning against Him). Still, this love had a level of purity like I had never felt before.

That's when I saw Jesus in a white robe, sitting in the chair next to me. I wept, and He comforted me. He had me lay my head on His lap. It's interesting because usually this would bring up feelings of fear or violation, but those fearful feelings dissipated in His presence with His love. It seemed I had been laying in His lap, crying for years, and He just sat there with His hands on my shoulder and head, comforting me.

He was completely without distraction or any outside pressure calling Him away. His only purpose in that moment was to comfort me. Then, He stood to His feet, and I felt Him wrap His arms around me in Spirit. Not even a second later, Julie came up beside me and hugged me as hard as she could. I turned into a puddle of tears. God made what I had just felt in the spiritual manifest in the physical. Julie held me while I sobbed and then she leaned over and said, "I was standing in the back of the church when Jesus said to me, 'Go hug My daughter.' So here I am."

Had she done this sooner or later, it would not have been as nearly significant. Her action highlights the importance of obedience, specifically *timely* obedience. When we draw close to the Lord, we can hear His voice much more clearly—for ourselves and others. When we respond quickly to His direction, it can profoundly impact a situation.

During my time on Oahu, Jesus was drawing me in with His unconditional love and gentleness. The next morning, I woke to a beautiful Hawaiian sunrise with a full heart. I genuinely *knew* that Jesus loved me.

NEW WATERS

Living on the island definitely had its luxuries. The water was always warm. Double rainbows draped the tropical skies regularly. I could hear dolphins and whales underneath the waves at Waimea Bay. A ukulele was consistently being strummed somewhere in the background. The smell of pineapple filled the beater cars on the way to North Shore. Hitchhiking with surfboards was normal, and the drivers were always kind. I loved being surrounded by tropical electric greens and soft blues.

I grew to enjoy Tuesday fasts and scrubbing a wall for three hours on community clean-up days because "it built character." I stopped feeling like I was going to catch fire (in a bad way) every time I walked into a church. I began to wear little bits of God's peace like jewelry. This trip was not hell after all; it was just me jumping through a ring of fire onto holy ground. Oftentimes, God will pull you backward like an arrow to gain momentum, just to send you flying into the next chapter. I was willing to give God territory in my life.

Shortly after my encounter with Jesus during that night of worship, I decided to fully dedicate my life to Him. I believed now, so naturally, that baptism was the next step. I had been baptized before, once when I was nine because I wanted to be dunked underwater in front of a crowd, and another time, when my Satanist ex-boyfriend said we should get baptized at some megachurch's Easter event. Neither of those times were authentic for me—but my next one would be.

Our internship was divided into two groups: one would go to Maui and the other would go to Molokai for outreach. I was selected for Molokai. Molokai is extremely rural. There are no hotels or flurries of gift shops. Everything closes at three in the afternoon, and there is just one movie theater on the island. The only shop open late was a bread shop window. A woman on the island made the most ridiculously delicious sweet bread and made her treats available into the night hours. I've never had anything so tasty in my life!

On Molokai, most people who travel there either know a native or rent camp space. During my stay there, I began to experience extreme spiritual warfare, which I honestly did not understand and was not equipped for, and neither did most of the staff. Post-traumatic stress disorder (PTSD) symptoms from my past began to creep into my life like bugs under my sheets. I was having chronic nightmares, increased suicidal thoughts, flashbacks, little to no sleep, and intensified physical responses to touch, especially if I was touched on the back of the neck. I fought hard to not to let these symptoms consume me.

We spent our time volunteering with a local church community there. We hiked barefoot in the jungle, ate that famous Molokai sweet bread, and camped in the rain. One night, at a small church gathering, I sat in the pew listening intently to Pastor Jonas. As he spoke, I heard an audible whisper, "You should get baptized."

Not even a moment later, the pastor shouted, "God wants you to get baptized!" My jaw dropped. I looked around to see if anyone else was experiencing what I had. After the service, I ran up to Jonas and Julie to tell them! It was a Christmas Day miracle! The traumatized, over-sexualized, hard-headed, bratty witch girl in the internship wanted to get baptized. Go figure, and way to go, Jesus!

Days later, our internship filed into a Molokai seafoam green bus and drove to a nearby beach. It was a gloomy morning, and my hair was in two French braids from the night before. Dark roots growing in and a makeup-less face. I didn't care. The group sat at the shore, and Julie walked me past the shore break. She then asked me what every person who baptizes another asks:

"Are you willing to give your life to Jesus?"

"Yes," I said.

I placed my hand over my nose, and Julie declared, "I now baptize you in the name of the Father, Son, and the Holy Spirit." Then dunked me beneath one of the small waves.

Cool, smooth water ran over my face like oil; all I could feel was peace.

Julie splashed me as I jumped out of the wave and lifted my hands in the air. We both moved as quickly as we could through the water back to the beach, laughing. And that's when it happened. As soon as my feet reached the shore, I cried; actually, I sobbed. The group gathered, blessing me with a lei around my neck. This lei was not one you could buy at a gift shop on Oahu or Maui—it was from a nearby plumeria field, handpicked and specially made for me.

Everyone put their hands on me, lifting up their voices in prayer. This type of intercession is called Korean-style prayer. It can sound like a bunch of noise to the person receiving it, but when you hone in on one voice, you can hear the individual's detailed prayer for you. It is extremely powerful for the person receiving it. Another moment of God dousing me in His love.

After all the prayers and embraces, Andrew, a native, began to sing beautiful Hawaiian worship music. Andrew's deep and powerful voice filled the beach that morning. As everyone sat on the sand worshiping, I walked in solitude to a place farther down the coast.

I could not stop weeping.

Time and again, I had witnessed many baptisms. I thought people were being dramatic or the church hired them when they came out of the water crying. Part of me thought it was all propaganda and somewhat embarrassing. But this, this was anything but that. Getting baptized was a life-changing moment for me—a major pivot. I wanted to die to self. I wanted to give up my life for a new one.

Sure, sobriety offered me a new perspective and a new route, but my spirit yearned for so much more. I craved freedom. Freedom from the bondage of self, from my addictions and habits, freedom from heartache and disappointments. Freedom from a life of dysfunction and a broken home. I wanted a new home. I wanted a new life. I wanted a new language, a new heart, and a new mind. This moment was that promise.

> *"For I know the plans I have for you," declares the Lord, "plans to prosper you and not to harm you, plans to give you hope and a future"* (Jeremiah 29:11 NIV).

Something was undeniably different. I had never felt this way before. I have such a heart for animals, and God knows this about me. I do believe that He designed me this way. Before Christianity, I had read Buddhist books about animals approaching monks without fear because of the inner peace they radiated. I loved that the animal kingdom could sense a person's heart.

As I sat there with tears drying on my salty, freckled skin, a baby crab walked over to me. I held out my hand in patience. The little crab approached me without fear, walked across my knuckles, and sat on my pointer finger. He was no bigger than my middle knuckle. I heard the voice of God at that moment, which reminded me of something out of the film *Pocahontas:* A peaceful moment in nature when Grandmother Willow speaks to Pocahontas through the wind. It's laughable but true.

"This is you," the Lord said to me.

I grew even more still. The worship music down the beach felt muffled as I leaned into the voice of God.

"This is you. You are an infant in your spirituality, but you will grow."

This creature was small and shelled, like me. In nature, a crab shell cannot expand. As crabs grow, they eventually need to leave their shell and move into a new one that fits. This process is called molting. How symbolic and significant.

When I put my hand back down to the sand, the little crab stepped off and ventured toward the seashore.

The group down the beach was getting ready to head back to the bus, so I stood up and walked over to them. Julie put her arm around me, proud.

"How do you feel?" she asked.

"Honestly? Like I have been walking around my entire life with dirt clods on me, and like I could physically feel them break off. That's the best way I can describe it."

"Rad." She smiled.

Major spiritual warfare hit as our time on Molokai came to a close and we flew back to our home base on Oahu. I was getting closer to God's will for my life, and the enemy didn't like that. Boy, was I about to enter another fight for my life.

When we arrived at our little apartment in Wahiawa, supernatural and disturbing things began happening to me. The nightmares, flashbacks, and restlessness increased. Paranormal activity began to stir up around me. Doors would open and close in the middle of the night; I had visions of disgusting demon-like creatures at my bedside, waking me up by licking my face with their rough tongues.

I was not the only one awakened in the night by our door opening by itself. One time I stood up, said a Bible verse out loud, and then said, "It's fine," to one of the girls in her bunk who was afraid. I tried to reassure her, "It's because of me. Don't worry. It'll go away."

This paranormal phenomena had followed me most of my life. It increased the more I participated in witchcraft, and it didn't go away just because I was baptized. Staff assured me that spiritual warfare after something like this was normal, but I still didn't like it.

Deliverance was not once mentioned to me within the five years of being saved. Many Christians do not have the knowledge needed to address this type of warfare, unfortunately, so some (like me) continue to suffer at the hands of the enemy. Why was this happening after I had made such a massive step in my spiritual walk toward Jesus? The best way for me to describe this to somebody who has no affiliation with witchcraft or experience in trying to get out of it is to compare it to a gang; in this case, a spiritual gang.

In the gang community, you cannot just leave when you want to. You are initiated in, and you are forced to suffer if you try to get out. This often includes harsh hazing to the point of beatings or even death. My ex-boyfriend had to do some horrific things to be initiated into the gang life, some things so terrible that I will not even mention them in this book. When you commit yourself to a gang, you commit for life. It's about loyalty.

In witchcraft it is the same thing. I had to be willing to participate in or be exposed to certain things to be part of it. I could not "just leave." Basically, you get jumped out if you even get out at all. This was the beginning of that warfare for me. Little did I know that my true freedom would not come for another four-plus years.

I had to fight, and I had to fight *hard*. This was before I knew that fighting "smarter" was more beneficial than fighting harder. When someone has true authority in Christ, the spiritual warfare may be annoying, but it's not as exhausting.

Before leaving Oahu, I had the opportunity to share my testimony. Everyone in my internship shared their experiences in coming to the Lord. Funny enough, I was one of the last interns to share, and for good reason! We had scheduled days and times for this when the staff was also present. People heard my story and thought it was sad, and some cried.

This was not an uncommon response when I shared my life in full detail. I was a year and a half sober when I was at Surfing the Nations and still had quite a bit of memory blackout from my childhood and adulthood, so I shared the pieces that I could recall. I thought sobriety was my destination for healing, but God had revealed to me more and more that was not the case. Sobriety was the starting point, the place where the light entered. Hawaii happened to be my stepping stone that followed.

After sharing my story, the group was given ten minutes to reflect quietly. Then one by one, interns and staff alike began to line up to share with me what God had told them during that time. This was called a time of prophecy. The ex-witch in me loved this. *Finally, some psychic stuff!* I thought. Christianity had been unappealing and seemed boring from far away.

So as a Christian operating from a place of knowing God and listening to the Holy Spirit, not demons, was intriguing to me. The gift of prophecy is designed to be encouraging. I loved that! And something I never knew Christians walked in.

Essentially, prophecy is hearing from God about someone or something. It is meant to uplift, edify, and encourage. In 1 Corinthians 12, the spiritual gifts are outlined, prophecy being one of them. Also, 1 Corinthians 14:1 (NIV) states, *"Follow the way of love and eagerly desire gifts of the Spirit, especially prophecy."*

There is a broad spectrum of prophecies—simple or profound. It can be someone experiencing God's love for you in that moment, sharing in it while speaking life to you, or speaking very specific details about your past, present, and future. In my opinion, when someone truly operates in the Holy Spirit, prophecy will never feel invasive or as if violating the person's privacy who is receiving the word.

The main difference between a prophet of the Lord and a psychic is the source and the exchange. Is it coming from the Holy Spirit or another spirit? For years, I practiced mediumship. I was able to receive accurate information for some people based on what was being revealed. These messages often came from so-called spirit guides or other familiar spirits. I was not always clear on who was speaking to me when I received these messages.

True prophesying comes directly from God, the only one true, living God. Make no mistake, there is no negative spiritual exchange when someone is communing with Jesus versus communing with other spirits. Spirits that are not of God are demonic! The source is the difference. The Bible tells us to test every spirit (1 John 4:1). When you are making exchanges with other spirits, you are giving the demonic access to yourself. I cannot warn people enough *not* to go to psychics, mediums, or energy healers!

I used to work with them and know firsthand that some have good intentions, but many do not. Regardless of the intent, when someone is eating at a table with demons, they walk directly into curses and turn their face from the blessings of God. I don't care who you are or what tools you use to protect yourself, if you are dabbling in the occult, you are making friends with deceptive spirits.

Seeing psychics is a waste of money, time, and peace. Guard yourself. As far as prophecy went, I had never experienced it before this moment. After my testimony, I stood at the front of the group with my short purple and blonde hair, jean cutoffs, a military jacket, and combat boots, palms sweating, nervous about what would be shared with me. Usually the interns shared their testimonies on stage in our church, but today we were in a forest of all places.

I remember feeling so vulnerable in those moments just after I had shared my story. Rosko, a staff member who also mentored me during my stay, asked if I was willing to sever all ties to witchcraft at this time. She asked if I was willing to make a public declaration that from this point forward, I would turn away from my witchy ways and make my way toward Truth and Life.

After returning from Molokai and having the sincere spiritual experience of a true baptism, I complied. Not because

I felt pressured or embarrassed but because something was shifting inside me from the instant I landed on that island. Something supernatural! I had walked away from my drug addiction and alcoholism, left the heroin-addicted gangster who was consumed in himself, and now was the time for me to throw in the occult towel.

After my declaration, the line of people began sharing with me what the Lord had revealed to them. Many spoke of my strength and my capacity to reach people. Others spoke about my creativity, and that one day I would paint scenes from the book of Revelation. Many of the verses and prophetic words were the same—God was making a point.

This moment of prophecy was an incredible experience. Not only was I seen and accepted like I had felt once before in the psych unit, but I was seen, accepted, and then filled to the brim with encouraging words that came straight from the heart of God.

It wasn't long after that when I booked my flight to LAX, and I would move back into my grandmother's condominium in Costa Mesa. My time on the island, far away from everything I knew, was the best thing for me, and I loved it so much. Unfortunately, it was time to kiss the island life goodbye with gratitude; I was truly thankful.

Near the same time, my cousin, Kat, had just experienced something on the other side of the country. We had never been close, per se; although close in age, we lived on opposite sides of the country and didn't talk much. Around the time I was halfway through Surfing the Nations, my cousin had been attending a church where the pastor began randomly prophesying and praying over her.

He called her out in the crowd, and as she stood up, he began speaking things about her life that he wouldn't have known without the Holy Spirit, and then said, "There's someone in your family who is being held down by satan right now. A relation of yours who is close in age to you. You don't really know her, but you want to know. God is going to deliver her from satan's grip, and she is going to have freedom and abundance."

This was *right* before I got saved, and ironically, as I write this, the word the Lord gave me for this year, the year I have finally completed this book, is "Abundance." I'm not one who asks God for a word at the beginning of each year, but on New Year's Eve, God spoke to me as I took a shower:

> *The thief does not come to steal, and to kill, and to destroy. I* [Jesus] *have come that they may have life, and that they may have it more* ***abundantly*** (John 10:10 NKJV).

Abundance goes beyond what we could even think or imagine; there is an abundance of everything in Christ.

My cousin Kat didn't tell me about this word initially, but during my deliverances, I grew very close to her. We would text and talk and pray on the phone often. Both of us were going through our own set of relationship problems and leaned on each other and prayed for our families. When she told me about this word she received, I was shocked, but it couldn't have come at a more perfect time, as I was halfway through my deliverance process then and needed encouragement. A word like that gave me even more ammunition to keep going. God was calling me.

BACK TO THE MAINLAND

Maura, a close friend of mine, picked me up at the airport in Los Angeles the next morning. I had taken the red-eye flight with little to no sleep and could not rest during the car ride home, so she probed me.

"Tell me about Hawaii, Jenny! What was it like?" she asked excitedly.

Maura was my closest friend in the recovery community. She had a bit more sober time than me and loved New Age culture, just like I did before Hawaii. She had come from New Jersey to California for treatment. Maura had kicked heroin multiple times, but this was the first time she was able to stay clean and implement the changes needed to create a new life for herself. We were pretty boundaryless and, therefore, very enmeshed. We spoke the same language most of the time, and I loved that about our friendship.

"Dude, Maura, it was like the most radical experience of my life. I literally love Jesus now."

Her smile dwindled and her demeanor shifted, but she was still interested. Though Maura may not always agree with someone, she is always kind. "Okay." She laughed uncomfortably. "What do you mean?"

I went on and on and on about the Bible, demons, prayer, the homeless, being of service, talking to God and hearing from God, prophesying over people, quitting witchcraft, being Spirit-led, praying for people in the streets, not swearing, changing the way I dressed, and so on. For two straight hours, I held Maura hostage in a Jesus prison. I couldn't contain the good news! She seemed put off and confused, but that didn't prevent me from sharing the Gospel.

"It's just so insane how God has moved in my life, Maura. Like, I wish you could have been there."

She smiled, her eyes glued to the road.

"So, remember when I did that photoshoot right before I left for Hawaii in Blackstar Canyon?"

"Yeah, kinda. But what does that have to do with anything?" she asked.

"It has everything to do with everything! You see, God has been so undeniably strategic with this trip to Hawaii for me, and it all started with *that* photographer."

"Okay? How?"

"Do you remember how he told me about his experience dating a witch? And that whole crazy story about a dream God had given him about the truth?"

"Yeah?" Maura was confused.

"And then told me to read that book about some witch doctor? He said I would get a lot out of that book. Remember?"

"Yes, actually."

"Well, I read that book, and it honestly changed my life. I ended up getting baptized, dude, and that book was the precursor for that!"

"What was the book even about, or, like, what do you mean?" she asked.

As I reminded Maura of my encounter with the photographer, I shared the book's details and the impact it had on me with her. Half of her was apprehensive, while the other half was completely enthralled by what I said. She was ripe in the spirit and hungry for God—she just didn't know it yet!

Here is a little backstory about how this book, *The Witch Doctor and the Man: City Under the Sea* by Bishop Samuel Vagalos Kanco, was introduced into my life. I had been modeling for years, and a few months before the STN internship, I had a shoot with a photographer I met through a clothing line I modeled for. As I got into his car one fall morning, I noticed a Bible in his backseat. I laughed and handed it to him as I laid down my collection of looks for the shoot.

"Is this your Bible?" I laughed at him.

"Yes." He looked a little embarrassed, taking it from me and putting it in the pocket behind his seat.

"What, do you like to read it on your lunch breaks or something?" I said mockingly.

"Sometimes," he shrugged.

Then this photographer began ministering to me. As he heard pieces of what I was currently involved in, he began to tell me about a witch he had unknowingly dated in high school. She had been dedicated to satan as a child. She put a love spell on him, thus entrapping him in a relationship with her.

I was captivated by his stories and how the Holy Spirit had revealed who she was and what she was doing to him. He told her he knew she was a witch, which was revealed to him in a dream. She denied this accusation repeatedly but eventually surrendered to the truth. Afterward, he left the relationship. God was looking out for him! He then went on to tell me about a book titled *The Witch Doctor and the Man: City Under the Sea.* The book was the testimony of a fourth-generation witch doctor from Ghana, Africa, who was radically saved by Jesus. I had never read anything like it before or since.

After our photoshoot that morning, I went home and read a few pages of the book. Interested but distracted, I closed out of the webpage and forgot about it entirely. Then, while in Hawaii, we were told to write two book reports. At first, I thought this was absurd. I read one book they gave me, unmoved by it. Staff told us we could select a second book as long as it was God-centered and approved by staff. I didn't have the finances to purchase a new book, but I suddenly recalled *The Witch Doctor and the Man* was online for free.

The following day, I printed out the story and got started. The first half of the book was heavy. The level of supernatural evil exposed in part one was chilling but—again—familiar to me. Part two related a man's personal accounts of deliverance and how Jesus, quite literally, came to him. An angel of the Lord pushed him out of his house down the street and into a church where he manifested demons and came to Christ! His story exposes the details of the demonic world for what it really is: wicked, deceitful, and seductive.

I couldn't hear a pastor, but I could hear this. I was so convicted I actually had to set down the book and walk away on a few different occasions because it was so gut-wrenching. The demons I had carried within me for years did *not* like this book. In one section of his book, he lists all the things of the devil.

I had practiced many of them without truly knowing what I had been involved in. This new knowledge upset me. I didn't think witchcraft was so serious; that book changed my life. Shortly after reading it, I was baptized and then shared my testimony. I had come to full terms with being a witch, something I had been denying prior to reading that book. I had rationalized white magic, necromancy, magic circles, etc. I had felt more comfortable with titles like "healer" or "white witch."

God placed that photographer in my path. I wouldn't be where I am today if it weren't for that photo shoot, that photographer, and that book! I could not contain this new fire within me.

Back in my island community, everybody was on fire like this. Yet, as I stepped off my pink Hawaiian cloud and walked back into Orange County where none of my friends were Jesus followers, I was quickly hit with major difficulties.

"Wow," Maura said as we pulled up to my garage. "You're so different now."

"You have no idea, dude. It's *all* Jesus."

"Or something." She laughed innocently. She kindly helped me unload my luggage, and I was back in my California home once again.

5

FLASHBACKS, FEAR, AND FALLING BACK INTO SEX AND LOVE ADDICTION

The two weeks following my return home were unexpectedly difficult. Going from a Jesus bubble back to my old life in California was a depressing adjustment. I wanted to stay on the island long term, but I could not make it work. During my island stay, I decided to remain celibate for at least one year.

In early recovery, celibacy and staying out of a romantic relationship are encouraged. I didn't do this in my first year, so I was going to give it a shot for my second. I wanted to stay on fire for God. The fire in me did not die out instantaneously. I had a lot of zeal, but lacked significant wisdom. There was a burning in me to bring Jesus back to the territories my feet had wandered before.

I went to raves and festivals—sober—and prophesied over people's lives. I set up a table on the Venice Beach boardwalk that said, "Free Readings." I used this phrase as a hook to draw people in, and then I prayed for them in Jesus's name. I was so excited. I even walked my best friend, Maura, through accepting Christ at three in the morning on my bedroom floor. A large part of me was committed to this new life. I *wanted* to be committed to this new life, but a darkness still hovered like a cloud at my back.

My PTSD symptoms did not disappear as a result of my pursuing God; in fact, they amplified. I needed deliverance, but no one told me. I knew nothing of it until five years after being saved. Repentance, though, is necessary for deliverance to even be effective. Repentance is making the decision to leave what God has prohibited and return to what He has commanded. It's walking in the opposite direction of what is hindering you and your relationship with God.

Sometimes, additional help or extra community support is required as one adjusts from their old life of sin to a new one. Twelve-step programs were the bridge for me. When I was delivered of demons, I actually left the program I was in; I was free.

People joke about the demonic, but if you've seen them face-to-face, you know that their only goal is to kill you; and if they can't do that, they will torment you endlessly. Even if someone gets free from the spirit of alcoholism, for example, it would be dangerous to pursue drinking or using alcohol again if it was cast out. Always seek the Lord on matters like this (Matthew 12:43-45).

For me, although the obsession to drink and the spirit associated with it has been evicted, I will not risk taking a drink again. Drinking and, of course, drug use open dangerous doors that I am not willing to revisit or test myself in again; I have a deep conviction about it. On a few occasions when I have been in a vulnerable position, a spirit of addiction has whispered, "You are so stressed out, you could use a glass of wine."

First of all, I never drank wine except on one occasion, and that was as a chaser. So this spirit knows that wine is something I never had the opportunity to "enjoy" and something that sounds a lot less harmful than shooting up cocaine or snorting pills, which is what my drinking would lead to anyway. Second, it has only come to me when I have been under great stress or in a vulnerable position.

Just like a predator in the wild will go after the young, the weak, the injured, or those on the outside of the pack, so will demons in the spirit realm! I call these demonic drive-bys. They are drive-bys because they come like a shot in the dark and are not always expected. As long as I do not take the opportunity to entertain or agree with these demonic thoughts, they will leave quicker than they came. They do not have permission to stay—*you* are the one who gives them permission to stay. That is why renewing the mind is vital (Romans 12:2)!

These are demonic drive-bys, not demonic drive-ins! They do not have access to drive into my life, park, and enjoy a meal unless I let them. I think if people could physically see the demons associated with their sins, they would bolt as fast as they could in the opposite direction.

Some sins and difficulties can take longer to turn away from for good, truly, and they may require additional work and support. You are a new creation in Christ; just believe it! And if you're reading this and you're not a believer, at least finish this book—you can experience freedom either way. Trust me, the Lord does not only have one way of doing things—He has a million ways of doing a million things. Hearing His voice for *you* is key.

Keep in mind, we are three parts: mind, body, and spirit, and all need to be cared for. Deliverance is a huge necessity that can heal us in mind and body, but it is important to devote care to each part of us.

In the majority of cases, spirits can lie dormant and stick around. In other cases, because of the pursuit of righteousness and the person's relationship with the Holy Spirit, the demon may leave during a Bible reading or worship service or in a church setting. We do not always need to make a "deliverance appointment" for a devil to be cast out, although I do encourage this, as many spirits hide. I personally do quarterly spiritual "check-ups."

One of my mentors and deliverance ministers, Stuart Greer, always says, "The most sincere and repentant people will get set free!" Repentance is key.

Unfortunately, there is a significant lack of repentance, healing, and deliverance in the church today. Many churches consider healing or deliverance an outside ministry. But that's not what Acts 2 says. These are walked out daily as a believer in Christ. People come to believe, but stay in bondage too often. If the Church were regularly moving in the giftings of the Holy Spirit, I believe a massive number of people would stop pursuing psychics for direction and would start pursuing the Almighty God (1 Corinthians 12).

Discipleship, mentorship, accountability, fasting, and prayer are primary spiritual resources necessary for the believer.

When it comes to the demonic, there are many ways they can access a person. One area of major attack is what I personally call emotional sins. This is not a condemnation of having feelings. We are human; we will have feelings, and we do not need to be ashamed of them. I have lots of feelings. However, emotions that are beyond our control that we feel consumed or enslaved by, choose to constantly entertain, or cannot escape from, actually indicate something else, likely spiritual, is occurring.

We are called to be led by the Holy Spirit, not by the flesh (our bodies and our emotions). If something unfortunate happens to a person, it would make sense that they would be very sad about it. But if the person stays in this emotional state too long, it can open the door to depression, addiction, self-harm, suicide, and an infinite number of unhealthiness. That emotional "sin" can give direct access to demonic spirits. We must be taking our thoughts captive, not letting our fleshly thoughts rule our emotions and our lives—that's honestly for our own protection. It takes practice!

Jesus wants every person on earth to be free of what keeps them bound and distant from Him; and sometimes, we don't even know we are bound. I definitely did not at first! Or at least not to the level I actually was. Coming directly to Jesus and getting free doesn't have to take years or decades; seeking and finding Him now is possible. However, I understand that people (like me) are confused, stubborn, and entangled with the world, so sometimes it takes longer.

If you're stuck in a place of habitually doing the same thing over and over that you know is not good, but you don't know how to change or don't feel too bad about it yet know it isn't right, ask God for the gift of repentance. Repentance sets you free, and demons will leave as a result. Ask the Holy Spirit to meet you in your room, or your car, or wherever you are right now, and deliver you. Whom the Son (Jesus) sets free, is free indeed (John 8:36)! God always shows up and is *always* on time—so hang in there!

As a new believer, I would see many people come to Jesus and remain entangled with their afflictions, me being one of them, obviously. I didn't always understand this. The Bible says we should consider ourselves blessed when we suffer for Christ; suffer *for* Christ, not suffer because we are under loads of demonic oppression and bondage like sin, flashbacks, anxiety, triggers, despair, insomnia, rejection, depression, guilt, addictions, and so on. So we say the sinner's prayer, and then what? Do we stay in our sicknesses and brokenness? Hide behind a Christian label yet live in secret sin? Put little effort into our relationship with God because we are "already saved"? Be ruled by all of our "issues"?

No, we shouldn't! Jesus offers freedom! We are not to be ruled by sin or circumstance! If the word *sin* confuses you, upsets you, or offends you, chances are you do not fully understand it, or there is something in your life that is violating your morals and God's standards.

There is so much more than all of what has happened to you or things you have done, or not done, for that matter. You don't have to be a slave. Imagine a long, winding staircase. When sin has ruled your life, you have taken step after step downward. When you look up, the staircase seems intimidating and impossible to climb, so you might either remain in the same spot, try really hard to climb the stairs on your own, or continue the descent.

When you truly give your *life,* not just your heart, to Jesus, He meets you on the staircase, throws you on His back, and carries you upward. If there is resistance on your part, He will stand there with you, continuously reaching out His hand to help you back up each step. You do not have to muster up your strength to climb these stairs, and you also do not have to worry about how far down you've gone and how far back up you need to go (Philippians 4:6). You just need to focus on the step you are on, the face of Jesus, and eventually you will get to the top of the stairs.

When our sin has consumed us, the untangling is a process. It usually doesn't happen overnight. Just my deliverance alone took more than a year and a half. Almost two whole years of regular sessions of having demons cast out of me. Can you imagine how I felt as I stood on that staircase? It was intense and very lonely at times. But Jesus loved me through it, reminding me that this was part of the untangling and that the freedom I so desperately craved was coming.

I am thankful for all the people the Lord placed in my life during this time. I had so much encouragement as I trudged up each step. Going downhill is easy! Climbing up the stairs felt hard and required a lot of one-on-one time with God. One of my favorite quotes of all time by the famous author J.R.R. Tolkien is, "Little by little, one travels far." I would tell myself this over and over again as I continued to move upward. Praise God for the little things that keep us moving!

In my Christian walk, I have seen so many stuck on that staircase, continue to be slaves to sin, or light up and then burn out. Why? Because they need deliverance and to actually understand their identity! They need a strong community! Their quiet time with the Lord needs to become the most precious focus in their life. Oftentimes, we come to Jesus, get baptized, and then continue trudging through life wearing shackles because it's what we are used to. We can hear the jingling of our chains but pretend it's jewelry—this is a form of pride. We are called higher. Deliverance, your secret place, and community will get you there.

THE TRAUMA IN MY BONES

When I moved back to California, I began working as a server in a restaurant. My PTSD symptoms were so bad that I had to ask all my coworkers not to touch my back or shoulders and always to speak up when approaching me from behind. If not, I would startle easily, have panic attacks, or swing and cover my head as a reflex. Not a good look behind a bar. When I went back to working in the school system, a child came up behind me one afternoon and tickled my neck; this triggered me to swing, thus bumping her behind me. Not hard at all, thankfully, but this was a wake-up call: I needed more help.

PTSD increasingly affected my place of work and my social circles; so naturally, I went back to therapy, this time pursuing a trauma therapist instead. Unfortunately, the next few years of my life grew very cataclysmic again. It was like something had its hand on a dimmer representing my life, and it kept dulling the bright spots until the darkness almost entirely consumed me. Again. This darkness was so familiar, but this time I didn't want it. It wanted me.

More than 18 months into my sobriety and approximately three months into my trauma work, strange memories began to surface. Intrusive images and dreams started occurring more regularly, and they went beyond just the abuse from my ex-boyfriend. As I sat with Marcia, my EMDR trauma therapist, I felt extremely uncomfortable. For me, this form of treatment was necessary before deliverance. It was almost priming my heart to get to the place of real surrender. Marcia and I checked in briefly that morning with small talk as I settled in on the blue linen couch across from her.

"So," she began, "Have you had any significant or recurring images or dreams this week?" She always asked.

"Actually," I started, looking down at my shaking hands, "I had three different images that kept replaying this week." I put my hands under my legs. My entire body began to shake. Not just minor shakes from nerves, but every part of my body convulsed. I could hardly speak. She noticed the shaking but did not react right away.

"Okay. Can you tell me what they were?"

"Um..." my voice was unsteady. "Yeah. One was of a man standing at my bedroom door in a towel." I began shuddering and shaking my head like I was trying to shake the image from my memory. Picture someone shaking beach sand from their hair. "And another was my mom putting baby powder on me, asking me if I had been hurt. And..." I swallowed, my speech noticeably slowing down. "The other was my childhood doctor touching my stomach, and I remember feeling terrified and looking over to my mom." My body began violently shaking as I shared these memories.

"Okay," Marcia said in her calm voice, observing that my physical response was clearly uncontrollable. "Now. Just because you are having these images surface does not necessarily mean something terrible, but I want you to know that what you are experiencing in your body right now is a trauma response. That is why you are shaking, but everything is okay right now," she said peacefully and lovingly.

I looked around the room and then down at my body in panic. That's when the present moment began to close in on me, and everything went black.

"No, no, no!" I muttered, covering my face. "No, no, please, no, no." I was crying helplessly, terrified, and alone. "Please, please, no." I began hitting the back of my neck like I was trying to get something off me, and then my voice trailed off, and I sobbed into my hands, covering my ears and my eyes, barricading my face with my forearms. *Somebody help me!* I yelled inside. It was like I was trapped in the jail of my own rib cage, and I couldn't get out.

I was not in Marcia's chic, modern Laguna Hills office anymore. I was in my childhood bedroom, crouched in a corner by my bed, with my favorite blue blanket over my head. I saw tan legs with dark hair on them inching toward me. "No!" I cried to myself. *I'm alone.* These thoughts circled my mind like razor blades.

I stayed in this memory for about an hour until I could eventually hear Marcia's voice calling me back. I was honestly surprised I wasn't admitted to the psych ward. She sat next to me on the couch, asking me to remove my hands from my face and open my eyes. She didn't make me look at her once I had pulled my hands away. She had me look down and asked me to name colors I could see in the actual room I was in, but I was totally incoherent, saying nothing.

She had essential oils in her hands and offered them to me. Still unresponsive, she put them toward my nose and asked me to smell them. Peppermint. No, lavender. I looked down at my red hands on my lap, then over at the pillow between us. Oftentimes, when people dissociate, they have either mostly or entirely exited the present moment.

This dissociation ranges from moderate to severe. Ice packs, water, things with different temperatures, essential oils, and even pets are all great tools to use when trying to re-enter the present moment. Spiritually, when someone is so accustomed to leaving their body, this allows demonic spirits to have access to the person. Unfortunately, this is not an uncommon response to enduring or recalling traumatic events. I had not experienced a flashback this ferocious before, and I was very confused.

"Jenny?" she said with concern in her voice.

Unresponsive, I kept looking down. Carpet. Tissues. A blue couch.

"Jenny, where are you right now?" Marcia inquired.

Sunlight. Silver glimmers. A glass table. The therapist's office. I wiped my nose. "Here." I finally said quietly.

"Where is *here?*" she asked.

"Therapy." I leaned over to the tissue box and grabbed a couple, dabbing my eyes and blowing my nose.

"Do you know who I am?"

"Marcia," I said.

Marcia worked as best she could to get me entirely back into my body before driving home. She had me count her fingers and do basic math, which I was terrible at even when entirely present. She had me stand up and walk around her office, then out into the hallway and into another room with a big mirror. She had me list aloud what I could see, hear, smell, and touch. She walked me over to a full-length mirror and had me look at myself, reminding me I was 25 years old and in a therapy session. It was like I was looking at myself, but didn't really know myself.

As we circled back into her office, we processed only a little as I remained fairly disoriented.

"What the heck was that? What happened?" I looked down, shaking my head, ashamed of myself. Still a little tearful.

"Well," she started slowly, "This was a pretty severe trauma response to those images you shared. What this tells me is there are some painful memories that you have compartmentalized, and they started to surface this week."

My eyes scanned different objects in the room.

"Where did you go?" she asked, tilting her head in curiosity.

"My room," I said. "It was the man in the towel." I felt sick to my stomach.

She nodded, "Okay. Well, it's good that it is coming out now. This means you are ready and strong enough to move through some of the pain."

"Yeah...," I trailed off. I appreciated people telling me I was strong, but hated it at the same time.

She gave me a glass of water and told me to hydrate the rest of the day. "You will most likely be very tired. Try to rest some." She walked me out of her office door and into the elevator. She came with me to the first floor. On difficult therapy days like this one, she would ride the elevator with me. She really was a great therapist.

I met with Marcia once a week initially and then twice a week as more detailed and disturbing memories bubbled up. I recalled sitting in McDonald's on Kamehameha Highway in Wahiawa, on Oahu in Hawaii, and prayer-journaling about child molesters, interceding on their behalf, begging God to purify them and to give them the help they need. *No one cares about them. Everyone cares about the abused,* I would think to myself.

Fast-forward six months from those journal entries, and here I was recollecting the sexual abuse from six different perpetrators, and a seventh to come. I recalled my intake into residential treatment in Tennessee almost two years prior at that point. I was asked then if I had any significant trauma. "What's trauma?" I asked, staring at the wall behind the woman at the desk.

"You know. Accidents, illnesses, deaths, molestation, rape, abuse," the administrator said.

"I don't think so," I shrugged.

My denial and suppression were *real*. Psychologists and neurologists attribute this memory loss to severe stress and trauma to the individual. I basically had amnesia my entire life until one day, I didn't anymore. The drugs, alcohol, and other addictions I struggled with effectively kept the unwanted memories at bay.

So, there I was, frequenting therapy rooms, getting honest about all of the secrets, and in so much pain. How was I to stay tender? It was like God was preparing my heart beforehand in Hawaii. My sobriety brought me to Jesus, and then Jesus carried me through the years of digging up trauma, which were necessary for my total freedom.

My brain could not take the distress as a child, which is why I had compartmentalized to the degree I did for almost two decades. When friends approached me and shared their stories of molestations, rapes, and assaults growing up, I couldn't help but feel like their assaults had been done to me. I would demand justice and cry for them, not sure why I was the one who was so emotional. I was completely blinded for years, and I was actually crying out for justice for myself, too.

Emotionally dysregulated and distraught most of the time, I continued to press in to Jesus as best I could. Mind you, this was without deliverance or discipleship. I read the Bible, went to church, and prayed as much as I knew how. I sought prayer and healing often. I begged God for my healing, and I continued to pray for the men who had taken advantage of me.

Unfortunately, after becoming so accustomed to being oversexualized much of my life, that was the identity I knew and felt most comfortable with. The magnetic draw back to that version of me was irresistible. The oversexualization had docked for about a year, but I soon fell back into my obsession with control and lust. So, my year of celibacy ended. The resurfacing memories only seemed to catalyze that side of me.

I had danced at a strip competition in Las Vegas, continued to watch porn, and exploited myself on the internet. I regularly attended strip clubs, which I was addicted to, pursued interviews at a few of them, and scouted the internet for sugar daddies. I was constantly putting myself in unsafe and high-risk environments. I was asked to be a nude model for Suicide Girls, but turned it down at the last minute.

Thankfully, there was what I call a "God cushion" present. He kept me from becoming fully lost in the depths of this evil, but I played at its shore. I never showed up for the auditions or pursued those men in person. However, the other aspects of my sex and love addiction were still very present. I was broken.

At precisely two years of sobriety, I broke my celibacy and regretted it tremendously. For the first time in my adult life, I panicked during sex, followed by a severe anxiety attack where I couldn't stop crying, and I could not breathe. I was sober but disoriented. *This reaction is new. What's happening to me?*

From a psychological perspective, I was acting out of my trauma and, as a result, was having amplified trauma responses. From a spiritual perspective, I had repented and walked away from my sin, only to do a full 180-degree reversal straight into the arms of destruction, and therefore, destruction is what multiplied and prospered. The few demons that had left my life as a result of stepping away from certain sins fled back with a vengeance.

> *When an impure spirit comes out of a person, it goes through arid places seeking rest and does not find it. Then it says, "I will return to the house I left." When it arrives, it finds the house unoccupied, swept clean, and put in order. Then it goes and takes with it seven other spirits more wicked than itself, and they go in and live there. And the final condition of that person is worse than the first. That is how it will be with this wicked generation* (Matthew 12:43-45 NIV).

As my therapy continued and I began to verbalize my experiences and not just draw them on paper or dissociate into an alter (remember, this part came with my trauma), I grew more and more angry. I grew angry with those men, with my family, with my current partner, with myself, and especially with God. I grew angry with those who hadn't been through what I had been through, or those who didn't understand, or tried harder to understand. I lived in offense.

I was assaulted again on a modeling job, which caused me to become even more bitter and afraid. My hate for men only grew deeper and thicker roots, while my fear amplified. My boyfriend at the time shared his past with me early on. He had also been molested at a young age, but carried that learned behavior with him and inflicted sexual abuse on two members of his family when he was younger. This enraged me, and I took all the pain and the injustice I felt out on him.

"People like you should just die," I would say to him.

There was so much unforgiveness in my heart. I wanted all men to die. I wanted to make every man pay for every time I was hurt. Even innocent men. I began fantasizing about killing my abusers, pressing charges against them, exploiting them to their friends and family, and vandalizing their property. Homicidal thoughts toward abusers are actually a common experience for most victims. Why? Because a spirit of unforgiveness often leads to spirits of anger and murder. And survivors stay tormented if they do not forgive.

Why me? I always thought. Self-pity was like a hot bath that I soaked in until I was pruned from the inside out. These thoughts sucked the life out of me, and I began isolating and losing weight. I would fall asleep on the floor in the corner of my room by the heater, where it felt safe; and sometimes, I would even crawl under my bed because I felt safer sleeping there. What a sad time in my life this was. My heart aches for people in this type of pain.

The memory recall didn't seem to ever let up, and I stayed in a constant state of trigger. The enemy was wearing me out!

Why couldn't *I* stop it? Why were things getting worse? Why did it feel like I had no control over any of the memories, and why did it seem as if God couldn't hear me, much less change my past or my current state? During that time, direct demonic attacks started happening again. I would wake to total body paralysis and strangling. I could feel an evil presence enter my room regularly. Brandon, my boyfriend at the time, had demonic experiences too.

I peed in my bed for crying out loud! I would beg Jesus for help, only praying in my mind because I could not speak aloud. I felt afraid all the time—afraid to sleep, eat, go to the grocery store, go to work, go to meetings. I was afraid to exist.

My therapist had me paint regularly to try to express the nonverbal emotions I had experienced at the age of three when the first abuses began, when words articulating my feelings were new. Because I assumed I could not access God anymore, and the support around me felt like broken arms were holding me, I went deeply inward. Marcia knew how creative I was and encouraged this aspect of me to flourish as a way to cope. Painting became my saving grace.

A lot of the time, I painted demons unknowingly. The revelation of that only came through deliverance years later when God directly showed me what spirits were possessing me. I could not paint, draw, or sculpt quickly enough during this era of despair in my life. It was like these memories had arranged themselves in an impatient, single-file line in my mind, and they all wanted to be chosen and expressed. I began having art shows and was asked to showcase my art at coffee shops, bars, venues, festivals, and the like. My art was selling like hotcakes, but I was miserable. People bought my pieces and loved them. Something about pain moves the public, and my pain was a deep well that felt like it trenched to the core of the earth.

At this time, I broke up with my current boyfriend and shortly after moved into another relationship. This was my pattern. This time, I found someone much older, much more successful, and beyond sicker than I was at the time. My draw to toxic men was undeniable. I didn't know who I was in Christ. This lack of identity is a common symptom: seeking outside validation from sick people.

I was almost four years sober at this point, and he was in the same recovery community. He had donated once to a dog rescue, which I was collecting for. He had asked me to speak at a meeting he ran in Orange County, which I agreed to, and he didn't seem to take his attention off me for too long.

When I spoke at his meeting, I didn't even recognize him. He approached me, and I assumed he was just another sober guy trying to hit on me—I mean, he was.

He walked up to me timidly, saying, "Hi."

"Um, hi," I said harshly, glancing at him and then looking around the room, not making eye contact.

"I'm Jay."

"Oh, okay, I'm Jenny, hi," I said inattentively.

"I asked you to speak here." He said, brown eyes studying me, his brows raised.

"Oh! Oh my gosh. I'm so sorry, yeah, yeah, hi! I didn't recognize you. I feel like a jerk!"

He smiled and showed me to my seat at the front of the room, where I would share my experience, strength, and hope regarding my addiction and getting sober from it. It was a good meeting. I was proud of myself and my speech. I was hardly affected by Jay and didn't think much about him. Little did I know that eventually this man would be a major stimulant in changing my life, both for the worse as well as for the better.

Even though I had turned my back on the Christian way of living, I still believed in Jesus and preached Him. God was not through with me yet! Isn't God awesome? No matter how much we mess up, He still loves us and wants a relationship with us (Revelation 3:20)! Now *that* is unconditional love!

For months, Jay and I spoke through social media and text. I had a million walls up. Still, he pursued me like he was starving, and I was the only person he knew who had a meal. His constant pursuit of me was like nothing I had experienced yet. Love bombing at its finest. My avoidance of emotional connection was stronger than ever, but that did not deter him in the slightest. In fact, it seemed to attract him to me more.

Boundaries had been crossed from the start. He would reach out regularly, ask me out to brunch, or try to get me to meet him somewhere. Because he was 15 years older than me, I was nervous. We would play around with the idea that he could be my sugar daddy, even sending me money before we first hung out, which I eventually sent back to him. He had never done that before, supposedly, and neither had I.

Both of us were desperate in our own ways. He for love and control, and me for anything that could distract me from my current pain.

Getting sober may help break a drug and alcohol addiction. However, many people who get sober without the freedom of Jesus either relapse or stay stuck in weird relationship patterns, sex and love addictions, eating disorders, gambling or shopping addictions, mental illness, torment from their past, and more.

If you're constantly being reminded of your past, you will remain ineffective in the present. Yes, we must acknowledge our past, but we should not be building a home for it and living there. Clearly, the desire to continue anesthetizing my past was strong. The Bible refers to the devil as *"The accuser of our brethren"* (Revelation 12:10 KJV). The devil always told me, "You will never be free"—and I believed it.

I had always felt defenseless. That was a lie, too. God was my Defender; I just had to move aside and let Him do that, but I wasn't ready yet. I was a slave to my cycles, and so was Jay to his—this was not going to be good.

6

TRAUMA AND THE TORTOISE

After Hawaii, I slowly drifted. The fire I'd felt for Jesus cooled into embers as disappointment, spiritual burnout, and old habits crept back in. Though I still called myself "spiritual," I was mixing truth with lies—chakras, tarot, and Jesus all in one breath. I didn't realize it yet, but I had unknowingly reopened the very doors God had once shut.

In January 2017, a dear friend of mine from Hawaii was tying the knot with her soon-to-be husband in Florida. Amanda was the first and only person I felt safe with when I began volunteering at Surfing the Nations in Wahiawa. She instantly embraced me with love and acceptance in a way that others truly could not at that stage in my life. She was the compass God used to point me in the right direction.

Amanda and Zeke had both been with other partners before meeting each other, but as a result of following Jesus full-on, they had decided to abstain from sex until marriage.

God was first, their bodies second. Their testimonies baffled me. I'm not kidding; it blew my mind to know that two people who were not virgins had decided to save themselves for marriage once they entered into a relationship! To be honest, I didn't really understand it, but I appreciated it, and it strangely inspired and convicted me.

A few years after Amanda and I left Oahu, a "save the date" showed up on my doorstep. Amanda and Zeke were getting married in Florida, and I was invited. I wanted so badly to witness a ceremony like this. Sure, love was great (mind you, I was still a cynic at this time), but what I really wanted to witness were two people with a story like theirs getting married! I admired how God was so important to them. Unfortunately, I didn't have the money to make the trip, so I let Amanda know that I sadly would likely not be attending their wedding.

A short while later, I was organizing at my boss's house when I found a fortune from a fortune cookie crumpled up in a drawer. I picked it up and peeled it open. The fortune read, "You are about to witness a miracle." I texted it to Amanda and said, "Imagine if that miracle was me actually making it to your wedding, lol!" I laughed it off, not overthinking it.

For years I had found fortunes everywhere, and I mean *everywhere*. Before I could truly hear God's voice in my life, I believe this is how He communicated with me and answered my prayers. I did not go buy a tub of fortune cookies, close my eyes, and then stick my hand in the tub whenever I wanted an answer. Instead, I would pray and ask God if I should leave a relationship. A day later, I would get into a friend's car on a sunny day, pull down the visor, and a fortune would drop into my lap with the answer. I found fortunes in pockets, under bus stops, in the grass, in the gutter, on a table.

I had even found one in a bush on the side of the freeway at night, when an abusive ex-boyfriend had kicked out my front windshield and thrown my purse out of the window. When I pulled over to collect what I could of my sprawled items, a fortune sat there, at eye level, in a dried shrub on the side of the freeway telling me to spend more time with friends. God utilized what He could to speak to me, because other than this, I could not hear Him. I knew that this was a way I received messages, so I was hopeful for a miracle—but I wasn't banking on making it to Florida.

Days later I was on the phone with my cable company trying to process a payment of $70. I knew I had $95 in my bank account but wanted to double check before I completed the payment.

"One second," I said to the cable guy on the other end of the phone. "I want to check my bank account before the payment goes through."

"No problem."

I logged into my bank account and saw that I had $2,800 in my account.

"What the heck!" I said out loud, shocked.

"Everything okay?" said the cable tech.

"Yeah, yeah. Oh, my gosh. One second, okay? I'm sorry."

"Sure."

I logged out of my account, then logged back in. There was still $2,800 in my account. I could not believe it. I thought my eyes were deceiving me.

"You can go ahead and process the payment," I said to the tech.

"Alrighty, you're all set."

I hung up the phone and checked my account once more. After further investigation, I discovered the money was a grant from the community college where I was enrolled. I figured they would give me a couple hundred bucks for textbooks since I was not a full-time student, but not this amount! I later learned the school had mistakenly given this amount to eight other students on the campus and could not revoke it. It was an accident for them but a miracle for me.

I texted Amanda and instantly booked my flight to Panama City, Florida. God was again setting something up. People forget the Lord is exciting, and He loves to surprise us and shower us with gifts! This surprise was special for me.

When I arrived in Panama City, I was freezing. Nobody, or maybe it's just me, thinks Florida can get cold, but it most definitely does! I was sick upon arrival but excited to witness a wedding like this one. Amanda and Zeke had a beautiful beach ceremony in the late afternoon, and it was filled with so much love. My little grinch heart grew three sizes that day. When I arrived at the reception venue, it was dark. Warm dinners were served, a dance floor was set up with string lighting, and a few of my peers from STN were in attendance, so I reconnected with them.

Then came the most dreaded yet exciting time of the reception—the infamous bouquet toss. *Women live for this, and probably die for this too,* I thought.

My inner commentary always made me laugh. So many Hollywood wedding scenes amplify this moment for women. I thought it was cute and kind of annoying, but that's about it. Amanda—in all her bridal glory—gathered the women and girls and led them to the dance floor. She turned around, pretending to throw her bouquet as the crowd said, "Aww!" She laughed, turned around, and threw the bouquet to the moon.

Women squealed and jumped up, lifting their arms into the air excitedly. And that's when it happened. Amanda's bouquet landed right on top of my feet. I looked down, then looked up at the crowd, confused, smiling. The three women in front of me pointed at the bouquet and then at me. "It's yours!" they laughed.

I awkwardly picked up the bundle of flowers and raised it into the air, laughing in embarrassment and shock. Everyone was clapping and cheering. Amanda bolted over and hugged me. The man-hater in me wanted to torch the bouquet, but the little girl in me was thrilled. Post wedding, Amanda sent me a handwritten prayer in the mail. It was a prayer for my future husband.

Two months after the boisterous bouquet catch, I caved and let Jay take me out. It had been a few months since I had spoken at his meeting, but our conversational chemistry was undeniable, and so was his insatiable pursuit of me. I agreed to a night out with him if it consisted of going to a 12-step meeting and then dinner with friends. The one-on-one idea terrified me, so this would be a good buffer to start. Looking back, those extreme butterflies weren't just an attraction—it was my nervous system recognizing what I had experienced in my past. It was just a different person this time. My mind ignored what my body could not—danger.

The fire between Jay and I was fierce. We had an electric connection. Honestly, it felt like currents of electricity were surging through my hands when I was with him. After a night of flirting and eating, he drove me back to my place, where I did *not* invite him inside. We sat in the car, conversing about our night. Clearly, we did not want to leave each other. Jay interjected as I began to hint that it was time for me to head inside.

"Wait! Do you wanna do that thing?" he asked.

"Uh, what thing?" I laughed, knowing exactly what he was talking about.

"Soul-gazing, remember?"

Boy, did I. Weeks prior, I sent Jay an article I had found about soul gazing. I was always researching new things on the internet and applying them. I was especially fond of anything that appeared spiritual in the slightest, and soul gazing seemed "spiritual." In short, it is the act of holding eye contact with an individual uninterrupted for four minutes straight or more. The end goal? To build or strengthen intimacy. This is not an uncommon exercise in New Age circles and tantric practices.

Eventually, you can increase the time. The idea is that it gives one the opportunity to be truly seen by another person. A practice that can supposedly be used in counseling and is also commonly used in "tantric sex" practices. Tantric sex is a vast range of practices carried out in Hinduism and Buddhism. Tantra exercises sexuality in a yogic or ritualized context. Something I would strongly advise against.

This was kind of intense for a first date, but it challenged my avoidance, so I was game. I constantly disregarded my internal alarm and often bulldozed through my own boundaries. I called it challenging myself, when in reality I was disregarding my spirit and disrespecting the "little Jenny" that just craved safety.

"Oh yeah. Soul gazing. Sure," I said, tucking my blonde locks behind my ears and then pulling them out again. It was an anxious habit.

I was so nervous and didn't want to do it, but I couldn't talk all this talk and then pansy out. So, there I was, in a car, with a new man, and about to become totally vulnerable for four minutes straight. What had I gotten myself into?

"Okay, let's time it?" he asked.

"Yeah, four minutes."

We sat in his car, our bodies mirroring one another, eyes locked. The intensity permeated the atmosphere. His dark brown eyes melted into my crystal blue ones. We didn't touch, but we wanted to. Our hearts were racing, and our eyes focused intently on one and then switched to the other while background music played.

After the timer went off, we talked about what we felt or saw in the other person while doing this. I could see part of Jay that felt lonely, desperate for real love, and not right or trustworthy, but I kept this to myself. Truthfully, we could have sat there for hours, but I gathered my things and reached for the car door.

"Well, thanks for the food," I said.

"Of course. When can I see you again?" He spoke softly as he smiled.

"Ummm," I laughed, "soon."

He didn't say anything. I opened the car door and then turned back around to face him.

"Are you gonna kiss me or what?"

"I want to; I just didn't want to be too forward," he said timidly.

"Then?" I challenged.

He leaned over to me, wrapping his hands around my neck, and we kissed our first kiss.

Fireworks. Seriously.

I went inside and immediately called my best friend to tell her all about it. "I'm pretty sure I just kissed my husband, dude," I told her, laughing. We talked on the phone like giddy girls for an hour, and I fell asleep content, excited, and in the throes of dangerously falling in love.

The following two months were mostly bliss. Within the first two weeks, Jay expressed his love for me on multiple occasions, which I bashfully evaded. Eventually, I told him I loved him too, and just like that, we were in a relationship. We soul-gazed every time we were together, building up to more than 30 minutes with uninterrupted eye contact. Looking back, I believe there was some sort of demonic influence happening. On one occasion, we both felt something supernatural happen; still, we liked it.

We couldn't get enough of each other. Most of my relationships moved quickly, but Jay and I were on the expedited fast track. There was no slowing down. Two months into our relationship, he moved into my condo. Our infatuation with one another was obviously unhealthy, but we didn't care. All we could see was the other person. We spent all our time together, texted each other whenever we weren't together, and he love-bombed me all the time by showering me regularly with flowers, cards, nice dinners, and gifts. He was obsessed with me.

Jay was willing to do and be anything for me, which I liked. His manufactured tenderness, though, triggered something else in me, and I began pushing him away, becoming closed off and even emotionally abusive toward him early on. In the same breath, I can also say that when someone is relentlessly pushing against a person's boundaries, especially a person who has been traumatized and has had their boundaries violated repeatedly, the pullback makes sense. Despite the psychology, toxicity was "my normal" then, and it was his too.

Clearly, my relationship with Jesus had dwindled significantly at this point. I would even go as far as to say that it did not exist anymore. Although I was and appeared very "spiritual," it was a worldly spirituality. It is sad that after such a profound encounter with Jesus in Hawaii I would turn away from Him or let other things take God's place in my life. My relationship with Jay was more tangible, so I pursued that. This is the power of sin and idolatry. Some may argue that this was just love, right? Wrong. True godly love will never pull you away from the Creator or push you into sin, and after all I had been through, I was still very weak in this area and my true default was to be detached and disconnected, although most of the world experienced me as lively, connected, and fun.

Three months into our relationship, we had our initial blowout. This, sadly, would be only the first of many physical altercations for years to come. My fear of true connection and his deep-seeded fear of abandonment and the need for control regularly triggered us both. I would run, he would chase, I would fight, he wouldn't let go, I would leave, he would beg me to stay—and the cycle repeated. It became more and more violent and equally retaliatory.

We both destroyed personal property, smashing objects and ruining clothing. We dumped out drawers, targeting anything of the other person's and went through each other's belongings. If I got into my car to get away from him, he would chase me on the freeway until my gas ran out or I pulled over. We would wrestle to the floor, and he would wrap his hands around my arms or neck, leaving bruises on my body.

His all-consuming need to prevent me from leaving would instantly activate my fight or flight response. I felt trapped. My cognitive mind would shut down, and survival instinct would light up. The abuse was horrible. Everything was a mess. Nothing was safe. There was so much dishonesty. We were constantly in fight or flight mode when we were together, but neither of us would leave. The physical chemistry kept us both addicted, and our mutual desire to get back to where we started (when we were in the throes of infatuation) kept us both in the relationship.

I didn't figure it out for years, but I was immersed in severe narcissistic abuse. Control on both ends was dangerous. Things felt sinister. We were welded to the merry-go-round of toxicity and were no strangers to the perpetual heartbreak that thrives in an abusive relationship. I became excessively cold and detached while Jay, although violent at times, tried to be tender. It was so confusing to be abused then showered with love and gifts.

I know now these were the building blocks of a trauma bond. The majority of abusers are not all bad, but will in fact have periods of what appears to be kindness, tenderness, and thoughtfulness. This creates cognitive dissonance in the victim, ultimately confusing them. Trauma bonds create a chemical reaction in the brain, leading to dependency in the relationship. Similar to substance addiction. Many people have actually used this term incorrectly, a trauma bond is *not* "bonding over trauma." It took years for me to recognize this in my own life. This level of manipulation was subtle and hardly detectable for me.

I was afraid yet addicted. Where was God? Can God be in situations like this? The short answer is: He was there, and yes, He can be. But the reality was we had so many open doors regarding our habitual and willful sin. Of course, being in trauma therapy during this time was questionable. Being in an abusive relationship while working through childhood abuse is as backward as it gets; then again, it was familiar.

Marcia, my therapist, had officially diagnosed me with C-PTSD and DID. She could identify three distinct "alters" or personalities in me (see Chapter 2) and questioned if there was a fourth. Jay knew about this diagnosis but did not understand it in the slightest. Him learning about my diagnosis sadly became a weapon he used against me.

The blackouts from the alter changes only added more dysfunction to our relationship. Although hypersexual, I would get triggered regularly during sexual contact with Jay, thinking he was an abuser and I was getting raped.

I would go into my "three-year-old alter" then cry and shake. When this started happening, of course, Jay was worried, and caught off guard. Eventually, he would become good at looking for the red flags during moments of intimacy and did his best to bring "Jenny" back. It was twisted. Then his sexual perversions entered our sex life, which was even more of a trigger.

Our relationship was sick, but Jay did his best to support me during these episodes. He helped, but I couldn't rely on him like I wanted to. He did the best he could to help me come back into my body after a dissociation. He would put ice cubes in my hands, put my cat on my lap, or put me in the shower. However, at the same time, he would also abuse me, which triggered the alter—*this* was my life with demons and it was awful.

Often in abusive relationships where trauma bonds have formed, the abuser will do anything to make their victim of choice dependent on them. Emotionally, financially, physically etc. The abuser will hurt the victim and then the victim will run back to the abuser for help. Once this becomes a regular occurrence, the abuser has been successful in creating a trauma-bond.

The trauma responses became so frequent that my therapist began to encourage me to seek inpatient treatment. I had come so far in my recovery, I thought, *How could this be my reality?* But Matthew 12:43-45 explains this. I was in the darkest pit of my life, and *again*, death came knocking at my door—this time with much more allure. Death seduced me and promised me that dying was the best and only solution, and I believed it. It promised me peace. It promised me silence. It promised me freedom. Death was promising me a "new life," and I was desperate for freedom, no matter what it looked like.

I believe in Jesus, so if I kill myself, I'll go to Heaven, right?

I began planning for my death date with fervor. I had not been this committed before. There was a suicide fantasy I kept close. I had first fantasized about this form of suicide when I was 15 and glamorized it in my mind, convincing myself that dying in this way was beautiful, artistic, and acceptable. (I will not share it in this book.) I started to get my affairs in order. I handwrote a suicide letter and typed one up as well. I was already fairly isolated but distanced myself even further from loved ones. I had a plan, the only thing that seemed to offer me any hope. I had twice attempted suicide, but this—this was going to be "the one."

I just want to say that our pain points and weaknesses are no secret to the enemy. He will move in and set up camp in our spirit's darkest, laziest, and most broken places. I did not have the spiritual knowledge at this time to figure out what was really going on. The demonic had legal ground in my life, and they continued to advance.

Although I tried praying and reading my Bible, no one had introduced me to deliverance or true repentance. Therefore, I remained alone and stuck. Still, I believed Jesus was real; He just felt very far away from me. Two days before we were to celebrate my four years of sobriety, I attempted suicide. I did not adhere to my original plan at all, which wasn't supposed to be enacted until later, but I was in so much pain that afternoon that I crawled into the darkest place of my soul.

I pulled into my garage, closed the patio and garage doors, and left my vehicle running. I had an older model car that emitted massive amounts of carbon monoxide. I researched this. My goal was to poison myself to death and die peacefully. Prior to the attempt, I texted two people: Jay and my dear friend Maura.

While in my car, I took massive gulps of air but remained mostly catatonic. I was frozen. My hands were glued to my lap and my eyes stayed fixated on the lights of my car. In that moment in time, I felt like something had taken over my body, and it definitely had. I didn't have a choice. I recall hearing myself internally say, *I don't really want to die*, and that's when Maura's name lit up my phone screen.

Pick up the phone, Jenny, I tried to tell myself. *Just swipe, that's all you have to do. Just swipe.* I was fully frozen. Did I really want to go through with this? If I killed myself here, my dad would be the one to find me. Did I really want that?

The internal lights of my car glowed and dimmed. I robotically moved my hand over to my phone and swiped. I couldn't even say hello and remained in a state of unresponsiveness. Still, tears filled my eyes and poured over my lower eyelids. *I am so sad*, I thought to myself. The million pieces of my heart had broken into a million more—if you have been in this level of pain, you know exactly what I am talking about.

"Jenny? Hello? Are you there?" Maura's voice sounded panicked. She knew how much I had been struggling during the last year and had just received my alarming text message. "I'm here for you. Are you okay?" she asked.

I couldn't say a word, but I could cry. Maura heard that.

"Jenny, I need you to tell me where you are. What can you see around you?" She had worked in trauma for years and was familiar with the severity of my dissociation.

I cried and finally got out the words, "I can't move."

"Can you tell me what you see around you? Did you take anything? Are you on drugs?"

The lights inside my car continued to flicker, and it sounded like my car was dying. For a while, I had trouble with this car, but at that moment, it felt like something was supernaturally working against my attempt. I moved my eyes over to the closed door that led to my back patio, a small sheet of light creeping in at the bottom of the door. My eyes gradually moved over to the left of me, and I could see my dad's work trailer that he kept in my garage.

"Jenny?" Maura's voice penetrated. "Jenny, where are you?"

"My car," I finally said.

"What can you see?"

Silence.

"Jenny!"

"My dad's trailer."

She was familiar with my home and knew exactly where I was.

"Is your car on?" she asked.

I began to cry even more while Maura walked me through turning my car off and getting me out of the garage. She picked me up that night and took me to a meeting, where I remained dissociated for the majority of it. It was what she knew to do to help.

When Jay learned of the attempt, he responded out of total fear, lack of understanding, and lack of control of the situation by angrily convincing my family that I needed to be admitted to the psych unit at a nearby hospital and that it needed to happen as soon as possible. He did not approach my attempt with love and gentleness but instead with anger. Verbal bullets of shame from him tore through my heart. He thought I was crazy. This was the same reaction I had experienced from my family before when I was suicidal at 17. More rejection, more anger, and even more disappointment. These feelings were hard to bear.

Long periods of time in these types of feelings are dangerous for many reasons. I understand that now; I did not understand it then. Jay and I were not well-versed in healthy reactions, obviously. My family knew I had been struggling but they weren't aware of the gravity of my situation until that evening. That is usually how it went. I refused to go to the hospital, but two days later I willingly boarded a plane to Ocklawaha, Florida, where I would spend a minimum of 30 days in a residential treatment center for trauma. This choice was another level of surrendering.

Both my parents and Jay drove me to LAX. My dad was mostly quiet, and somewhat mad, I thought. Jay made jokes along the way and my mom was more gentle than usual. As I entered the airport I began to panic. I didn't want to go. It felt like the first day of second grade all over again when I went to a new school and cried the moment I set foot into the classroom.

I hated airports. I hated sleeping in a bed that wasn't mine and a large part of me didn't want to be in a place where I wouldn't be able to escape the pain of facing my trauma every single day. I had to face it. I hugged my dad and Jay and looked over at my mom, tears in her eyes. She knew how scared I was, and she was scared too. From what I could recall, we hadn't had many times of genuine closeness or vulnerability, but this was one of them.

In Florida, I was picked up from the airport early that morning by a gay woman who shared her story of trauma and recovery with me. She was easygoing and made the transition less anxiety-provoking. She had been through the center I was being taken to and encouraged me that it would be a nurturing and comforting place for me. The LGBT community always made me feel so comfortable. I think it's because most of them have been through so much rejection that I felt accepted and seen by the majority of them. The common thread of rejection bonded us. It's a shame that some of the Church today continues to reject them instead of letting God be the ultimate lifestyle changer.

When I arrived on site, I did my intake and was sent to the medical building. For three days, I hardly slept and refused to be admitted into a cabin. I was terrified of cabins because I experienced both abuse and my first face-to-face demonic encounter in a cabin during my childhood years. There was no way I would stay in one alone, so the clinical team allowed me to stay in the medical building for the first few days until they found me a roommate.

I didn't want to talk to the other patients or make friends. I didn't want to eat in the lunchroom or walk around the beautiful property; I wanted to sit in the uncomfortable medical bed and hide. I could not afford to stay more than a month at this facility, so I had to make the most of it. My family had taken out a loan and had committed to making payments so I could get the help I needed, and that was even with a partial scholarship. I had no idea my family did this for me until years later—to think I wasn't loved by them was preposterous. I just wasn't loved the way I wanted.

During my time at The Refuge, I started to open up, share in groups, and sit with other people at lunch. My therapists were very sympathetic, and I soon felt a sense of belonging and safety with the patients who shared their traumatic experiences during process groups. Three days out of the week were focused on intensive trauma work where we would sit in group for six hours each day and move through our traumas.

In addition to one-on-ones with a therapist, there were many process groups; though it seemed like we were paired with others who had similar stories. I had felt seen before in the psych unit, 12-step programs at times, as well as for a time in Hawaii, but the level of vulnerability that was encouraged at The Refuge allowed me to express a depth I never had before. Knowing that others had experienced what I had brought me the most relief. I had felt alone my entire life, but there I was not alone at all.

One afternoon I stormed into therapy enraged after a phone call with Jay. He had admitted to watching porn after lying about it, which highly triggered the lack of safety I already felt in our relationship. There were so many lies all the time I couldn't handle it. He had struggled with porn addiction for a long time but didn't want to actually do anything about it. My anger felt bigger than the therapist's office that day, and I could not sit still.

"Why don't we go hit the tires, huh?" Leslie, my therapist, said to me.

"The what?"

"The tires." She stood up, walked over to her desk, and pulled an aluminum bat from behind it.

"Your anger is too big for this room," she said, "follow me."

The Refuge is a massive campus located within a natural reserve. There are beautiful trees and a ton of wildlife. There are long, winding, and paved roads that stretch from cabin to cabin, all doused in every shade of green you can imagine. It was quiet and humid. I loved being outside there. As we walked down one of the roads, we began to cut across the grass, making our way over to what looked like an actual pillar of black tires.

"See those?" she pointed over to the pillar.

"Yeah?"

"Well, when our clients have a lot of feelings that they need to physically move through, sometimes we take them to the pillar where they hit the tires with a bat until that energy has moved out of their body. We don't want that trauma to stay trapped."

At the tower of tires, Leslie handed the bat to me, smiling.

"I want you to take a deep breath, hit the tires as many times as you want, and then scream as loud as you can for as long as you can."

I looked at her. I was willing to hit but not scream, so I hesitated.

"I'll scream with you the first time, okay?"

I wiped each of my palms off on my pants, wrapped my hands around the bat's padded handle, took a deep breath, and began swinging as hard as I could against those tires. Dink, dink, dink. The sound of metal hitting metal was muffled but echoed outward, still. The tires were placed on the outside of a pole. If you hit them hard enough, you would hit the pole on the inside and make a sound. Dink, dink, dink. A group of clients down the way looked over and cheered. I stopped and looked at Leslie.

"Deep breath, then scream," she said.

We counted to three and then screamed as loud and long as we could. I took a few more breaths and then picked up the bat again, this time with tears in my eyes and even more anger than before.

"It's deeper than the issue with Jay. This is about betrayal, Jenny," Leslie said.

I began to swing harder, clearly winded and losing momentum. I stopped and screamed for as long as I could and then I began to fold and cry. The heaviness in my stomach evolved into a lump in my throat, which eventually poured out of my mouth like a whimper. That deep well of pain began to move up and out of me like a geyser. And just then, a huge tortoise appeared out of nowhere and walked right between Leslie and me. I dropped the bat.

"Oh, my God," I cried, looking at the tortoise, tears melting off my face like hot wax. Then through my tears, I told Leslie about my baptism in Molokai, when the small crab approached me, and the Lord told me that I was an infant spiritually but that I would grow. I told her that I was vegan and had a huge heart for animals. I told her I felt God used them to demonstrate the different stages I was in my life.

"Last time it was a crab, and it was this small." I demonstrated the size of the crab with my fingers. "And now, here I am facing the pain of my past and my fears and another shelled creature shows up. It's like God is saying, 'Here you are! You have grown,'" I sobbed.

Leslie had tears in her eyes, "You're going to make me cry," she said. "In all my time working at The Refuge, I have seen so much wildlife, but I have never once seen a tortoise here." She shook her head in disbelief. "Just wait until God shows you an animal that is no longer shelled, Jenny." Her words encouraged me, and I clung to them.

I cried and processed through the pain of perpetual betrayal in my life, while also saturating myself in thankfulness for this experience with Leslie. In suffering and in rejoicing, God always seemed to be right on time.

7

THE LORD WEPT WITH MY DAD THAT DAY

When I returned home from Florida, Jay and I took a road trip to visit his family, who lived in Oregon. I knew I needed more time at The Refuge, but unfortunately, funds and insurance keep you there, and I had neither after 28 days. I was thankful for my time there. A feeling of *finally* being seen was common among most clients, and I will never forget the inclusivity and acceptance I felt because of that.

Trauma is a strange thing. It takes you through a tunnel of many different emotions: shame, guilt, rejection, loneliness, despair, disconnection, discouragement, resentment, anger, fear, and the list continues. To get to a place of acceptance of my past while also being genuinely accepted by others who understood and related to the Rubik's cube of the complex emotions of trauma was truly a gift from God. I believe the Lord allowed me to walk through this so I could deeply understand it before He radically healed me.

People go their entire lives craving a sense of belonging. We most desperately need a union with God, but most of us don't even know or understand that until we fully pursue Him. We all long to be reconciled to our Creator, our Father in Heaven, whom our souls knew before He sent us to earth for a mission. Once we realize our true identity in Jesus, a sense of belonging becomes natural. However, for many, it can be a long road. Fortunately, there is no condemnation for that. In my case, it wasn't about how long it took me to get there—it was that I got there.

All that to say, I was still grateful to have had a month in Florida where I did feel a sense of belonging among the other patients. Although bummed to leave after just four weeks, I was excited to see Jay again. We were electrified to see one another and spend time together, but unfortunately our usual cycle of abuse picked up where it left off on our trip. I did not expose the abuse in our relationship while I was at the trauma center. I didn't want to believe I was in another abusive relationship, so I just pretended I wasn't. Denial was a long-term survival pattern of mine—I swear I could write a book on that alone.

We returned home to California two weeks later and would once again make an effort to push down all of our trauma and pretend it wasn't there. A therapist at The Refuge stopped me once when I was walking by a pond of water with a ball nearby.

"You see that ball?" he randomly asked me.

"Yeah?" My eyes squinted against the sun to look over at it.

"That is your trauma."

I was listening.

"If you push that ball underneath the water for long enough, what happens?"

"Um, it comes up?" I laughed.

"Right. You can push a beach ball beneath the water's surface and manipulate it under the water for a time, but then it pops up, and you have no idea what direction it will go."

"Totally," I said.

"When we push down or bottle up our traumas, they will eventually come out, though we can't always predict the direction."

"Wow, that's a really good analogy." I looked over at the ball at the water's edge and pondered. That example spoke to the poet *and* the traumatized parts of me.

Trauma is that way. It can manifest in so many forms when not dealt with. Sometimes, it may be addictions, self-harm, or eating disorders, while for others, it may be angry outbursts, control, OCD, and similar behaviors. It can also be fear and regular bouts of crying, perfectionism or working harder than others to prove their worth. It is a shame that we do this as humans.

It saddens my heart that I spent so many years holding the beach ball under the water just to retrieve it and shove it under the water again and again. What saddens me even more is that I have witnessed people in my life who have done the same thing. I wish people could just watch somebody else struggle and decide not to do the same thing, but most have to experience it on their own before real change comes. Some people cannot see the beach ball, and others *choose* not to see it.

Some refuse to admit to the pain caused by the events in their life, or they just accept how things are and will be. It's true; this is the way things are for many. But it doesn't have to stay that way.

Jesus endured pain, too. He endured heartache and sorrow and betrayal and trauma. He had moments of desperation when He prayed to God the Father and asked Him, "Is there any other way?" He knew that dying on the Cross was a prophecy He was destined to fulfill, but it did not deny the human in Him who felt gut-wrenching agony:

> *And he* [Jesus] *went forward a little, fell on the ground, and prayed that, if it were possible, the hour might pass from him. And he said, "Abba, Father, all things are possible unto thee; take away this cup from me: nevertheless, not what I will, but what thou wilt"* (Mark 14:35-36 KJV).

The Bible even says Jesus was in such emotional turmoil that He sweated blood in the Garden of Gethsemane the night before going to the Cross:

And being in agony, He prayed more earnestly. Then His sweat became like great drops of blood falling down to the ground (Luke 22:44 NKJV).

Jesus knew everything that was going to happen, He knew His future; and even with all His knowledge, He still had sorrow and hoped for an alternative solution. He also stayed in God's will despite it all. Can you imagine? So many people only see the God side of Jesus. But Jesus was 100 percent God and 100 percent human. Meaning, He felt emotional, mental, and physical pain like you and me—but it didn't cause Him to sin. Although He was fully without sin, He was not without feeling, and His life was not easy in the slightest.

Jesus was led by His Spirit and the Holy Spirit, not His emotions. When He went to the Cross, He knew what He was doing. He knew one of His closest friends would betray Him and He would endure great torment. So many people wonder: *Why did God do this to His Son? What kind of God is that?*

Well, He did it for love. Keep reading.

CURSED IS EVERY MAN WHO HANGS ON A TREE

Christ hath redeemed us from the curse of the law, being made a curse for us: for it is written, Cursed is everyone that hangeth on a tree (Galatians 3:13 KJV).

Jesus took upon himself all the curses of the world, so we didn't have to. Before deliverance and through my time in the witchcraft world, I had multiple curses put on me. When I came to Jesus and spent hours upon hours being exorcized from demons, you know what broke those curses off my life? Jesus Christ—His blood, His name. Demons connected to those curses left my body when I acknowledged His work on the Cross and claimed His blood against all curses set against me.

Jesus did not die on the Cross just so we can continue doing whatever we want and remain suffering, although many do. He died on the Cross as a sacrifice. And He leaves it up to us if we want to embrace that sacrifice and be set free, or ignore it and pretend "It's just for those people." God sent His Son so that when He died and rose from the dead, His Spirit (the Holy Spirit) would be released to dwell in all believers.

Jesus died so we could be reconciled to our father in Heaven, have eternal life, and so much more!

Despite this wonderful Good News, many still reject God—and, sadly, rejecting God leads to hell. Hell is a choice. Following Jesus is also a choice.

God does not send people to hell; He allows them to make their own choices, giving each person total free will. Each individual makes their own choice between spending eternity in Heaven or hell. On earth, we can experience both God and satan. I'm sure everyone can look at their life and see bits of good and evil in themselves. In Heaven, there is no evil, no wickedness, no trauma, no disease, no mental illness, no pain, no fear, etc.

In hell, however, there are the highest levels of these tragedies and even more unthinkable and awful experiences.

On earth, we seem to live out both good and evil. God gives us many chances in this life to accept Him. If people want to reject Him their entire lives, they receive hell, which is giving people what they want—total separation from God. The ultimate rejection of Him equals no relationship with Him. God will not force anyone into reconciliation with Him. At the root of this disinterest, anger, or doubt is pride. It says, "I know best," and pride in any form is never good.

God doesn't want to control you, ever. His heart cries out for every soul. The most controlling person I have ever experienced was the least loving person I knew. God differs from people like that because He is love (1 John 4:8). If someone loves you deeply and truly, that person will not try to control you. If people could grasp the revelation of who God really is, much of their pain and desperation for other things would dissipate. They would understand that God wants to protect and love them, never to control them.

And, God longs to heal His children. If a mother sees her child running out into a street full of cars, she will run after that child and stop him, sometimes even yelling or grabbing the child ferociously. The child may even cry or fight back. Is this control? No! It is love! She sees something the child does not. She wants to shield the child from danger and death. It is the radical love of a parent.

This is like God. He doesn't set up rules that we must abide by, or else. He sets guardrails in place for our protection from ourselves and the enemy of our souls. Everything in the Bible and everything God does is always, always, always out of love.

If you have been ill your entire life, and one day someone gave you a pill that could instantly make you healthy, wouldn't you take it? When you immediately recovered, wouldn't you want to tell everyone who was sick to take it? Because you were ill for so long, wouldn't people notice that now you are completely healthy?

You would tell everyone you know because you have been set free from your lifelong affliction and want the same for others! That is why I cannot stop telling people about Jesus. It's not because I'm some religious weirdo or because I get a gold star on a chart each time. It's because I was in such desolation; only Jesus could set me free! It wasn't my ideas, feelings, and hard work that changed me. He did that—the only thing is, I was desperate and willing.

My circumstances were shifting—not exactly in the way I would have ordained them, but they were nonetheless. As Jay and I returned home after our road trip, I was reunited with my dad who regularly stayed with us at our condo in Costa Mesa a few days out of the week for his work. I enjoyed my time with him, more so when Jay wasn't there. It was special when it was just me and my dad.

My father is an incredible artist and builder. He is detailed in all he does. He worked as a landscaper as his main job when I was growing up, and his hands were calloused from decades of manual labor. His skin was red and leathered from days, weeks, and years under the sun and his eyes were like glaciers, an ice cap of blue. If I looked into his eyes long enough, I could see a deep sadness below the surface. At the same time, he seemed to have a strong passion for justice. I can see his tender heart within those glaciers.

I noticed these things as a child. Although my dad has experienced many heartaches in his life, he loves to laugh. He really knows how to get a crowd going and make people enjoy themselves. He is the neighbor who always has his garage door open with people always stopping by. Like all of us, he is multifaceted and his humor is a gift. Growing up, people were always at our house or just stopping by to "Say hi to Steve."

He liked his alcohol, so people who liked to drink would stop by for a drink and some laughs. Sometimes his drinking was fine; other times it was very hard on our family growing up. There were times in my younger years when my mother would be at school and I would find him passed out on the couch with all the doors and windows open and every TV and stereo on.

At eight years old I could not comprehend the severity of his drinking; I just knew that when my mom wasn't around, he liked to drink more, and when he liked to drink more, he was typically more upset. He would have outbursts or shut down. Often I would stand at the end of the hallway and call for him.

"Papa? Papa!" I would yell, holding my dog's collar in my hand to walk with me down the long hall.

Sometimes after finding him asleep, I thought he was dead. Eventually, I learned that the drink made him sleepy and that he would wake up at some point. Sometimes, I would even try to put him to bed. I loved him very much, and still do. As a young girl, I felt like his heart was so fragile. I believe children can see things that adults cannot or choose not to see. Regardless, kids still feel it. I remember holding his face in my little hands as he drunkenly cried into them after an altercation with my mom—I was only three.

As a little girl, I so desperately wanted his pain to go away. Though, his hardships did not get in the way of my love for him. As I got older, this changed, and my mother and I grew resentful about his inability to look at himself. At age 13, I called a family meeting to try and get him into rehab, a desperate effort for a child. My attempt failed. His happiness was not contingent on what I did or didn't do, but I didn't know that at the time. He was my dad and I just wanted him to get better and I wanted our family to be happy.

Early on, I wanted to see others healed, happy, and free. Being born into my family and facing the adversity I have is no mistake. It has given me a huge heart for healing and loving people. Many parts of this book have been painful to write; however, I believe the Lord has continued to cheer me on through this writing because it may become someone else's survival guide and hopefully turn them back to Jesus or introduce God's love to someone for the first time.

God does not create our dysfunction, but He certainly can use it.

I also want to share that I am writing this from a healed place. I do not have any resentment or unforgiveness toward my father, and I honor who he is and his walk in life. He is an incredible person. Sharing this is not to expose my difficulty, but my heart and the heart of children who are much more aware than we may think.

Children want healed parents. They want their mother and father to be happy, just like a parent wants their child to be happy and healed. Kids have so much innate faith in their parents, which I think is why Jesus uses them as an example when He tells us to have "childlike faith." Children typically do not worry about rent or food because they trust their parents will keep a house for them and get them food. They just trust them.

When you sit on a chair, do you check it every time you sit on it? Probably not. You trust that it is going to do its job and support you. Why can't we give God the same trust and childlike faith? It is one of our biggest challenges as humans. I know that most of us are all doing our best. And if we aren't, we usually know it.

When I returned home from my road trip with Jay after treatment, my father sat me down and shared something rather heavy with me. During the two weeks Jay and I spent in Oregon, my dad reached out to my childhood abuser, someone we knew who I have chosen to call Barry in this book. I did not share who had abused me until two weeks into The Refuge through a phone call with my Florida therapist. She phoned my therapist's office in California, where my parents were, because I needed support in that conversation, as did my family. My dad was in shock upon hearing who abused me as a child. He let it sit for a few weeks, and then he acted.

After the road trip, my dad told me he had met Barry at a nearby restaurant and told him he had learned about the abuse I endured growing up. Despite Barry's denial, my dad believed me, defended me, and told him never to contact me or my family again, which, to this day, he has not. Doing this was bold and painful for him. I believe that God has recorded my father's incredibly hard and noble act in His Book of Life to honor him later.

The years of abuse were not just a betrayal for me but also a deep betrayal for my father and mother. My 57-year-old dad went into that restaurant restroom and cried after their confrontation. When he came out, Barry was gone, and my dad mourned the lost childhood of his daughter and his newly discovered deceitful friendship of many years. He went to a nearby church, sat there for a while, and wept. I know the Lord wept with my dad that day.

I cannot write this or even reread it without tears in my eyes. Not for myself but for lost and broken-hearted people.

Betrayal in any form is devastating. If you are reading this and that is you, I just want you to know the Lord loves you so much. He loves you through your brokenness, chaos, weariness, sickness, trauma, lies, and weaknesses. The Lord does not look at you and see what you see; He sees the truth, beauty, and redemption.

You are highly favored by God. He loves you, me, my dad, and my abusers, with more resilience and passion than you could ever imagine or get here on earth from a person. You cannot "work" for His love. Despite our iniquities, His love remains steadfast regardless of what we do or don't do. Did you know that? His word says:

> *For I am sure that neither death nor life, nor angels nor rulers, nor things present nor things to come, nor powers, nor height nor depth, nor anything else in all creation, will be able to separate us from the love of God in Christ Jesus our Lord* (Romans 8:38-39 ESV).

You, dear reader, are so loved. I know many survivors of abuse rarely have someone who believes them and someone who also faces their abuser on their behalf. Having my dad take this action was indeed very special for me. However, this did not make the feelings surrounding my abuse any less complicated than it was or any less painful. Although proud of my dad, I still felt like I was treading water in a lake of heartache with bricks tied to my ankles. I was sad for myself and my father.

About a week later, I went to a meeting to try and get some relief from the heaviness of my situation. The betrayal of sexual abuse often affects more than just the victim. That night, Jay asked if he could pray for me. This wasn't a common theme in our relationship, so it meant a lot.

We sat across from one another at the dining table. He reached his hands out to hold mine and asked God to give me the peace I so desperately desired and the strength to move on. I stopped him mid-prayer. My voice cracked, and I could only get out, "I just want my dad." A lump swelled in my throat. My dad happened to be at our condo that night, so I ran upstairs and knocked on his door.

"Pop?"

He awakened and sat up in bed.

"I just want to hug you," I managed to say before I collapsed into his arms in tears. At that moment, I needed my dad more than anything in this world.

We held each other and cried, trying to hold back the tears and failing tremendously. We hardly spoke a word. The pain was so deep for each of us, but the light and love of the moment was undeniable. Light is not always something you can see, but light is always something you can feel. And that night, the light of God was an embrace for the both of us.

8

THE CHAPTER I DON'T LIKE

I continued to work through the damage of my past, pursuing another 12-step program that helped me focus on boundaries and my behaviors connected to love and sex addiction. My identity was not yet in Christ, but these programs offered me community support. I had Jay move out of the condo, and after significant pushing, he eventually pursued his trauma work and recovery, but it didn't last.

Sadly, much of my encouragement led him to do things that weren't authentic but manipulative. It wasn't personal; it was just how he was, which took me a long time to figure out. Many people want healing without the work and pain it often takes to get to a healed place. I understand. Many just want to be liked, so they do what they have to for approval, but if it isn't an authentic desire to change, the person doesn't change. You can only heal to the degree that you can be honest with yourself and others.

Our relationship was complex. Unfortunately, with both of us being constantly activated by the other's pains and defects, the cycle of abuse, and a massive lack of focus on the Lord, our relationship came to a slow and painful end. Our habits were too embedded in both of us. I could not stop allowing his behavior, and he took full advantage of that.

Even though I had changed and stopped my abusive behavior, he could not. I even remember our therapist congratulating me on my ability to adapt to the abuse. I had stopped physically fighting back and began to turn limp during fights. This limp effect seemed to slow down the abuse. I wasn't fighting or running; I just started taking it. This response is known as the fawn effect, which is a main symptom of battered women syndrome and one of the four responses to abuse. Fight, flight, freeze, or fawn.

We had traveled overseas for his work, and I believe this trip snapped the remaining thread that held us together. While in the UK, I spent a day alone in Birmingham. It was a mostly gray day, reflecting my inner world, but a little sun broke through the clouds as I walked out of the cathedral where I had just attended a 12-step meeting. Isn't that just like God? A beam of light in our darkness. God's a poet for sure.

The cobblestone roads circled the area, and vendors were out on the streets selling food and goods. Though it looked like a lovely day it was painful for me. There seemed to have been many of those, though, hadn't there? A group of people was in the road with chairs just outside the church's main doors.

Walk over to them, I heard in my heart, so I did.

"Hi, what are you guys doing?" I inquired.

"Oh, we are out here offering prayer. Do you need prayer?" a woman with dark hair asked me.

"Yes. I need so much of it," my heart sank.

"Come take a seat," she said.

I walked over to the plastic folding chair where two women and one man stood. They asked if they could place their hands on my shoulders.

"Anything specific we can pray for you?"

"Yes," I replied and went on to tell them all about my abusive relationship, how horrible this trip was, and how abandoned I felt being here in a foreign country. I shared in detail about our love, how conflicted I was, how Jay's heart was full of greed, and how his coworkers were the same way. It was like I was with a band of narcissists, and I was the only empath (someone with an empathetic personality). I felt like the odd man out; because I *was* the odd man out. I rarely ever felt like that because I've always had such an easy time getting along with people. I was likable, and I loved people.

This group we were traveling with was not that way, though. They were mean, they hated God or didn't believe in God, and all they cared about was money. I can't say I had ever been around so many people of this nature before. Honestly, I could not connect with them on any level; and because of the abuse in my and Jay's relationship, I felt ashamed and secretive, which also played into a lack of connection, I'm sure.

Many victims in domestic violence situations may actually come off aloof or disconnected. They are trying to survive. At this time, I knew Jay hated me. Jay seemed to hate women altogether. I didn't understand why he wanted to keep trying in our relationship other than being addicted to the chaos and having some form of control. Any love was just a memory at this point. I was hanging onto a memory and not the reality of our situation—typical love addict.

The people on the street looked at me with soft eyes and concern as they began to pray. I cannot remember everything they said, but one woman shared a vision she received. She said, "You think that you are in jail. You think that you are trapped. But God is showing me a vision of you inside a jail cell, and the keys are in your hand." Man, I wish I had honored that vision when I got it; it would have spared me a lot of turmoil.

I thanked them with tearful eyes and lengthy hugs before venturing to my hotel room in the city alone. This woman's vision confirmed what I had been feeling in my heart. To stay was gut-wrenching, but so was leaving. Yet, I had a choice. After flying home, we had "no contact" for two weeks. This "no contact" was a common practice in the 12-step program I was in for addictive relationships.

Afterward, we continued in our couples counseling, and I had gone almost two months without acting out abusively.

At this point, I was just receiving it. One time, Jay and I were separated at an event by four security guards. Then, a week later, a friend of mine called the police after he broke into my house, followed by an angry outburst that had me cornered in our garage. This friend had lost her dad to suicide, right after he tried killing his ex-girlfriend and her new boyfriend. She said Jay's behavior reminded her of her dad.

"This is not love anymore! This is an obsession!" I cried out cowering beside the washing machine, "I can't do this anymore, Jay. Our relationship is so unhealthy and has to stop! I can't be in this relationship with you anymore!" Terror and heartache swirled inside of me as my inner child screamed for safety. His fear manifested as anger, and my fear resulted in a shutdown. He scoffed and walked quickly out of the garage, throwing his garage door opener on the ground before getting into his car and speeding off. The police came, and we filed a report.

I was so tired—my heart was exhausted. Our relationship had come to a final halt. After attempting to leave so many times, this was it, or was it? I had been diligent in my work, and I wanted his efforts in his own recovery to match mine, and they just didn't. There were still things he was unwilling to look at and change and we needed to be separated for the betterment of our own health and safety. We both had done so much damage, and I needed to continue to look at and take ownership of my actions. I wanted to be close to God again like I had felt in Hawaii.

For days after the breakup, I paced the house, burying my face in one of Jay's shirts and crying into it. Jay was an idol to me. When something or someone is an idol, life comes crashing down all around you when it is removed. We had moments of "breaking up," but this was not one of those. It was like he had died this time. I grieved for our love and the hope of our love. It's almost easier to move on from someone who dies because you know they are gone. In breakups or divorces, it's like they died, but only to you. It can be such a lonely place, depending on the circumstances.

If you are currently in this place, I promise God is right there with you. He is nearest to the brokenhearted and those who are crushed in spirit (Psalm 34:18). I struggled so much in our relationship and wondered why we couldn't make it work. It dumbfounded both of us. One week later, we spoke on the phone. I told him that if he completed his 12 steps in his program for our relationship addiction, then I would speak to him.

I assured him that I loved him and so badly wanted to be with him, but I needed to see him do this work before any reconciliation was possible. Jay needed to do real, honest work on himself, which was always the case; but when pride is your master, that is impossible. We committed to not seeing anyone else and to focusing on ourselves during this time, then hung up the phone. I was anxious but hopeful.

Four months went by, and I had never done so much work on myself in such a short amount of time. I was still in the zone of doing all the work myself, instead of fully surrendering to God. And, Jay was still an idol even though I tried deceiving myself into thinking otherwise. Regardless, this time period was healing, and a lot of that was because I had been away from the mind-bending that is born out of narcissistic abuse. I was actually regaining a sense of peace and my sense of self. My relationship with God also felt like it was gaining strength again and I was committed to healing on a different level.

I stuck to my agreement with my mentor that I would have zero contact with Jay unless he completed his steps. Jay would send a message periodically, telling me how much he loved me or a dream he had about me, or message a mutual friend to share how far he was in his 12-step work. Not directly replying to him devastated me, but I was committed to the work.

During these four months of no contact, I soaked myself in the Word of God. I went to as many meetings as I could, continued therapy, joined an additional small group at church, was of service to as many addicts as I could be, spoke on panels and institutions more often, fed the homeless biweekly, prayed for all who needed it, and stopped watching regular television. I immersed myself in affirmations, audio sermons, and self-development videos. I even slept with these things on in hopes of reprogramming my subconscious mind, as the subconscious mind never sleeps.

I wanted to change! Although I felt connected to the Lord again, I was still doing things by my own strength in many areas, but I didn't understand that—you don't know what you don't know, until, well, you know! I was trying to control the outcome of our situation big time. I was so committed to changing the way I felt and the way I thought. I did not want to be who I had been my entire life.

A big part of me was trying hard to change in hopes of restoring the relationship with Jay. It was for Jay, not for God. Man, was that a hard lesson. Sure I was proud of myself for how far I had come, but much more work needed to be done, and I wanted to follow through until total healing was mine. *Could total healing actually be mine?* I often wondered.

Before I even knew 2 Corinthians 10:5, I practiced taking every thought captive to the best of my ability during this time. I thought Jay was a faithful partner. He had his demons (literally!), but he was loyal and did not cheat in his relationships from what *he* told me. I think deep down, I knew how much deception there really was, but I wanted to ignore that internal ping. The fear that he could be out there doing whatever he wanted, despite our spoken agreement, terrified me. Dreams of him with other women came periodically.

I had to kick fear out of the driver's seat of my life and take the wheel. It's interesting because this type of thinking can be a good thing unless someone is completely blinded and a slave to denial—which I was. The truth was, he had indeed cheated in many of his previous relationships yet lied to me about it. Regardless, I trusted that he was doing the work, and I kept turning the focus back to myself or back to God whenever anxiety-provoking thoughts would try to infiltrate my mind.

Still, I was unsettled in my gut. Your gut is your second brain, you know? It is the only place in the body (besides the brain) where brain cells actually reside. Your gut *is* your second brain. I was so thankful though for my sponsors at this time. My mind was *finally* healing. Years of therapy and reprogramming my thinking through 12-step programs, and other things I listed previously, were working and I could see it! The work was catching up to a degree!

As I sat in the presence of God, I felt over and over again that Jay would become my husband, but there was also the consistent theme of letting go as well. Was it just me who wanted him to be my husband? Was another spirit telling me he was to be my husband? Or was it actually God? Two different people in two different states who had no idea what I was facing, messaged me at random saying God told them to tell me to "Let go."

I held on to these supernatural encouragements from God, but something still felt estranged in the natural. God was trying to tell me to actually let go, but my denial had me hanging on. Self-will run riot! I eventually prayed that God would remove Jay from the throne of my heart and place Jesus there. I even prayed that Jay would lose his business or money so he could truly find God.

His gambling addiction was out of control. I had witnessed his business and pocketbook grow during our relationship, but I knew that his greed was a massive barrier between him and God. In that, I knew Jay was, unfortunately, a barrier between God and me. We were both so used to making our relationships our higher powers and living in our own will. What a pitiful place to be! When someone or something else is your god, there is no room for Jesus to reign.

God *will* shatter your idols, if not immediately, eventually. The first Commandment says, *"You shall have no other gods before me"* (Exodus 20:3 NIV). It is to our own detriment that we make other things or people our gods.

Come November that same year, I learned from my roommate, Sarah, that Jay had been actively dating another woman. As soon as Sarah told me, I broke my no-contact agreement and called him directly. We spoke for about 30 minutes, my hands trembling the entire time. He confirmed this was true and was "shocked" I had actually been celibate and committed to do my work the last few months. My word was usually good, so I was put off by his remark. He knew how hard I always worked on myself, so this also felt like a cop-out. I was confused.

"You left me, Jenny," he kept reiterating.

"We talked about this, Jay. I needed you to do the work. What about our love? I thought you wanted to get married."

"I do," he said.

"Clearly not, if you are in another relationship." Beads of sweat formed at my hairline. I wasn't even angry; I felt confused and rejected. I had never been in this position with a man.

"But you abandoned me. We could have just stayed together. *You* left."

"No, we couldn't have, Jay. It was too abusive. You know this."

The rejection, my level of vulnerability, and grief were too much to bear. My entire body began to shake as I tried to keep my voice as even as possible.

"Well, I really hope you're happy now," I said and ended the call.

This brought back memories of my high school sweetheart cheating on me. My body remembered the betrayal history. So many betrayals by so many people by the age of 27. I recalled falling to my knees in my bedroom during my senior year of high school. My best friend had called to tell me my boyfriend, who I had lost my virginity to, had been cheating on me. It was so out of left field back then, and this felt the same—the utter and total heartbreak of something so unexpected.

Betrayal burns no matter the age.

For the next two hours, my roommate and my best friend held me while I cried and deleted more than 800 pictures on my phone. This betrayal cut like nothing had before. I was blindsided. In a way, I had chosen to be blindsided. Denial will do that to a person. No amount of sexual abuse from my childhood, heartache from past lovers, or hurt from seeing my dad struggle compared to this anguish. Despite the separation, I had chosen to trust Jay's words—that he would do the work and stay committed to me.

For years I had refused to trust him, but because I wanted to change this about myself, I had chosen to trust him fully on this. Those who have experienced total trust in a person and then total betrayal know exactly what I am saying. It was like having my entire house burn down before my eyes without being able to do anything about it. It felt like such a loss. I had put all my hope in a person. Therefore, my hope was not entirely in God, and that burned.

Two long days dragged by, and the tears felt like endless streams. Then I made a decision. I did not want to do the work anymore. For me, this included communicating with God. You see, God still was not on the throne of my heart, and the next few months following proved it.

I was curled up at the edge of my bed one evening, replaying my past and imagining the love of my life with someone else, and my heart went from flesh to stone. At that moment, I heard God's cry for me. I had listened to the audible voice of the Lord before. I had heard Him speak directly, firmly, gently, and kindly, but this time was much different. This was the voice of the Father. It was like His voice cracked in pain. To this day, I have never heard His voice quite like that. I wasn't even praying to Him when He spoke to me.

"Come back to Me, My child," He said painfully. I sat up on the corner of my bed, looked up at my ceiling, and with a defiant and rebellious heart, I said, "No," and grimaced. The tender heart for which I had worked so hard, calloused over again instantly. Although much of my story is about seeking God and running from Him, this period of rebellion was much different. I began hating God. During this time, God was a liar. God manipulated me. God betrayed me. God was not good. Was God even real?

I had never felt "tricked" by God before through all the difficulties of my seeking. Didn't He say Jay would be my husband? What was happening did not show that. I wanted control over the situation but had none. I stayed angry and distant from Jesus for half a year. Which felt like an eternity, honestly. I looked back into my past and felt like God had deceived me multiple times. The enemy was having a heyday with my mind. I even thought my trip to Hawaii was some manipulation by God, that He had tricked me into salvation.

In truth, Hawaii had been one of the best and most spiritually prosperous times of my life. I spiritually regressed to viewing God as an Oz, as a being who sought power and control but was without love. This thought was not the truth and will never be true! This is what looking at life through a bitter heart does. It is a broken lens. It makes it seem that everything and everyone is against you. Bitterness, in and of itself, is a devil. Naturally, I instantly began dating someone whom I choose to call Crew.

This new relationship was abundant in sin, as I was doing anything and everything to keep my mind off Jay and to separate myself further from God. I wanted to be as numb as possible.

Shortly after my phone call with Jay, he reached out to me again, this time in the middle of the night. He begged to see me and talk to him, to which I eventually agreed. He was supposed to be in Thailand with this other woman for two weeks but then flew home after only five days. I never got the actual truth about that. But his month-long heartthrob had dissipated, and he came back to me looking for another chance.

Although I was already in another relationship, I spent two hours with him in the middle of the night. I hadn't seen Jay in months, and as soon as I walked out of my condo and toward his car, he broke down. I had never seen him cry like that before—collapsing in total and utter desperation, regret, loneliness, and instability. He embraced me and could hardly get out a coherent sentence. Yet my heart was hard and my spirit confused. I missed him, *and* I hated him, but he was not well.

"I'm so sorry," he said again and again.

We got into his car and drove up and down the Pacific Coast Highway. It was one in the morning. He begged me to marry him and forgive him. I didn't say much. Nothing was right. Around two in the morning, he dropped me off. As he tried to kiss me goodbye, I reiterated that I was still seeing someone else. I loved Jay so much, but I wanted to forget him. The damage had been done.

Before I got out of the car, he said, "Whenever you are done with this guy, reach back out to me."

I gave him a blank stare and then slammed the car door. I walked up the dimly lit alleyway to my front porch, more confused than ever. As I made my way up the stairs, a small part of my heart yearned for him. I got into my room and cuddled up with my apathy.

Months passed, and the simmering relationship I was in with Crew, burnt out. Same me, same pattern. I needed out of the relationship I was in. It was a quick fix that didn't fix much. Less than 24 hours after breaking up with Crew, I contacted Jay. I knew I was fully submerged in my sex and love addiction, but I didn't care. I knew that Jay was not doing well, but I didn't care about that either. I submitted to my apathy.

Jay had gambled his business away, embezzled $42,000 from his business partners, and lost most of his friends. His porn addiction acted as an anesthetic, and his entire demeanor had shifted. Or had it? Maybe I was just seeing what had always been under his facade of seduction and charm for the first time. I saw a gray and dying man where there was once some life. His skin was literally gray. We were both very, very spiritually sick. He began losing weight, and whenever he stayed over at my house, he spent most of the day in bed in my spare room; quiet, disheveled, and lifeless.

I learned later that he was messaging other women. This was a sad existence. It felt like he was slowly passing away, and I was taking care of him, which drew any life I had left out of me. It seemed like I was reenacting my childhood. If I could just heal a sick man, I would be worth something! This motive kept me in one sick relationship after the other. Identity in Christ, however, breaks such destructive cycles, even lifelong ones that feel deeply embedded in a person.

This situation with Jay frustrated me. I was angry. After such a betrayal, I felt I deserved more. *Didn't I?* Where was the Jay who had such a knack for sweeping me off my feet and love-bombing me? Reality check: since that happened only during the first two months of our relationship, that man he originally presented to me didn't exist. The term psychologists use for this type of manipulation present in toxic relationships is actually called *mirroring.* They will manufacture *your* perfect partner, but it's not real. Jay was not well, and I couldn't expect someone in that position to care much about anyone else.

So in a moment of desperation, I sought God again. I recognized that my situation was extremely unhealthy, yet there was part of me that felt like I was moving in the right direction to some degree. I hadn't felt that way in months. I was confused. Was my trauma steering the ship, or was God?

Whenever I reached out to the Lord to ask for His guidance regarding Jay, all I heard was, "Wait." One night I lay curled up in bed by myself, and my body turned toward my single-paned window. My room was cold. I scrolled through my past social media to the posts where I was Holy Spirit-filled, God-centered, and undeniably full of life. I missed that version of me. It was even a prettier version. I wanted to portray that version of me online. It was exhausting.

I missed my connection with Jesus. I was so dissatisfied that I prayed another angry Jenny prayer. "God, hello? You keep telling me to wait. I'm so sick of waiting. You told me to wait before, and then Jay broke my heart. This is not fair anymore! 'Wait, wait, wait,' that's all You say! You need to tell me right now what the heck am I waiting for? (except I even used a lot more "colorful" language) How long am I to wait? Is it even worth it to wait? You need to tell me what I am waiting for! Seriously. Thanks, amen."

It felt like I had chewed God out over the phone and then hung up on Him. I don't encourage prayer like this, but most of us have had it a time or two, or even more. It was authentic to say the least. This was before I knew the Lord as my Friend. Less than an hour later, I shut my eyes and drifted off. Shortly after that, I awoke to an audible voice.

"Wait seventy-two days!"

That would be Easter Sunday, as I counted the days. Was this God or satan? The devil comes as an angel of light (2 Corinthians 11:14), meaning he can come, creating extreme deception. He can even come to a person after a genuine prayer to God with an answer that isn't from our heavenly Father but seems like it. He can make things sound right and good. He did it to Jesus in the desert multiple times! The enemy even quoted Scripture to Jesus to try and prove his point and make Jesus stumble! Of course, that didn't work on

Jesus because He knew the character of His Father in Heaven. I did not.

If the enemy did it to Jesus, he would do it to us. Hearing the true voice of God coexists with righteousness. If you are not walking in righteousness and have open doors to sin, don't expect every voice you hear to be the Lord's. In my case, it was a familiar spirit, not God's.

Despite ongoing bitterness, betrayal, and spiritual confusion, God clearly instructed me and Jay to give each other up for 40 days. During that time, Jay entered treatment for his addictions, and I spent much time in prayer and reflection. I received a prophetic vision: Jay was on the bathroom floor cracked in half, like an egg, with hundreds of bugs pouring out of him. Then I saw this invisible power, like a wind, blow over him. There seemed to be a barrier. I didn't know it at the time, but God was warning me about his demonic infestation.

At first I interpreted this prophecy wrong because I saw it with my eyes, not God's. I knew that Jay was broken, but I was hopeful because of his newfound connection with Christ during rehab. On Easter Sunday we reunited, with hopes of a new beginning—this time anchored in Jesus.

9

WHEN ANGELS DRIVE OUT DEMONS

During those 40 days, I had a very interesting encounter. Little did I know this would be the beginning of some major supernatural—both demonic and angelic—meetings. I worked part-time and drove down the same streets at the same time almost every day. I knew what events were going on at the schools on the street, what time traffic was thickest, and what each and every church sign said and when it changed.

As I drove home with my dog, Gary, one evening, I saw a church sign that read, "Free Prayer Inside." I loved stuff like this, so I did a U-turn and pulled into the church parking lot. As I hopped out of my car, grabbed my little white fluffy dog and put him on my hip, I was hopeful that I, and maybe even Gary, could get some prayer support. I had faith in Jay and me during this no-contact period, but I still could use some encouragement. There definitely was still some fear.

I walked to the front glass door of the church and knocked. I saw a man through the window in his office wave and give me a "I'll be there in a second" gesture.

As I entered, the man said hello and motioned for us to sit on a bench just outside the sanctuary.

"Hi there. What can I do for you?" he asked me as he clasped his hands together. White hair, pale skin, gentle smile.

"Yeah, this is so crazy. I literally drive down this street almost every day and I've never seen that sign out there! The prayer one."

"Oh really? Yep, it's out there every Thursday," his words felt patient.

"Amazing. I drive past here every Thursday. I don't know how I've missed it."

He smiled.

"I guess I could use some prayer. Maybe my dog could, too; he's kind of aggressive." I laughed. Anyone who knows Gary knows.

I briefly told him about Jay and me. He nodded. I wasn't trying to take up too much time. I had to get home and get some things done, but it was like he had nothing else to do but sit there with me. Very rarely had I experienced someone so present.

He sat across from me and prayed. He didn't say anything super profound but as he prayed, I felt warmth surround me, actual heat. Then something ever so softly touched my back.

It felt like two hands on my shoulders, and it was radiating peace.

If you can envision what holding peace in the palm of your hands would feel like, it was like that. Like a very subtle but undeniable vibration, if I could put it into words. The prayer ended and that touch on my back lifted. He prayed for my dog, too, as silly as it was, and I thanked him and told him I probably would be back next Thursday.

The following Thursday, the sign wasn't there. It wasn't up the following week or the week after that. I never saw the sign again. I even called to ask about it, but there was no response. I wondered if I had heard him wrong or if there was a shift in scheduling. Regardless, the experience was comforting and has made me wonder since.

The next week, I was driving through Huntington Beach when I took a wrong turn. I passed by a tent on the side of the road that again read, "Free Prayer." I was so excited; as I said, I loved this kind of stuff. I pulled over, and a woman and a man prayed for me. They were so happy and encouraging. They prayed about Jay's time in rehab and my resilience. I could tell they were happy to be of service, really happy.

I wasn't a burden to them; they weren't getting paid for their prayers. Even though they were praying for *me*, it felt like they were doing it because they loved *God*. They were honoring God by looking after His people. If more people loved God, wouldn't the world be a better place? Prayer is extremely powerful. Never underestimate the strength of an encouraging word!

As I write this, I can't help but think that God knows everything we ever do. He sees it all, the good, the bad, and the motive. The motive may not matter to people, but it matters to God. In my study of near-death experiences (NDEs), which I have been passionately researching as of late, I have found something similar among many people's heavenly experiences—and yes, people experience both Heaven and hell.

Some people have mentioned that after dying, they were shown a timeline of their life when they entered the heavenly realm. These people saw the times they lived for God, the times they didn't, the times they raged, the times they forgave, the times they bullied someone, the times they helped carry someone's groceries, the times they stole something, and the times they gave something. And with all of that, God exposed the motive for each. It was all laid bare, and I'm talking *everything*. Nothing is hidden from God's sight (Hebrews 4:13), and in that moment with God, you know it. People judge the outward appearance, but the Lord looks at the heart (1 Samuel 16:7).

This revelation alone has made me reflect more intently on my life. What am I doing daily? What are *you* doing daily? Who are you living for? Or what are you living for? What is taking up space in your life, mind, and heart? What is consuming you? The Lord sees you pass up the homeless person when you have two dollars in your pocket. He sees you brush off the friend who is having a bad day. God sees your secret prayers and secret cries; He sees your love for humanity or maybe even your lack of love. He sees you do things with a bad attitude or a grateful one. He sees your heart surrounding finances.

He sees you holding the door open for that mom and her three kids. He sees you helping the overwhelmed person at TSA. He sees you leave out a bowl of food every night for the stray cat. He sees you spot someone in the grocery line who doesn't have enough money for what they've purchased. He sees your donation.

He sees you prepare a meal for your family and give everyone else the better plate before yourself. He sees you in all these things that are possibly unseen by others and even mundane. He sees you pick up trash as you walk into the supermarket. He sees you help your elderly mother or father when they are bitter or depressed and hard to be around. He sees you look at your faults before finding them in your dysfunctional family or friends. He sees you in your selfishness and your selflessness. He sees your true feelings behind what you do.

Nothing is hidden from His sight! You cannot hide your heart from God, even if you have grown successful at hiding it from others and yourself.

These things should make you think. Who are you living your life for? What is on your mind the majority of the time?

In a 12-step program, somebody told me that your higher power is what you think about most. So, who (or what), is your God? Can you honestly answer this question to yourself? Can you zoom out and see beyond your next paycheck, bill, or next potential dilemma?

Side note: Your "god," idol, or idols may not seem like a big deal. Sometimes cleaning is my god! Of course, cleaning the house is necessary. And I love stewarding what God has given me, but if I feel the Lord is calling me to sit and pray or read or worship and I'm choosing to go over all my baseboards with Mr. Clean's Magic Eraser first—at that moment—who or what is my god?

While this is not always the case for me, it is sometimes. As mentioned previously, your crossed-off to-do list isn't going with you to Heaven. I encourage you to invite God into whatever space this is in your life. Ask Him to show you where you can improve if you don't already know. And then ask Him for the strength to do it because changing is hard.

Changing a habit and a mindset is not typically instant. But making a decision definitely can be. Ask God if you're not aware of any offensive or wicked way in you. He will answer, and it will be kind.

Additionally, if you are thinking of someone else you wish would change as you read this, I get it. I *totally* get it. My question for you is, are you praying for them? If you are, *how* are you praying for them? In times of confusion and frustration with people in my own life, when I don't know what or how to pray, I will either pray in tongues (Acts 2:4) or ask the Holy Spirit to lead me in prayer.

Praying this way can take focus and quietness if you are new to praying. The Lord will literally say, "Repeat after Me," then He will walk me through a prayer, line by line, about a person or situation, and I will pray this out loud. Prayer like this typically highlights ways my heart is not right in the situation, and it demonstrates God's true love and mercy for the other person.

If there is someone(s) in your life who resists change, ask the Holy Spirit to help you pray for them, and ask Him if they are to be in your life. Sometimes they are, and sometimes they aren't. If they are stuck in a habit, a mindset, or an addiction, your prayers will not return void. Be persistent! God's ways are above our own, and sometimes our prayer life needs a spiritual defibrillator. Jesus can do that. Just ask Him (Matthew 7:7).

I did much personal work on myself before God came to me and delivered me. Because I had done so much work, I have often wanted other people to do the same—to use the tools I was given to help them. I would lay them out for people; some would take them willingly and apply them, while others ignored or were offended by them. This was a hard lesson for me to learn— not everyone wants to change, not everyone wants help, not everyone is willing to be honest with themselves or others, and I cannot change anyone; that is a job for the Lord.

I always think of the story in John 5 that I discussed in Chapter 3 of the paralyzed man at the pool of Bethesda, and when Jesus approached, he asked the man, "Do you *want* to be healed?" Jesus told the man to *"Rise, take up your bed and walk"* (John 5:8 NKJV). The man who had been paralyzed from the waist down met the Savior of the world that day and was healed and filled with joy. You can too.

I know the first part of changing is a desire for it. For a long time, I would offer people unsolicited advice because I wanted them to be free from their suffering. Sometimes, this is necessary. When I hear the Lord tell me to speak something to someone, even if it's uncomfortable, I do. Other times, it amounts to straight-up pride on my part, and I'm later convicted. I think that I know best when sometimes I do not.

This is one of my most regular prayers: Eradicate all pride completely from me, even if it's the smallest amount of pride; I don't want it. Asking God to prune us and cut off our defects can feel challenging, but it's always worth it. If there is an aspect of myself that I know is extremely hindering, and I'm angry about it, I will quite literally tell God to burn it or gut it out of me, no matter how painful.

We are to be image-bearers of Christ. Do you think Jesus had a bad attitude or self-righteous demeanor? Heck, no! And He most definitely was not prideful, He was straight up humble.

The Bible never says to pray for humility; it says to "humble yourself," meaning it's an action and something you have a choice about. The nicest people I have ever met are also the most humble. Kindness is a gift, and a free one at that. God will honor your heart as you pray for assistance in this area. He is glad when you have humbled yourself enough to look at your character honestly.

Prayer has changed much in me and can change much in you; maybe it already has. Authentic prayer alone is humbling, and praying for a lost and dying world will also tenderize your heart. I often find myself led to pray for the rejected, the suffering, and the demonized, including people who are on their way to hell. That said, prayer has many facets.

There are different types of prayers for different seasons or difficulties. One form of prayer that I've seen radically shift things in my own life includes what I call, "war prayers." When I know I have come up against the devil and his demons, and I'm being attacked from all sides, or someone in my life is being attacked horribly, I step into my authority in Christ and I go after it. I am a warrior on the battlefield, and my opposition is trying to take my land. I stand in the defense as well as the offense. Let me explain.

I fight my battles in the Spirit now, doing my best not to argue with people about what I think they should do or shouldn't do. Instead, God will lead me into the little closet in my downstairs bedroom or my prayer closet upstairs to pray and wage spiritual war. The Lord has an army of angels, and our prayers can dispatch warring, guardian, and ministering angels. Praying on the defense looks like rebuking devils and telling them to leave in Jesus's name.

We should absolutely be doing this. But we can also pray in the offense, asking God to dispatch His angels to help us fight the battle and to pray for a place of victory because Jesus has already won. There are warring angels for a reason; they war with us and on our behalf! They fight off the evil present with us now or that has come our way before now. Do not be confused, though; I am in no way telling you to pray to angels!

The Bible strongly advises against it, as do I from personal experience before getting saved. (I was calling on angels and speaking to them, but they were fallen angels, and that was revealed to me later.) We are to call on the Lord and *only* the Lord; and if it is in His will, He will send His angels out to aid us.

I had no clue about all the people who had prayed for me for years before coming to Jesus, and I still don't fully. But what I do know is that not one of those prayers got shot down like a bird in the sky and fell dead to the ground. Each prayer reached the throne room of God the Almighty and the angelic were sent to me before I knew what was happening. I knew I had a heavenly encounter that Thursday afternoon when that man prayed for me with my dog, but I thought it was just a special moment when I felt an angel of the Lord. Later, I learned that God was giving me these encounters as encouragement before the legion of demons would try to terrify me before they were cast out from my life.

While Jay was still in rehab for gambling, he would come down for a day or sometimes the weekend if he had a pass from his treatment center, and we would go to church. One Sunday night, we went to Rock Harbor church in Costa Mesa. The messages were good, but during worship at night the Holy Spirit would radiate through the room.

On this particular Sunday night, I had invited a longtime friend, Ashley, to church with Jay and me. She sat on my right and Jay sat on my left. As worship began, I mentioned to Jay that he should go up front for prayer, nudging his elbow and smiling. Shaking his head he said, "Nah, I'm good." That was so like Jay, resistant! God works with resistance, though. Did you know that? Resistance may bother or intimidate a person, but it doesn't scare God.

"C'mon. Really? Your back hurts all the time, and you're in a difficult situation. Just get prayer," I said.

"I don't think so," he replied as he turned to face the band. I prayed, asking God to change his heart so he could open his heart to prayer.

We were sitting in the front row on the right side of the stage. I didn't usually sit toward the front, but we did this day. As we each settled into our place of worship, I closed my eyes and raised my hands. Instantly, I saw two similar looking angels. One stood behind me, and one stood behind Jay. They weren't necessarily tall, but their wings tips seemed to almost reach the ceiling. They stood in total peace behind Jay and me. Right then, I felt the same hands pressed against my shoulders as I had felt in that "Free Prayer" moment in the church.

If total healing and love created a physical sensation, I was experiencing it. One angel stood directly behind me with its hands on my shoulders; there was a masculine touch. The other stood directly behind Jay, positioned in the same way but with a more feminine aspect. This moment was comforting, yet not a normal experience for me. My entire life, I had experienced the demonic from tormenting and attacking spirits and ghost-like spirits that caused fear and violation. To see and feel an angel of the Lord is entirely different.

As I stood there being saturated in this feeling, I saw three demons inside me. One resided in my left shoulder, where a majority of my chronic pain radiated from, and it looked like a black line or worm-like thing. Another one lay at the base of my skull toward the right side that looked like a beetle, almost like a leech-beetle. The third was inside my womb, which looked like rotting roots. *Whoa,* I thought to myself. I had never seen anything like that before.

In that moment, I heard a man's voice. "You ready?" the angel said to me. I didn't even have time to respond or think about what "You ready" could mean. Then I saw the angel behind me with a tool that reminded me of what is used for traditional stone sculpting. He had this tool in one hand and a hammer in the other. He hit the tools together on my left shoulder. Instantly, a solid black wormlike serpentine creature flew out of my shoulder.

A breathy "Oooahhh!" left my mouth. My shoulders shuddered forward, and I gasped for my breath out loud.

"Oh, my God," I said under my breath. Holding my chest, I looked around to Ashley and then to Jay. Their eyes were closed as they were in their state of worship for the Lord. Did they not hear me? My mind started racing, and my heart was pounding. I was freaking out. What the heck was that? I was trying not to have an anxiety attack. I just prayed and prayed and prayed.

As worship came to an end and we sat down for the message, I could hardly focus on what the pastor was saying. I can't even recall any of it. I didn't want to tell Ashley or Jay what I had just experienced, so I just sat there ruminating internally. As the pastor ended his sermon, he asked everyone to close their eyes.

He said, "If you are in this room tonight and you feel like you are currently without defense, please raise your hand." People silently lifted their hands. "Keep them up high," he said. "Now, I want everyone to open up your eyes. If someone near you has their hand up, please walk over to them and, with their permission, lay your hands on them and begin to pray."

Jay's hand was up.

Haha! I thought to myself. He didn't want prayer, but God is giving it to him anyway!

Five people approached Jay, worship music began again, and the people in the room prayed for those who needed defense. We all prayed for Jay in our own way, and slowly, each person lifted their hands off him and went back to their seat, while Jay stayed seated for a while. *Maybe he's just soaking it all in,* I thought. After some time, he finally stood up and worship ended.

The lights brightened and everyone began socializing and moving out of the sanctuary.

"You didn't want prayer, but God gave it to you anyway!" I laughed. "See?"

He smiled and said. "You know, something really weird happened," Ashley and I were listening. "Everyone had their hands on me praying and I could feel people move their hands off me, but one person's hand was there for the longest time. I just thought, 'Wow, they must be praying really hard,' and when I opened my eyes to look over my left shoulder, no one was there."

I was a deer in headlights, and my eyes widened and my jaw dropped.

"It was a thin hand—gentle," Jay said.

"Dude. It was an angel," I replied. "At the beginning of the service, I saw two angels behind us. One behind me touching my shoulders and one behind you!"

Ashley, Jay, and I just looked at each other in amazement. Whoa.

"Crazy! I believe it!" Ashley said in her bubbly, high-pitched voice, laughing.

I told Jay about my experience with that wormlike thing afterward.

You ready? I couldn't get those words out of my head. What did that even mean?

10

THE BRUJA AND MY SKYLIGHT TO HEAVEN

It's wild to think that for so many years, I prayed a specific desperate prayer, and then when God came down like a rushing flood to answer it, I was surprised and caught off guard. His power intensified, surprising me repeatedly during the year and a half when I was being delivered. I wanted freedom so badly that I prayed for it all the time—sometimes even demanding it. But when God served it up, it was hard to accept it in some ways!

In the back of my mind, I just wanted the Lord to pick me up mid-race and drop me at the finish line where I could lift both hands and shout in glory, have others see me, and maybe even get a trophy. Things were still about me. I thought that was how He was going to provide my freedom. Instead, I ran the race, out of breath, exhausted, with bloody feet, seriously dehydrated, alone most of the time, and barely keeping a jogging pace. And when I finally reached the finish line, I fell to my knees and went face-first into the gravel.

It didn't look like a victory to the world because it was a different kind of victory, which I like to call "total surrender." I finally surrendered to the will of God in my life. This was a hard place for me to get to, but one worth all the previous sufferings. Surrendering is humbling.

CURSED

A few weeks after the angelic experience Jay and I had at Rock Harbor, something strange began to happen. I had always struggled with anxiety on and off since I was in elementary school, but through many years of therapy and support groups, I learned ways to control it and minimize it, yet it still existed in my life. I became skilled at recognizing the signs of an anxiety or panic attack and preventing it, which I also applied to flashbacks. I had lots of tools in my toolbelt.

However, one day, while getting sandwiches in L.A. with Jay, I suddenly became extremely anxious. Nothing happened, no triggering conversation, no thoughts in my mind that I was aware of that could cause the response, but I found myself growing more and more nervous. I hate that about anxiety. It's like the more you become aware of how anxious you are, the more worried you get, and it just builds until a panic attack erupts.

I could feel the onset of it about to cripple me, and I needed to get away from people. I couldn't eat my sandwich, so we wrapped it up and headed to the car. I began driving him back to his treatment center in Venice Beach. He stayed in rehab for gambling recovery for almost seven months.

"Are you okay, babe?" Jay asked. He had seen me through so many things and couldn't always tap into empathy, but he seemed genuinely worried this time.

"I don't know. I just feel so anxious. I don't know what's happening." I started to cry as I switched to the carpool lane, my hands shaking on the steering wheel. "I honestly feel like I'm cursed, Jay." Those words couldn't feel truer coming out of my mouth. Then, the car fell silent.

As I dropped him off, he gave me some words of encouragement and kissed me goodbye. I drove the hour or so home and went to bed.

That night, I had the same dream three times over. In the dream, I walked into a room with a marble staircase. It wasn't a particularly clean or beautiful room, with boxes and miscellaneous things crammed into some corners and little messes here and there. I hardly noticed anything else because I was mainly focused on getting to the stairs to climb them.

I ascended the marble staircase, stopped three steps from the top, turned around, and then the dream would start again. The third time I dreamt this, I saw something as I turned around. A woman was at the bottom of the stairs, off to the side. Her chin pointed down to her chest, and she had medium-length black hair covering most of her face. She seemed to look at me through a sliver of space between strands of her hair. She outstretched her thumb toward me and was cutting it with a blade, causing it to bleed, muttering words I couldn't hear.

It looked like she was trying to do something to me, so I turned around and looked directly at her. "Hey! Are you okay?" I asked her.

She jumped! It was as if I couldn't see her, and in a way that implied she had just been caught. As I woke up, all I could hear over and over again echoing throughout my room was "Bruja, bruja, bruja," as I woke up. *Bruja* is the Spanish word for witch.

The dream haunted me for days. I couldn't get the image of what she was doing out of my head. Since my teenage years, I have been skilled in dream interpretation. I usually don't have to think much about the symbolism; I just know. In high school Spanish class, people would come up to me after roll call. There was usually a vacant seat next to me, so they would sit and tell me about their dreams. I would tell them what I thought, discuss it, and then interpret the symbols.

Back then, I had a large dream book to which I could refer. Since coming to Jesus, however, I no longer use these kinds of books as I feel the symbolism isn't always in line with what the Holy Spirit says, so I trust my inner knowledge of what things mean as God reveals them to me.

However, this dream with this woman baffled me. I felt afraid but also like I had known her before, or rather, she knew me and watched me; I just wasn't as aware of her. The one thing I did innately realize was that someone had or was currently cursing me.

So I reached out to a gay friend I had been with the week before at a sober birthday dinner who told me his family was involved in Santeria. I wondered if this was connected to him. I had not been active in witchcraft for years, so this was off-putting. The friend didn't seem connected to what I was experiencing, so I let it go as best I could. As I wondered about the dream and didn't fully understand, I decided to Google what a thumb represented. I discovered it represented control.

Without the thumb, holding or doing anything with the hand is hard. *So, something has had power over me,* I thought. (Note: The heart of witchcraft is always control and manipulation. Whether white magic or dark magic, the desire is to control something.)

Days later, I had my prayer-healing appointment at the church, which I described in Chapter 2. When I sat down with the ladies, I shared the dream, and they all read the notes they had received about me from the Lord.

"You know, I feel like I have been cursed," I said nervously after quickly describing the dream's details.

Sue acknowledged what I shared and agreed this could be possible. Still, due to my level of demonic manifestation in that first session, there was no opportunity to approach this topic until later. As I shared at the beginning of this book, I felt so much freedom after my first deliverance. It wasn't planned, by me at least, but God definitely planned it! When I walked out of that church, it felt like I was floating on a cloud as I walked to my car.

The weight of the demons in a person's life is unknown until exorcised out. I felt exhausted for about a week after a deliverance like that, but it was combined with so much peace and contentment. I felt joy. Real joy. I ordered an acai bowl afterward from one of my favorite coffee shops called Milk & Honey and contacted my friend Amanda from Hawaii. She was the first person I shared this experience with, and she quickly told me that if I didn't have the energy to write it all down, I should record a voice memo instead so I wouldn't forget it. Which is what I did days after the next angelic encounter. I was glad she suggested that.

I assumed after this type of freedom that I would sleep wonderfully. Not so. That night, when I fell asleep, I was tossing and turning. The Lord spoke to me and said it would take three days, and then I would sleep well. So for three nights, I struggled to get to sleep. The third night, I woke up, and in my half-awake, half-asleep state, God revealed something very interesting and bizarre. I saw an angel approach me and extract a beetle out of my neck. It was like I could see it in the spiritual sense. Almost like a dissection, the angel separated part of my head and neck, removed the beetle, and then put me back together. The beetle was the same demon I had seen in my body that evening at Rock Harbor.

After this, I fell right back to sleep. When I woke up the second time that night, I encountered something I had never experienced. It was a choir of angels. I did not see them, but I heard them singing all around me, as if a hundred angels encircled my bed. It seemed the Lord had opened a skylight to Heaven and I could hear inside as they fully surrounded me.

Peace—abundant peace. My mind, my spirit, and even my body could feel the peace, releasing a physical sensation. I felt the most relaxed I had ever felt in my life, which spoke volumes, considering I operated in a hyper-attuned state after experiencing abuse, rejection, neglect, and shame. I was always in fight-or-flight mode, on guard for the next attack. My body was sore!

This default of my system didn't exist at this time in my room. I was wholly and entirely safe. I would fall back asleep and wake to the same choir and peace, and then it was like the Holy Spirit Himself was speaking different things to me. To be honest, I can remember only one: "I bestow My peace upon you." Hearing these words, I could see them above me and then watch them fall and sink into my heart like warm honey. They were going into my spirit as I lay on my bed. It was a supernatural experience.

I often liked sharing my spiritual experiences with people, but my deliverance and my angelic encounters felt uniquely sacred. I wanted to keep them close before sharing them with anyone. For a week following my first exorcism, I was exhausted. I mean *really* exhausted. I assumed this to be expected on the first day, but I was so tired all week.

I began doing personal research on people's deliverances, what their manifestations were like, and what they felt afterward. No one in my life had ever gone through a deliverance at the time. This was all new to me, so I researched quite a bit. I learned that apparently, after a deliverance, it is common to feel lethargic, and after a *major* deliverance (like the one I had), being tired for a week was quite common.

Just two days after my freeing experience, despite my exhaustion, I went to church on Sunday and prayed for people after the service. However, the night before, I had another dream. In the dream, I saw a man who wore a red baseball cap with a rope-like accessory over the front of it sitting at a table. In the dream, he asked for prayers from his family. I stopped him and said, "Are you sure you don't need prayer for your romantic relationship?" I also saw the first letter of his name in the dream: M.

The following Sunday morning, as I stood in the front of the church after the service, a flood of people came down the left aisle and out the main doors. I stood there smiling, expectant for anyone to approach who needed prayer. Praying for others was always exciting for me. It's funny how drugs, witchcraft, and chaotic relationships used to get me high, but now I was getting high off what I did with God! And it's a high that lasts.

After the service, looking through the sea of people, I suddenly saw the man from my dream. He had a red baseball cap and a rope accessory across the front. He had a prayer written down on a piece of paper. We offered this form of prayer to those who did not want to be directly prayed for. They could write down their prayers, which would be distributed to the prayer team so we could intercede throughout the week. I saw him walking toward the prayer wall with his rolled-up prayer request in hand. My heart was pounding. He didn't see me.

"Hi!" I said. "Did you need some prayer?" I reached toward him.

"Me? Oh, yeah. I wrote one down," he said, shrugging his shoulders.

"I would like to pray for you though. Is that okay?"

"Sure," he said with a half-smile.

"I have to tell you, the Lord showed me you in a dream last night. He showed me your hat, the color, the design. What exactly do you need prayer for?" I asked, even though it had already been revealed in the dream.

"Well, I don't know. My fiancée and I are having a lot of trouble. I don't really know what's going to happen." I watched his heart sink.

"Oh, man. I'm sorry to hear that. What's your name?"

"I'm Matt."

"God wants to speak to you today. I don't want to weird you out, but He also showed me the first letter of your name and that you needed prayer for your romantic relationship. I'm glad you're here." I smiled. "Is it okay if I touch you?"

"Really?" His eyes widened, a glimmer of hope. "Wow. Yeah. This is so cool! And yeah, that's fine."

I placed my hand on his shoulder, and we shut our eyes. As I prayed for this man, I could feel the Holy Spirit radiating through me as each word fell from my mouth effortlessly. I didn't know what I was saying exactly, but that is the beauty of prayer when you are connected to the Lord. I was just a conduit. This connection is my favorite thing about God and having a relationship with Him. He cares so deeply for everyone, and because I have a relationship with God, He speaks to me in ways that can encourage and help others.

His love is an endless river, and He can use anyone to display that love. I get excited when I get to be the person God uses. When we are available to God, He can do amazing things through us! As I closed the prayer, I looked up at Matt. Tears ran down his bronze face. I squeezed his shoulder.

"I'm so glad the Lord showed me you. I have a lot of hope for your relationship, Matt. God loves you very much," I said to him.

"Thank you so much. This was really incredible. I have to bring my fiancée here. Could you pray for us? Are you going to be here next week?"

"I won't. I'll actually be out of town, but maybe I can catch you guys the following week. Have a good rest of your day, Matt!"

"Thank you!" He wiped his tears and walked away smiling.

Hope. So many of us just need *hope*. Our circumstances don't always need to be perfect, nor do our bank accounts or relationships, but when hope is added to any situation, it makes such a positive difference. Hope changes our perspective, thoughts, and language—thus changing our hearts and lives.

I never saw Matt again, but will always remember this encounter specifically because although it was an opportunity to show up for this person, God was revealing something very special to me. One, the closer I get to the Lord by humbling and purifying myself, the more my gifts will develop, which in turn helps me love His people better. Two, my deliverance brought me much closer to God.

Dreams, visions, and prophetic prayers for others increased as I was delivered. The enemy always wants to stop what God is doing or could do in a person's life. As the demons were being evicted from my mind and body, clarity broadened and the capacity to see, hear, feel, and know God grew.

After this encounter, God gave me a vision. In this vision, I was swimming in a pool at night. When I ducked underwater, I could see a light on the side of the pool, but I couldn't see anything else. If you've ever gone night swimming, you know what I'm talking about. Everything is blurry; you can make out some things but can't see much underwater, especially in the dark.

Suddenly, I was submerged in the pool during the day, again without goggles. When I was underwater, it was brighter outside than before. I could see the shapes in the pool, knowing which direction the underwater lamp was, and so on. Objects were still cloudy, but I could make sense of them. Then I had a third vision that superseded the previous two. This time I was underwater wearing goggles at the brightest time of the day, and I could see everything perfectly.

"This is life after deliverance," God spoke to my heart.

As I stepped into deliverance, God gave me a sharp clarity of what things were and why they were there. I could suddenly see everything. Nothing was hidden or distorted because the light of the day, combined with the purpose of the goggles gave me the ability to see. The light of God exposes evil, and our relationship with Him gives us eyes to see.

First Corinthians 12 discusses the eight irrevocable spiritual gifts of God. If you are unfamiliar with this, I encourage you to read this chapter in the Bible. It's one of my favorites. The Lord assigns spiritual gifts to us when we're born that are given to us after salvation. We are to earnestly desire the gifts, and we can actually ask God for ones that don't come as natural to us; they are all available! The Lord cannot take these away from us as they are gifts, and these gifts are without repentance (Romans 11:29).

In other words, God's calling on our lives is irreversible and it is up to us to decide what we want to do with it. For example, I have sensed a prophetic calling over my life since I was a little girl because I could see spirits. However, God's intended calling over my life was warped through my witchcraft practices and trauma when I used it to glorify the devil by necromancy (engagement with the dead and demons) and other divination practices. These things were not glorifying God, they were glorifying myself and satan.

When I came to Jesus, I asked the Lord to take this dark ability from me and replace it with a Holy Spirit-restored version when He saw fit. For a few months it was inaccessible and then awakened again as I stepped out at a festival to pray for people with a friend for others raving. God was helping me then.

All that to say, the closer you get to God, the more you seek Him and become available to Him, the more real and available He becomes to you. Sometimes people become so focused on the gift that they forget to gaze into the face of the Gift-giver. Scripture says to *"Seek first His kingdom and His righteousness, and all these things shall be added to you"* (Matthew 6:33 NKJV). Meaning, everything else will be added—including spiritual giftings, direction in difficulty, discernment, blessings, and so on—when we simply seek God.

God sees our motive. When our motive is to know Him, our lives and our perspective shift. Seek Jesus and He will use the call over your life to better the world and the people in it. He loves you so much.

11

BED-WETTING AND THE HAUNTED HOUSE

There are spiritual giftings from God, and there can be occult giftings from satan. In my experience, occult giftings come with torment, and there is little to no control; God's giftings come with peace. The godly spiritual gifts revealed in 1 Corinthians 12 include: wisdom, knowledge, faith, healing, miraculous powers, prophecy, discernment of spirits, speaking in tongues, and the interpretation of tongues.

The Lord will place callings on people's lives, but it's up to them to bring them to fruition. As a child, I experienced occult gifts, often stemming from generational spirits. In reality, I was just opening myself up more severely to the demonic realm. Satan is an expert in offering the counterfeit version of God's call on a person's life. Example: God has called me to walk in prophecy, healing, and discernment. The enemy enticed me with witchcraft, leading me into divination, energy healing, and necromancing.

Now, let's press in a little deeper to prophecy and the discernment of spirits. Prophecy is biblically encouraged to be the most sought-after spiritual gift. Its main function is to edify the Church (1 Corinthians 14:1,5). There have been times in my life when I have received a prophetic word or just a word of encouragement, which shifted something in me. It always fills a person with hope or faith, sometimes more than we know. For instance, being told you're a good mom when you feel like everything is falling apart can change your day!

The Church needs encouragement, and the Church needs prophecy! We are commanded as believers to *earnestly* pursue the spiritual gifts—not to evade them entirely or leave them up to the more "mature Christian." If you are a believer, *you* are the Church, and you are called to be set apart! Seek and you *will* find.

Often, I can approach a person and instantly pick up on a spirit or spirits that are oppressing the individual's life. Sometimes I can see what soul wounds they have and can also pick up on motive. Either the Lord reveals it to me, or the demonic actually manifests, and that tells me what I need to know.

I don't see this in every person, but only in some people God highlights to me. Other times, I can sense what they are oppressed with by feeling their emotions or physical pain in a moment, or through a sense of knowing. The gift of discernment can also recognize motives behind what people are doing and saying, whether good or bad.

God doesn't always release me to approach the person; sometimes, I just go into intercessory prayer for the person. And truthfully, sometimes I forget to pray and then repent later! Other times, the Lord tries to protect me by warning me about an individual. And then there are times He opens the door for me to pray with the person, and He delivers them.

I don't always mention the demonic presence I see. If the person does choose to pursue deliverance, more spirits always surface. This happened to me when I was delivered, and I know it to be a common occurrence in this line of ministry, because I see it all the time. Some Bible-believing Christians also agree that the gift of prophecy offers an enhanced level of discernment when prophets of the faith speak.

This discernment creates a deep knowing of whether or not the prophecy is in line with the Spirit of God or another spirit, such as that of antichrist, a Jezebel spirit, etc., or just the flesh of the person where they are speaking out of pride, emotion, or even their own soul wounds. The weight of these gifts without Holy Spirit-filled guidance is chaotic. If something is not in line with the Word of God, but rather goes against it, it is the enemy.

What I thought were "giftings" growing up was actually demonic oppression. My "gifting" of sight into the spirit realm terrified me as a child, pre-teen, and teenager. Wherever there is torment, there is a demon! My God-given identity growing up was not fostered by a Christian, a family member, or a pastor who understood or knew what I was facing.

My grandmother would pray with me in moments of torment; however, what I was facing truly required deliverance and someone who knew how to do that. This did not feel like a gift, but the New Age world, psychics, and occult healers said it was, so I tried to look at it that way when, honestly, I was exhausted by it.

While I am discussing the seeing and hearing of spirits, I also want to touch on psychosis and related disorders, and what I have seen as a minister of deliverance. The spirit of kundalini can cause these disorders through the kundalini yoga practice and transcendental meditation that focuses on aligning the chakras (what occultists believe to be the energy centers of the body).

When this serpent-like demon is "awakened" from the base of the spine in the root chakra, it shoots through all the other chakras, aligning them, opening the third eye, and the person will begin to have heightened psychic abilities—which is demonic possession. And because it is a witchcraft spirit, it brings with it "occult giftings" as well as torment and psychosis for many. (Psychosis is a severe mental condition when a person loses sight of reality.) It doesn't always cause psychosis, but it can and I've seen it. I personally have been delivered of the kundalini demon without the psychosis, yet I was still tormented.

I believe that many witches practicing the craft today actually have a prophetic calling. However, just like my own journey, without direction and without Jesus, this gift doesn't come to fruition the way God intended. The enemy imposes his counterfeit "gift," leading to destruction. The last thing the devil wants is for a person to be saved, know who they are in Christ, and walk out a real on-fire Christian life.

Baseline Christianity should look exactly like the book of Acts! Baseline. If the church you're attending now doesn't operate just like that one, find a new church. I understand lukewarmness. I got saved, was burning bright for Jesus, went back to my old life, and fell into the lukewarm category for the few years leading up to my radical and life-changing deliverance in 2019.

I fully believed in Jesus, but didn't look like Him, even though I talked about Him. If you've fallen back into your old sinful patterns, only have a relationship with God on Sundays (and that's if you even make it to church), there's no time like the present to call on your heavenly Father, who loves you more than anything. Ask for His help in coming back to Him. Recommit your life to Jesus. You don't have to wait for a special moment. You can do that right now.

OCCULT OPPRESSION AS A CHILD

I was very demonized growing up. Meaning, I was oppressed, could see the demonic and was attacked demonically on a regular basis. I was sensitive, traumatized, and introduced to witchcraft early on. This made me an easy target for the enemy. I had frequent supernatural encounters and could often step into a building and know instantly if there were spirits there, what types, their names, and sometimes their functions. This was necromancing and divination. I did not have the Holy Spirit guiding me.

Before Jesus, this occult gifting led me straight into the world of mediumship, Wicca, and necromancy. It wasn't until I was 18 and received a palm reading where it felt like I finally heard answers for everything I was dealing with. But it wasn't from a godly source, it was from a witch. The Bible is not opaque about this topic. It clearly states:

> *Do not turn to mediums or necromancers; do not seek them out, and so make yourselves unclean by them: I am the Lord your God* (Leviticus 19:31 ESV).

Sadly, many people do it anyway, Christians included. They then become bound in ways they don't even know or understand.

When I walked into this psychic's home, there were three women present. One of the women spoke directly to me, saying, "Whoa. You are very psychic!" as she reached for my palm. Her warmth caught me by surprise. This witch was different from some of the practicing psychics and witches I would get involved with later. Regardless, she was still deceived in her practice, and this encounter with her led me deeper into my deception. She was beautiful and glowing. She had short brown hair tucked back behind a white handkerchief on her head and wore a large 1950s-style Rockabilly skirt.

The three women were doing psychic readings, and they were all related. A generational line of witches! The mother, who appeared to be the owner of the home, intimidated me. She was in the same room doing a reading on a friend of mine. *I got the nice lady,* I thought to myself. My original intent was not to get a reading, but after being convinced that it was *just* $5, I submitted.

As the young witch pointed out what she thought I was gifted with, my face lit up.

"Really? Psychic? You think so?" I responded. My desperate 18-year-old self yearned for any sort of validation.

"Yes, you are psychic and very gifted. You should pursue this as it is so natural to you. You would be very good at it!"

"Whoa, cool. That makes a lot of sense." I felt strangely hopeful.

"Yes," she smiled. "Just envision a white light around you at all times for protection. It also looks like you have a lot of stress coming in your *very* near future." She continued as she followed the lines on my hand. "You have quite a bit going on right now." Her face was troubled, and her fingers traced the grooves in my palm slowly and then quickly.

She offered to continue the reading for a price. I declined but thanked her for the five minutes, and my friend and I left. This immediately opened the door for a curse on my life, as if my life wasn't already cursed enough. That same day, I returned home and was kicked out of my parents' house for possessing and selling drugs. They gave me an ultimatum. Either go to a rehabilitation program or get out.

"Why don't *you* go to rehab!" I yelled across the table to my father before storming down the hall to my bedroom. A pot calling the kettle black. Naturally, I packed up all my art supplies, my midriff tops, and my bad attitude, making sure to tell my parents to go to you know where themselves as I walked out of the front door. I jogged down the street to my friend's car, shaking my head in disbelief. I hated being there anyway.

"They're insane!" I said as I threw my things into the back seat of her small two-door car. "Is this a joke?" It felt like a movie scene.

"Dude. Yeah, that's crazy," she said as she flipped a U-turn and sped off toward her mom's house.

I stayed with that friend for a short time before I hopped to the next place, and then the next place. My addiction never let me settle anywhere for very long. I would later refer to myself as the "traveling gypsy who never left Costa Mesa." Ironically, I am now writing this from my bedroom close to the beach, on the East Coast.

As addiction controlled the next four and a half years of my life following this event, witchcraft too was warmly welcomed. Powerless people seek witchcraft. Prideful people don't want to submit to God. And I was just that. Powerless and prideful.

Although clearly under enormous self-induced stress, there was part of me that felt encouraged after getting my palm read. It was the first time someone could acknowledge this part of me happily and then actually give me direction for it. I had zero direction at that point in my life. No Christian had told me what I was facing or had given me any type of solution for seeing spirits all the time. Maybe they didn't know how to handle it, to be honest.

When I had shared my "ghostly" encounters with a pastor in high school, he just looked at me wide-eyed and seemingly afraid. I believe he and his wife tried their very best with the knowledge they had to help me. And truthfully, I'm not sure I would have been ready to receive help then anyway.

So, I walked through my teen years regularly seeing spirits that I thought were "ghosts" and occasionally what I thought were demons, as they presented themselves to be "darker." Now, in case you don't already know, there are no such things as ghosts! There are only angels who serve the Lord and demons who work for satan. Demons can shapeshift depending on function and authority in the spirit.

Two demons I encountered (which I discuss in the next few chapters) changed their appearance multiple times to me. However, they were the same spirit trying to accomplish the same thing. Some can even mimic dead loved ones. That's right; if you're seeing your grandpa who passed away walking around your house, it is a demon, and you need to shut all open doors that are allowing the demonic in your life. That is a familiar spirit, meaning it is a spirit that has been in your generational line. Kick it out of your house by commanding it to get out in Jesus's name and then anoint your entire home.

You see things like this on television and social media, often with psychic mediums or shamans who are tapping into the spirit realm. The reality? Your past loved one is either in Heaven or hell. They are not still roaming the earth or in a place of limbo or purgatory. Anything claiming to be a deceased loved one is a demon, and I know this from personal experience and also from the Bible.

Again, these are known as familiar spirits or what I call familial (family) spirits. They are generational demons. Remember, the devil comes only to steal, kill, and destroy. These spirits want to weasel their way into your life and destroy it in any way possible. There is always going to be some sort of lack in your life when you are pursuing witchcraft in any form. Deception is the key these demons use to unlock the doors of your life so they can invade your space and create chaos.

I currently have a friend whom I believe to be cursed. Curses can come upon us when we are living in sin or have been directly cursed by a person, and of course, generational curses are very real. This friend has regularly sought out mediums and other energy healers to contact people in her life who have died. I have warned her against this, but at the end of the day, it's between her and God.

She always seems to be comforted for a short time, and then the issues arise. She has had so many setbacks with finances, accidents, addictions, relationship problems, health, family, children, and the list goes on. She is not ready to close the doors she has opened to the spirit realm. In her case, demons have legal rights to her life. I did this for a long time as well, until the Lord opened my eyes to it completely.

Sometimes, you just don't want to give up what you know is not right. And that is your free will. And in other cases, you actually don't know what is wrong because you don't know God and don't know His Word. When it comes to the topic of spirits, we hear various words: ghosts, spirit guides, gods, goddesses, departed loved ones, marine spirits, orbs, etc. They are all demons.

As Christians, we are given the gift of discernment. If you are entertaining spirits, you are deceived. Ask God to reveal the demonic in your life, and He will. Ignorance is not bliss; ignorance is bondage. I encourage you to ask God to reveal the demonic agenda in your life, and He will. When you know where the pest is and how it got in, you can poison it with the Word of God and evict it by seeking deliverance and living a righteous life.

I understand the allure of the supernatural. God is supernatural, which is why we are so drawn to it. However, testing every spirit is vital. You don't know what you don't know, so if you have meddled with the occult, don't be afraid or self-condemning—seek the Holy Spirit. God is good. He has delivered His people from demons since the beginning of time, and His grace is unfathomable.

I was submerged in this lifestyle for a long time before it turned on me, and I began to recognize its evil works in my life. Still, on occasion, I make mistakes when I choose to ignore or brush off my discernment. For example, receiving a gift and bringing it into my home when I shouldn't have, or watching a show with an undertone that glorifies sin. It's not religious, its discernment. And what may be safe for some may not be for others.

Personal conviction is biblical; however, the Bible is clear about all things witchcraft. Each time I have personally watched a show in my home that glorifies witchcraft in any way (whether outright glorification or subtle), demonic attacks happen. I am very sensitive spiritually and am hyperaware of this, thanks to the Holy Spirit. Many people experience demonic attacks and don't even know what that is, or if they do, they don't know why it's happening or what to do about it. Don't let the enemy into your home!

Growing up, I was always hypersensitive and aware of things that others were not, or if they were, just not as intensely as I was. I often found myself in homes that were "haunted." I could see, hear, feel, know, and even smell things in the spirit realm. I figured it was just a "sixth sense" because I had seen the movie.

I'm going to do my best to explain something here that may be over your head, or you may easily understand exactly what I'm saying. I was considered an "indigo child." The term indigo children was coined in the 1970s when a parapsychologist and psychic claimed she could see auras around children.

Without going into too much depth on this term and its background, in short, certain children who had a "heightened consciousness" in addition to being highly creative were known as indigo children. Basically, psychic kids. This was me. When I was in witchcraft and the New Age, this was a very big deal and felt like a badge of honor; however, what it actually translates to spiritually is occult gifting, which is actually demonization.

The "giftings" I had as a child were not from God. They were a result of familial and generational spirits and curses passed down to me through my bloodline. Children who are introduced to and participate in witchcraft at a young age often have generational witchcraft in their generational line, whether they know it or not. This was also my experience, as I was introduced to it at the age of seven.

So while the world viewed this as a gift, it was actually demonic oppression because I was not under God's covering. Due to not being raised in a Holy Spirit-filled home, but instead one that was full of sin, I was very oppressed in many ways early on. When I entered middle school, the torment increased. During my junior year of high school, I opened the door to tarot and oracle card readings. Angel cards, by the way, are all about *fallen* angels—which are demons!

I encourage you to look into Doreen Virtue's testimony on this. She was one of the most famous occultists in the world of witchcraft and is now a born-again Christian! A majority of the really popular oracle cards were designed by her before she was saved. She speaks directly on this, refusing product royalties and downsizing her life significantly since the publishing company refused to stop producing her cards and books. She now calls her once "angel cards," demon cards.

As a teen, my draw to witchcraft amplified. I started picking up various witchcraft books and spent much of my spare time sitting in front of the witchcraft or spirituality section in libraries and bookstores for hours on end. I attended parties and events with large crowds of people asking about my paranormal encounters.

Multiple times I had rows of peers sitting down and listening, enthralled by the scary stories I would share. My body would shake as I described my first face-to-face demonic encounter in middle school. I was clearly traumatized and oppressed by a spirit of fear, but people craved the stories. Part of me did not want to share this encounter in this book because I do not want to glorify it in any way. However, the Holy Spirit has encouraged me to share details of my experiences in hopes of exposing the evil that can erupt through the choices we make as well as the things we do because we lack spiritual knowledge.

When participating in "spiritual" things out of ignorance, our spiritual defenses come down (and that's if we even have any to begin with). Picture this, a hedge of protection (an invisible forcefield) surrounds us. Sin creates holes within that hedge, and demons come in. What could start as just the point of a needle entering our hedge of protection could eventually expand into a doorway. If we are not spiritually discerning or aware, we can be taken advantage of and put ourselves in vulnerable situations where we are susceptible to demonic attack. I did this again and again and again.

The Bible tells us in Ephesians 6 to put on the *"full armor of God."* That's not just one or two pieces, it's a full spiritual get-up. This is a well-known Scripture to most Christians, and an even more powerful one if your eyes have been opened to spiritual things. When I first heard this Scripture, it didn't mean anything to me. It seemed like poetry, or another Bible verse used to make people who believed in this stuff feel better about things. Now that I have been delivered from *more than a thousand* devils, I know firsthand the importance and weight of this Scripture. It reads:

> *Finally, be strong in the Lord and in his mighty power.* **Put on the full armor of God** *so that you can take your stand against the devil's schemes. For our struggle is not against flesh and blood, but against the rulers, against the authorities, against the powers of this dark world and against the spiritual forces of evil in the heavenly realms. Therefore,* **put on the full armor of God** *so that when the day of evil comes, you may be able to stand your ground, and after you have done everything, to stand. Stand firm then, with the belt of truth buckled around your waist, the breastplate of righteousness in place, and your feet*

fitted with the readiness that comes from the gospel of peace. In addition to all this, take up the shield of faith, with which you can extinguish all the flaming arrows of the evil one. Take the helmet of salvation and the sword of the Spirit, which is the word of God. And pray in the Spirit on all occasions with all kinds of prayers and requests. With this in mind, be alert and always keep on praying for all the Lord's people (Ephesians 6:10-18 NIV).

The following are different aspects of the armor that protect your spirit:

- *Salvation:* Salvation is the helmet that guards your mind. Being saved and believing in Jesus, making Him Lord of your life. If He truly is your God, no demon can take His place in your mind. You have to make the honest choice to follow Him and keep following Him and reading His Word to renew and transform your mind.
- *Righteousness:* Righteousness is the breastplate that guards your heart. Getting *right* with God and operating from a pure heart. If you are doing something you feel might not be right, it probably isn't. The deeper your relationship with God, the easier it is to become aware of what keeps you from being right with the Lord. Righteousness can seem hard at first, but peace always blossoms as a result. Honor your own convictions, even if they are different from someone else's.
- *Truth:* Truth is the belt around your waist. You shall *know* the truth, and the truth will set you free. Not an experience

of the truth, but knowing it fully and believing it. The more guarded you are in truth, the less likely you are to sin. Guard yourself from all sexual impurity!

- *Peace:* The shoes that carry you readies you for the gospel of peace. The gospel of peace is what we stand on as believers. We walk in peace, we carry the Gospel, and we share the love of God. We are called to tale the Gospel to all peoples of the earth, and with that, peace will be reaped and sown!
- *Faith:* Faith is the shield that protects you. Faith is a shield. When you are shielded, you are covered and protected. Radical faith opens the door for healing and deliverance. Fear cannot come against true faith. The lies and attacks (or flaming arrows) of the enemy dissipate against your faith in God. Faith shuts down demonic strategy every time.
- *The Word of God:* The Word of God is the sword that defends you. God's Word is your defense. When things are problematic, speak His Word. When you get that medical report or diagnosis, when you experience a trauma, a heartbreak, or whatever, you need to come against that evil with the Word of God. If you are under demonic attack, the Word of God is your sword. It *will* slay demons. I have seen Scripture literally freeze, taze, and harm demons in the spirit. It puts them in a chokehold!
- *Prayer:* Prayer brings life and change! We are called to pray in the Spirit (speak in tongues) and to pray regularly for one another (the saints or other believers). The tongue brings life or death. When we speak life out loud through

the power of prayer, the atmosphere shifts! And when we speak in tongues, we are edifying ourselves and speaking a language to the Lord that the enemy cannot understand.

The full armor of God is not just a Scripture to encourage, it is a battle plan! If you go out into the battlefield (the world) without one of the elements that make up your armor, or without any of them, you practically have a target on your back! At one point, I felt like I kept getting attacked. I had just moved out of state with my family and hadn't built a community yet. I was in an abusive marriage (which is definitely an open door for the enemy by the way!), and I knew my armor wasn't rightly worn. I wasn't living in sin, but I had a feeling something was off, beyond my relationship issues.

I asked the Lord to show me my armor. He gave me a vision. It looked like everything was intact from the front. Then He showed me the back of me. There was a huge gap behind my right shoulder—a massive hole in my armor. My back wasn't covered. Had I been on an actual battlefield, with arrows, gunfire, or swords coming at me, I would have been stabbed in the back.

Now this vision is much more prophetic than I recognized at the time I received it.

I brought this vision to my mentor, Sue, and said, "Doesn't the breastplate go all the way around? Shouldn't it cover my back, too? I'm confused because I am walking in righteousness, so why would there be a hole in the back of my armor?" She then explained Roman army formations to me and emphasized the importance of building community, "The enemy always attacks the vulnerable," she said.

If someone is isolated, that person is vulnerable. Period. When it comes to Roman army formations, they operated in groups, where the person behind covered the person in front's back with a shield. The shields were made of leather and soaked in water so that when actual flaming arrows came firing down, they would be put out instantly. One person can only cover or defend themselves so much; so in war, someone is there to cover your back. Community matters! Church matters! But this vision actually had a double meaning.

In marriage, the husband is called to be a covering for the wife, and oftentimes, a mother is a covering for the children. Love covers a multitude of sins. If the husband is not covering the wife, and is in fact abusing her, acting in habitual sin, mistreating her, or not loving her as Christ loved the Church, there is a lack of covering that comes through love and prayer. I was not being covered and was therefore open to attack.

Later, after this vision, I discovered multiple betrayals. At the time of the vision, this wasn't revealed to me, though it was later. If you don't have revelation, ask the Lord and wait for His answer.

So there was a hole in my armor. I didn't have community, I didn't have a God-fearing husband, and I was alone and vulnerable. Once I built community and things panned out differently with my husband, the Lord showed me I wasn't just fully covered, but completely hidden away.

Eventually, God fully shielded me from the abuse, which I am so unbelievably grateful for now after enduring abuse much of my life. I had to fully surrender to God. And He rescued me. God is your defender, He will fight your battles, and He will rescue you. You need only be still (Exodus 14:14).

FACE-TO-FACE WITH MY FIRST DEMON

Although I grew up with a believing grandmother and a dad who would take me to church for a period of time in grade school, I was not taught about the deception of evil, the dangers of magic, what sin actually was and why it was bad, or the importance of being spiritually protected. I know this topic is heavy for some people, but these concepts are especially vital for children to understand. It can save their life!

Satan loves to entice children into his kingdom by using books, tv shows, movies, and video games. If you search the internet for the statue outside of the Church of Satan, it is a baphomet next to two children looking up at it. That clearly speaks for itself. If we don't teach our children, they will be destroyed for a lack of knowledge (Hosea 4:6).

As I progressed through grade school to twelfth grade, I had no knowledge of godly discernment or an understanding of spiritual protection. So when I awkwardly paraded through middle school, I did what my friends did for the most part. My identity was rooted in wanting to be accepted, like most middle schoolers. In eighth grade, I signed up for a camping trip through a club. I joined this club because my friends did, and

I signed up for the camping trip at some cabin in the woods because my friends did. I hated camping and anything to do with the wilderness.

I also had a crippling fear of spending the night in places, which I now attribute to the abuse I endured growing up. At that time, I was unaware of that connection, of course; I just knew I was 13 and embarrassed by this fear and wanted to get over it once and for all. My parents were on board and encouraged me to go on the trip. It was a two-day, one-night stay at a location seven hours from home. I would go with a busload of kids from my class, and I figured being with so many friends might make me feel more comfortable.

This was a grave mistake for me. Whenever we make decisions to appease someone else or to prove ourselves, that indicates that something is out of balance. Obviously, I was in the eighth grade and had a broken inner compass, so I don't blame my younger self. I feel badly for her.

I packed an overnight duffel, and as our bus drove through forests and rocky terrain, I began to deeply regret my decision. There was no going back. *What have I done? I can't go back now,* I thought. We had been driving for hours. I began to tense up, my fear getting the best of me. *It's only one night,* I thought, my hands profusely sweating. *Why am I so nervous?* I tried to soothe myself to the best of my ability. Looking back, this absolutely could have been a trauma response, and may have been partially, but I knew deep within me that this was not going to be the trip I wanted it to be.

It is important, of course, to face our fears as we grow up, but it is also important to listen to our God-given intuition. When we don't know ourselves well enough, fear and intuition can feel the same, or we can be fairly removed from it. Because my intuition was not developed or fostered by a godly adult, or at all really, I overrode my bad feelings time and again.

Part of this was also because I had been molested for many years, and my abuser would convince me that it wasn't bad, even though I knew it was. The level of manipulation, violation, and gaslighting that a victim experiences is astronomical.

Eventually, the survivor will tell themselves things like, "It's not that bad; I'm making a big deal of this; It was my fault; I'm just dramatic; I should have known better; It was just a dream; It wasn't real," and so on. Sometimes the denial can be so deep that survivors will convince themselves it didn't even happen to get through it. Gaslighting degrades a person's spirit over time. Growing up, I had become so accustomed to shutting down my discernment that it formed into a habit of not trusting myself. This habit eventually led me into some very dark places where I suffered as a result.

As we got closer to the cabin's location, I grew more and more nervous. The school bus pulled into the dirt parking lot, and I looked through the window at a two-story cabin. My skin crawled. *At least we aren't actually camping*, I said to myself. All the kids began whooping in excitement. While I tried my best to fake my excitement, fear invaded every cell of my body. We filed out of the bus, pushing past one another and then up the stairs, into the front door of the cabin.

A Native American woman with black and gray hair greeted us. She smiled a cold, fake smile. The moment I stepped foot inside the cabin, I paused and surveyed the living room and kitchen. My eyes scanned the granite countertops. "GET OUT OF HERE!" An evil voice shook me to my core. I had never heard a voice like that in my life, and it caught me *very* off guard. I knew it was not my voice or my fear speaking. This was another entity entirely. I was in for it, and I knew it.

As I got older and immersed myself in psychic mediumship, I became pretty desensitized to voices like this (which are demons by the way). The spirit world scared me less and less over time, but at this age, the fear was all-consuming. I grabbed the little Cross I wore around my neck that my mom let me pick out from Tiffany's. We were not a lavish family in the slightest, so to be able to spend $120 on a piece of jewelry for my eighth-grade graduation was a huge deal.

It was a small crucifix I wore mainly for protection. I thought objects could protect me. I thought the symbol alone of Jesus could protect me. I knew Jesus was a real God. I didn't think then that He was the *only* way, as I had also been involved in the Hare Krishna Temple while growing up and worshiped Krishna and Rama too. Yet, Jesus always felt safest to me and for good reason.

My friends and I rushed into the bedrooms to try to find the perfect room so that we could all be together. We settled for a room with four bunks. There were five of us, so one girl would sleep on the floor. That afternoon, we played weird games where we were blindfolded and taken to different parts of the surrounding land. This was supposedly a team-building exercise. I was led to a tombstone.

Apparently, a man had died there when he had mysteriously fallen off the cliff next to the house. My group put my hands on the gravesite and then tore the blindfold off me, laughing.

"Ahh!" I screamed, jumping backward. "Dude!" Everyone got a kick out of my reaction, and we moved on to the next activity. I felt dissociated the whole day. At nighttime, we sat by the campfire where, naturally, ghost stories were being told. I covered my ears while my friends poked and giggled at me.

The adults also laughed. This felt like bullying. I was not typically a scared person; in fact, I usually acted quite the opposite, unless I had to present a project to a classroom full of peers. Then I was mortified. But I was a risk-taker from a very young age, and I was always bold about it. This, however, was my weakness—the supernatural. It was unknown to me, and it felt out of control. I saw and heard things I did not want to see or hear. I was tormented because I was demonized. I could have honestly used a deliverance as a teen!

The majority of my life before ten years old was a blackout. I have very few memories of those years, some of which are good, some are scary, and some are very sad. As I mentioned earlier in this book, psychologists attribute such blackouts to severe traumatic events and dissociation. Blotting out time to survive it. Experts in deliverance attribute it to major demonic possession, which can happen with trauma, among others like occult rituals and such.

Trauma was an entry point for the demonic, and sadly, due to no fault of my own, a huge door had been kicked in and left wide open for many years of my early life. So when I would enter into a place like the one I was in, it was as if demonic spirits flocked to me. The fear did not help either, because that, too, is an open door. Just like predators in the wild feed off fear, so do evil spirits! (See Isaiah 41:10.)

After the campfire, we went into the living room, where again, more ghost stories were told. The Native homeowner looked at me with evil in her eyes. It felt like there was such hatred there, and it was as if she was enjoying my squirming. I thought that was so bizarre. Before bed, she warned all the kids, "Oh, and if any of you hear or see anything in the night, don't worry about it." She walked into her room smiling. All the boys went downstairs and settled into their bunks, as did the girls upstairs. When it was time to turn out the lights, she wandered to each bedroom to turn off the light.

"Hey," I said as the owner poked her head into our room to shut off the light. "Do you have any night lights or anything like that for us here?" She looked through me, gave me a firm "No," and closed the door. I thought it was odd that she seemed almost hateful to me. A friend in the room let me keep her flashlight, so I fell asleep with it in my hand right next to my teddy bear.

Thud. I woke up. Thud, thud, thud, thud, thud. The soft pounding began to amplify into a louder pounding that went all around the room. Fear gripped me again, and this time harder. *It's probably just the boys messing with us*, I thought. Then the pounding circled the room and was getting louder and quicker. My head was pressed up against the wall as loud thuds passed behind it. I pulled away from the wall, trying to make myself smaller in my bed.

I tried to fall back asleep as best I could, but the adrenaline was pumping through my body so intensely that it was impossible. My hand gripped the Cross around my neck. "Jesus, if You are real, make this stop. Make this stop," I said internally over and over and over again. Our bedroom door was open partway, and then the room got very quiet and still. Slam, slam! The screen door and glass door down the hall opened and closed, a light turned on and off in the bathroom, and the mirror, which was on a hinge in the bathroom, creaked open and shut.

Slam, slam! The screen door and glass door opened and closed again. This happened so quickly that it would be humanly impossible to move that fast. I knew that if, in fact, it was a person doing it, there was no way it could have been just one person; it would have had to be two people. I lay there frozen in fear, staring through the bunk ladder at our open bedroom door.

"Jesus. If You're here. Please help me, please help me." I fell asleep. Then the pounding began again, and I was startled awake from my short slumber. It was *so* loud. I was shocked that the entire upstairs was not waking up because of it.

"Hey!" I whispered loudly, "Get up!" I was on the bottom bunk, so I kicked my friend's bed above me multiple times. She was out. So I turned to my other friend to the right of me, "Hey!" I said. "Hey! Wake up!" But nothing. Everyone was sound asleep, and I was too scared to move off my bed. Then Bree, my friend who was on the floor, woke up, rubbing her eyes. The pounding stopped and started again. "What the heck is that?" she said. It was amplifying.

"Dude, I don't know, it has been going on for a while, and our door is open now."

"What? Do you want me to come up there with you?" she asked.

"Yeah."

Bree crawled out of her sleeping bag and got up on the twin bed with me. We lay there, paralyzed and frozen together, silently panicking about the constant pounding. "Bree, there's no way this could be the boys. They are downstairs; this is going all the way around our room."

"That's true...," she trailed off.

"It's going behind our heads," I whispered. "There are no rooms on two sides of this bedroom."

Before bed that evening, the boys got on their bunks downstairs and began banging on the ceiling until they were told to settle down and go to sleep. This was not that. The bedroom we were in was upstairs, down the hall on the far right.

The hallway and another bedroom shared two walls with our room, while the other two walls did not have anything next to them. It was *naturally* impossible for a pounding like that to encircle our room. We were dealing with the demonic.

We both curled into each other and remained in and out of sleep the entire night. I woke up a time or two to the pounding, and one time in a very lucid state, I woke and thought I saw an apparition near our bed. I fell back asleep. I woke again to an extremely eerie feeling; I almost felt drunk. I looked over at my friend's bed to the right of me and swore I saw something.

I blinked a couple of times, but I wasn't sure what I was looking at. A creature with a large head, with coal-black eyes that seemed deep yet went nowhere, and a huge smile starting to form on its face. This thing was lying on the bed across from me, and it was perched up on two hands, just staring at me, smiling. It looked like it only had half of a body. I remember being so out of it, questioning if what I was seeing was even real. I fell back asleep again.

"Jenny, Jenny!" Bree's elbow prodded my side. Her voice was hushed and panicked.

"What? What is it?" I said, opening my eyes and looking straight up at the mattress above me.

"He is looking at us," she said quietly with a shaky voice.

"What?" My heart sank into the pit of my stomach, and cold sweat began to form on my hairline. I gripped the Cross around my neck.

"Look over at Sarah's bed. He is right there," she said.

"No. Wait, is he perched up on two elbows staring at us right now?" My voice, too, trembled. I kept staring at the mattress above my head. I did not want to look at it. Bree slowly turned her head to the right and then back to me.

"Yes. And he is smiling at us."

Fear. Indescribable, tormenting, and entrapping fear. We lay there, entirely frozen, eventually drifting off to sleep once more. At 4 a.m. I knew that somebody was actually awake, so I got up shortly after. Our eighth-grade history teacher, who was one of the chaperones for the trip, was lounging on the couch, barely waking up. I felt safe now that somebody was actually awake. Bree and I shared our experience with the teacher.

"Did you hear the pounding all night?" we asked.

"What pounding? You mean when the boys were on their bunks pounding on the ceiling?"

"No, we knew when they were doing that. But later in the night. Like, the whole night? The pounding all around the house? You didn't hear it?" I asked, confused. "It was so loud."

"Yeah, and we saw some creepy ghost thing on Sarah's bed last night, too," Bree added. Mr. H. laughed in disbelief, shaking his head.

"Oh, I'm sure." He rolled his eyes, rubbing his face tiredly, coffee mug in hand. We shared the full details of what had happened with the girls in our room. They laughed at us and, for the rest of high school, would make fun of the time we "saw a ghost on Sarah's bed." This was triggering on multiple levels for me. I hated not being believed. The bus ride home felt like it took a century.

When I arrived home, I shelved my teddy bear in my bedroom closet and took off the Cross around my neck. *These things don't even work.* An innocence broke in me that weekend. The little bit of faith I had slipped off me as I placed my necklace in my desk drawer. You see, faith and protection don't come from objects; they come from God. But I didn't know that then. All I knew was that I hadn't been protected much of my life, and I didn't know why.

Partway through my shower that night, it felt like a presence had entered the bathroom. *What is happening now?* Fear, again. Did this *thing* follow me home? That night I slept in my parents' bed. I tried to tell them about my experience, but it seemed inconvenient and unimportant to them. At 13 years old, it felt like every traumatic experience I had ever endured was insignificant and invisible to everybody else. A core belief I would carry on my shoulders for well over a decade to come: *I was insignificant.*

Loneliness, depression, anxiety, and self-hate crawled into my life like a spider up a drain. That night, at 13 years old, I wet the bed.

12

RITUALS, OCCULT PRACTICES, AND THE LEGAL RIGHTS OF DEMONS

This face-to-face demonic encounter was pivotal for me as a teenager. As my loneliness and depression grew deeper and the little faith I had in God was practically gone, I began to shut down in many ways. Something in me changed after that event. I suddenly started seeing spirits regularly, hearing them, physically feeling and sensing them; fear always came with it. I could never shut it off after that!

Before this event, I had a few encounters, like when I was seven and played with a Ouija board. After this, a switch turned on that I could not turn off. I only had one friend who understood, and her cousin who would do automatic writing at funerals (something I would later practice on my own). Automatic writing is when you channel a spirit and write down what it has to say.

A person is often completely taken over by a spirit of divination while doing this. What you are watching if you witness something like this, is a demonic possession. Familiar spirits are demons and they are mentioned in the Bible. Familiar spirits like families. Think "familial." Spirits of witchcraft, addiction, or unforgiveness are just a few examples that may plague an entire bloodline.

My friend Pearl, who had similar experiences, was depressed like I was and self-harmed like I did. Pearl, my friend Janie, and me, all had a notebook we'd hand off to one another during passing periods. It was dedicated to the discussion of self-harm, suicidal ideation, and all the ways we wanted to die. Darkness clung to us and brought us together.

We were sad girls who felt alone. Death seemed like a savior to us. Pearl had ghostly encounters in her house, like I did, so we felt safe with one another because we knew what we were experiencing was very real. As we transitioned into high school, our friendships shifted. I started hanging out with a different crowd who drank and did drugs. I began identifying more as a party girl. That party girl façade, I hoped, would cover up how deeply sad, insecure, and scared I was.

I became popular in school, except many in my circle strongly rejected the part of me that saw into the spirit realm and would tease me because of it. Some, however, did embrace it. Most of my friends, though, thought I was just living in a made-up supernatural story world. It felt like I was walking in two worlds. I remember being called "schizo-girl" by a girl on the cheer team because I could "see and hear things that weren't there." I had thick skin, but statements like that bothered me. When people hung around me long enough, they too would have spiritual encounters, so the label was quickly debunked. The truth of the matter was, I had been cursed.

I want to mention that a mental health diagnosis is not God's will. His will for us does not include anything that falls under the umbrella of mental illness. God does *not* give illness. It is a by-product of the fall of Adam, and it is often a spirit or a curse that has attached itself to a generational line. Many people diagnosed with one or more mental illnesses often have an unloving home life.

There is no ceiling on what God can do, and just like the well-known Bible teacher Priscilla Shirer says, "We do not have the capacity to wear God out." Therefore, He does not grow weary of healing and delivering His people! I have been free from my torment for seven years now and off all psychiatric medication since my first deliverance. If God can do it in me, He can do it in you.

The enemy always wants to shut down what God wants to show off. Before I came to know Christ, I believed everybody had their path, and it didn't matter what you chose as long as you were a "good person." That is probably the biggest lie of the devil, next to the deception that satan doesn't exist. Every person has a different idea of what a good person is. Therefore, being good is a matter of human opinion.

Unfortunately, we are not the judges of what *good* is. That is where the Word of God comes in. The Bible is helpful, pointing out the ways in which we can descend into sin and can ascend into righteousness; His grace makes that possible.

When we accept Jesus, we are in His righteousness. The Bible is not a baseball bat to beat people with—it's a pillow to rest on and a sword to fight evil with. You *have* to know that you have an enemy to defend yourself against one, right? Until my high school graduation, I sometimes prayed to Jesus or went to worship nights down the street. There was definitely a piece of me inherently drawn to Jesus—not the words a pastor spoke but a feeling that I couldn't get anywhere else. I was caught up in the world of me and was a slave to sin, but I still wanted peace. I just looked for it in all the wrong places.

Jane Goodall, the well-known ethnologist and conservationist who studied chimpanzees her entire life, speaks about a spiritual peace she found in the jungles with these creatures. She says that the same sense of spiritual peace she felt among the trees, she has also felt in old cathedrals where people have gone to worship year after year. This peace is the presence of God, and it usually comes in the form of a feeling, not words. Jane's experience is what I am describing.

As a teen, I encountered God's peace on worship nights. However, it wasn't enough then for me to stick around. My allegiance to self and satan was much more entrenched than my occasional awareness of God. Not long after meeting with the witch who read my palm at 18, I crossed paths with another diviner outside a grocery store.

"Hey!" a man hollered at me as I walked out of the store. "Do you like whales?"

I laughed. He caught my attention. "I love whales!" I began to walk past him, groceries in hand.

"Awesome! Me too!" He walked over to me with a clipboard pressed to his side. He was working with an environmental nonprofit. I hardly had any money to my name, but I weakly signed up to be a monthly donor. I loved animals, I cared a lot about the environment, and I didn't want to say no.

His black hair touched his auburn skin and rested on his shoulders. He had interesting beads and crystals around his neck and wrists and his hands were adorned in rings.

"You're an Aquarius, aren't you?" he asked. That was his in.

"Yes, I am! The most unique sign of the Zodiac." I laughed. "How'd you know? Looking back, he probably saw my date of birth on the form I had just filled out, but I was being *seen* at the moment, which, again, meant everything to me at that time.

"I could just tell. Let me do a reading on you, yeah?" he asked.

"Oh, no. Sorry. I have, like, no money." That was true.

"No, no. For free. I want to." His dark eyes wouldn't let me say no.

"Wow, really? Yes!" I said.

He smiled and reached for my hand. "You are an artist, huh? Very creative."

He continued in his reading, which went on for quite some time. He spoke about my home, current and future partners, stress, gifts, and so on. I was enthralled. This reading, however, did not come without a cost. Ten years after our first meeting, I would have demons cast out from my body that were connected to curses put on me or transferred to me by this very person.

I had a feeling that his practices were dark, but a magnetic draw pulled me in. I had questions, and he had answers. After meeting him, I began to experience increased paranormal activity in my home. I would hear humming in my room, my closet door would open and close every night at the same time, and my roommate with whom I shared a bed even woke up one night sitting straight up in bed like a zombie with her eyes wide open, saying, "She is here."

"What! Who is here?" I woke up, terrified.

"You know her," she replied. Still sitting straight up, stiff as a board, eyes staring vacantly forward.

"Dude, where? You're freaking me out!"

"At the edge of the bed. She is here," Abby said, laying back down as if what just happened, didn't. And she went right back to sleep.

"Abby! What the heck!" I shook her and shook her.

"Wake up! What are you doing?"

When I finally woke her, she vaguely remembered what had just happened. We both were afraid and confused. On Friday the thirteenth, green apparitions appeared in my room along with hissing. I did not like this as it felt violating and uninvited. The truth was, though, that I did invite it in; I just didn't mean to. A Scripture that comes to mind here is Hosea 4:6 (NIV): *"My people are destroyed from lack of knowledge."*

After my first reading with the warlock, I contacted him periodically. Years later, I sought him out during a panicked situation when my friend Nick was close to death. The friend was a past lover of mine who was lost in a canyon in Orange County and had been missing for days. Friends and family formed search parties looking for him and the girl he was with.

In that situation, I hurriedly traveled to the warlock's home at night. I wanted to do everything I could in this situation, and what I knew that worked, was magic. As I approached the warlock's house in the canyon, he greeted me at the front door and had me follow him up a flight of stairs to his room. He had altars set up with objects I hadn't seen before. I figured it was some African mysticism or something native.

The objects were strange, and I found myself not wanting to look at them. I was nervous. This warlock was practicing a different kind of magic. He did a reading and sent me home with directions regarding my friend. I always seemed to ask psychics and witches of different kinds if they believed in God. I literally asked every person who had ever done a reading on me that question.

They would say in a roundabout way that they believed in a creator but would often go on to speak about other spirits, guides and ascended masters. Sometimes, they would mention

Jesus only as a teacher, prophet, or master. I also would ask them occasionally if they did readings on Christians. They told me they did often. Knowing what I know now, I assume these to be lukewarm, desperate, or backsliding Christians—because a Spirit-filled believer would never step into this.

The warlock told me multiple Christians sought him out. As I sat across from him, I felt like something occurring in the supernatural wasn't right, but I could not resist my draw to things of this nature. I felt afraid yet intrigued as if I wanted to hide yet be seen. I wanted to delve deeper into occultic practices and refine my knowledge of the spirit realm. I wanted to pursue mediums and be pursued by others for readings and information.

So many things had happened in my life where I felt totally and completely powerless. When it came to witchcraft, it felt like I finally had control over *something*. I had no idea that what I was actually doing was giving up my control to demons that needed a host.

When I left his house in the canyon, he told me to do a ritual in my home that night. I went out and bought candles as directed, and I wrote things on pieces of paper because I did not have an article of Nick's clothing or any of his hair, which was directed to me as a second option. I laid out some herbs and repeated a chant-like spell repeatedly to a specific saint. I had no idea I had just partaken in my first Santeria ceremony. This type of witchcraft blends practices from both Roman Catholicism and Yoruba.

Santeria literally means "the way of the saints." How deceptive is that? Unfortunately, many worship saints and pray to them as they believe they will intercede for us. For some, the lines get blurred with elements of witchcraft. I performed this ritual with a friend and began to get visions.

The next morning, my boyfriend Greg (ex-satanist and gang member) tore off a piece of a cardboard box and made a Ouija board out of it. We joined the search party that day in the canyon and took the handmade board with us. I would not put my hands on it. However, Greg did. Someone approached me, asking me to help lead, and I was then taken on a helicopter to search.

I felt purposeful in my psychic pursuit, but it still didn't feel right. We were given information by the demonic, but we were not the ones to find my lost friend. The coordinates we got were not far off. However, Nick and the other girl were found alive and admitted to the hospital!

You see, although I was given some supernatural information, it *always* came with a cost. Each time I partook in an occult ritual or ceremony, it widened the dimensions of a spiritual door in my life for the enemy. A significant unseen damage occurred in my soul even though I thought I was doing the best thing at the time. Asking a warlock for direction who had been right about things in my life before felt like my only option. I was desperate and didn't want my friend to die.

This deception, to me, is one of the saddest facets of witchcraft. It draws in the desperate, and then it keeps them in bondage. I was only increasing problems in my life, not solving them. I remember some girl I used to party with in my late teens telling me I shouldn't be seeing psychics.

"What do you mean, why?" I laughed at her as I cut through the McDonald's parking lot on the way to my apartment.

"I heard it opens a door," she said seriously. This caught me off guard, considering the group of people I was hanging around with had little to no morals, let alone knowledge about the supernatural.

"What do you mean?" I asked.

"I don't know, it's like bad luck or something. That's what my mom says."

Her face was so serious, and I was confused by it. So, I chose to ignore the warning. *People just don't get it,* I thought to myself. I couldn't say no to readings. If I had $25 in my bank account, it was the psychic's money. I was desperate for direction, answers, confirmation, and compliments. I saw another witch in Venice Beach who was upfront about her dark magic.

"I hex those Christians who walk by here all the time," she said in her bitter voice.

I side-eyed my boyfriend and sat down. When I walked up the steps and into her home, I could feel the pressure of evil in that house. It felt like a hundred invisible black ghosts were swirling and hovering over us. It was almost like I had to duck to move through that place; the room was thick with them.

It was an eerie experience. I left that day instantly knowing something negative had just happened. She gave us bad news, and as I walked out, I said to my boyfriend, "Man, I feel like something was just taken from me. That was weird." I shook it off and then went home and got drunk.

Increased paranormal activity was happening yet again, this time in a new apartment. My roommates always experienced the wild stuff too. It was a regular occurrence, and it seemed to be amping up. Because the demonic activity typically centered on *me*, I wanted to do what I could to shut it off. So as a result, I began using drugs and drinking more to fall asleep.

Chaos always broke out. Strange people slogged in and out of the many apartments I had, bringing all their baggage with them and leaving it inside. My home was a revolving door for the lost. When I look back and think about some of the people who came into my house, I can't even believe it.

Through the many diviners and witches I encountered on my detoured quest to Jesus Christ, I became entranced by herbal magic and crystal healing. I spent my free time in occult shops where I made connections with the psychics there. I felt at peace in these places, one of which I would phone at least every two weeks for information. She was good friends with another medium who became my teacher.

This medium, whom I will call Katy, was related to a woman I had occasionally worked for in the past. I loved this connection. Katy was older and beautiful. Although highly immersed in her craft, she was sensitive, kind, and warm in many ways. She did not practice black magic, but white magic. I appreciated this at that time.

The difference between white magic and black magic? There is no difference at the root of it. Witchcraft, by definition on Google, is "the practice of magic (especially black magic) or the use of spells." In a modern context, it is a religious practice involving magic and the affinity with nature, usually within a pagan tradition. It is also "bewitching or fascinating with charm." Truly, any form of manipulation and control is in the realm of witchcraft.

In a simplified sense, white magic is typically socially acceptable, whereas black magic is less so. The line between them denotes the intention to cause harm and have major control over situations (black magic) whereas white magic is deemed more selfless, and there isn't usually intentional harm or control per se.

The idea of white magic is very misleading. I had an easy time convincing myself that Wiccan practices, white magic, and goddess worship were acceptable in my life because I was never trying to harm a person intentionally. I wanted to do mostly good and bring good things to myself. It was however, deeply rooted in self, which should always be a red flag.

Although my intentions were not to harm people, the people I brought into readings and practices were definitely harmed spiritually. They were seduced into opening a door to the demonic in their own lives. You can't involve yourself in occult practices, or sin for that matter, of any kind and not leave unscathed.

Some occult practices include black magic; white magic; Wicca; goddess; god; or saint worship; false religions; nature worship (yep, that includes burning sage and palo-santo); Satanism and Luciferian practices; astral projection; voodoo; Yoruba; Santeria; herbal magic; crystal/stone healing; divination through crystal balls; magic mirrors; altars; the third eye; transcendental meditation; kundalini, other forms of yoga, channeling; pendulum uses; light language; chakra cleansing, centering, and healing; any form of energy healing; reiki; the casting of spells whether upon oneself or others; the New Age; potions, consulting witchdoctors, psychics, and mediums; and necromancy, including communicating with extraterrestrial aliens (which are demonic spirits) as well.

Candle magic, sex magic, and blood magic are also all demonic. Some feminists are attracted to variations of blood magic because they believe it celebrates their monthly cycle and femininity. Again, deception. More occultic things include Ouija boards, seances, tea leaf or coffee ground reading, palm reading, aura reading and practices, magic circles, opening or closing portals, rituals and ceremonies including moon ceremonies and the use of hallucinogens during ceremonies, astrology (enneagrams were also created by an occultist), the use of any type of tarot or oracle cards including but not confined to standard cards, angel, goddess, animal totem decks and the like. Sadly, Disney has even started producing their own decks.

These are only a short list of the many occult avenues that satan uses to entrap people. If you have meddled in these areas, even if it was just once, repent now. I say this out of all of the love in my heart for people in bondage (known and unknown) and from a place of true freedom from witchcraft. I lived it. It looks pretty, and it sounds nice because witchcraft in all forms is designed to be alluring!

Lucifer himself was once one of the most beautiful angels. He is attractive in many ways, but it is all a facade (Ezekiel 28:12-15)! If you are practicing any of these things listed, you have been manipulated and deceived by the master deceiver, satan. There is always a trade-off when it comes to satan. The devil will take advantage of every opportunity he can. If you do not give him access to your life, he cannot control it.

However, when you open a door, you essentially give the enemy legal rights to your life. Not all open doors look like witchcraft, though. Alcoholics or very heavy drinkers have an open door. If you are having sex outside of marriage, that is an open door. If you are frequenting places of other religions and engaging in their practices (like I did in Krishna, Buddhist, Unity, and Goddess temples), that is an open door. Excessive gossiping can be an open door. Abuse of any kind is an open door.

Constant anxiety and fear are open doors. Even what we watch or listen to can create open doors. Some are less obvious than others. This is where a relationship with Jesus and the power of the Holy Spirit comes in. Also, being part of a church body is extremely important! Conviction—that feeling you get that you should or should not do something—is enhanced as you get closer to God.

I once practiced magic, also known as magick, and used intravenous cocaine without much thought about it. Clearly, those were two very serious doors I opened in my life. Now I have developed such an intimate relationship with God that I repent if I have so much as a judgmental thought toward someone. I even gave up caffeine per my convictions for a period of time. If we want to live out the life God has planned for us, following our convictions from the Holy Spirit will get us there.

Regardless of all the freedom I have experienced, this doesn't mean I do not struggle. God is regularly pruning His garden (us) so we can bear new, fresh, and healthy fruit in our lives. We live in a fallen world, but sin starts as a thought. Keep your thought life pure, and your life will be positively refined in many ways.

I have mentioned the legal rights of the demonic a few times. So what does that mean? In a simplified sense, legal rights essentially are laws that protect people, right? It is illegal for me to break into your house and steal from it. If I do that, I will go to jail. Laws are set to ensure everyone's safety.

Legal rights apply to both the natural and the supernatural. Demons don't break in, they are given access. If I lived with you, my name is on the lease and I have a key, the reality is I could steal from you if I wanted to. I've been granted access and you trust me.

This same example applies to the demonic. If a demonic spirit is given a key or allowed in, they will not only enter but also steal and destroy whatever they can. If they have entered a person, they will do anything possible to deteriorate the mind, body, relationships (especially with God), and materials or finances. They have one motive, and that's to steal, kill and destroy. They will do anything to keep your heart away from God. Another easy-to-digest this example would be: if I left my front door open all day and all night long, what would come inside? Maybe some bugs, a mouse, maybe a rat or a bear, or another person. Even if I just left the door open a crack, things would eventually come in. This is what we do with our spirits. "Oh, I'll just watch porn this weekend while my wife is out of town." "I'll just let the guy I've been talking to spend the night." "I'll just open one more credit card." "It's just weed, I won't try anything else." "I just want to feel better, aligning my chakras is okay." Every time you partake in sin, you are cracking the door open.

The Word of God gives us commandments. The commandments are not a prison sentence but laws for spiritual safety, which can also evolve into emotional and physical safety. If the laws get broken, that part of your life no longer belongs to you but to satan.

When a police officer arrests you, you are under that officer's authority. You are put in jail and subject to the rules and regulations of the penitentiary until you are released. You no longer have total control of what you want to do. That is exactly how it works in the spirit realm, except Jesus is the One who releases you. The demonic doesn't happily give you up. Their objective is to keep you imprisoned your entire life, take over your soul, and bind you to hell for eternity. Their agenda opposes God's plan and purpose for your life. When it comes to Jesus, Revelation 3:20 says that He stands before us, knocking on our door.

It is up to us to let Him into our hearts and lives. So even God Himself respects these spiritual laws and operations He has implemented. When you open the door to Jesus, miraculous things will occur in your life. If sin comes knocking at your door, and you don't get out in a reasonable amount of time, demons now have legal rights to you, and destruction multiplies. The point is, your free will and choice remain in both of these circumstances.

If you have ever read the whimsical tale *A Wrinkle in Time* or have seen the movie of the same name, the main character Meg, her brother Charles-Wallace, and her friend Calvin are taken through time and space to find Meg's father. They find themselves starving when they enter an alternate universe (which I feel represents hell). They come to a beach crowded with people and are then approached by a man who recognizes them and offers them a meal.

The children are unfamiliar with this man yet are strangely attracted to him. He is the enemy and enticing at that. A banquet of food suddenly appears before them, "Eat up!" the man says, capitalizing on their current weakness (hunger). Meg is apprehensive and watchful, but the boys dig in. As Calvin halfway devours his sandwich, Charles-Wallace stops after a few bites and complains of the meal tasting like dirt. Just then, their sandwiches disintegrate in their hands, leaving them with sand running through their fingers.

The thing that was supposed to satisfy their hunger was false. Then, Charles-Wallace begins to separate himself from Meg and Calvin and becomes prey to isolation and manipulation by following the enemy, who points out how "different" he is from those around him—thus luring him in. "You're different like me; follow me." The enemy deceives. Charles-Wallace has always been so different from everyone else; deep down, he just wants to belong.

This perfectly illustrates what the devil does. He deceives! The enemy recognizes the weakness in a person and goes after it by offering something they need or want. He then uses it to harm them, creating a legal right in that person's life for the demonic to enter. What we actually need is God, not what the Enemy is offering us.

Having a *real* relationship with the Lord is extremely helpful. This truth can be seen through my testimony and worldwide. Consider people like Heidi Baker, Todd White, Jessi Green, and Billy Graham. What began as a purely personal, individual relationship then grew into huge ministries that have helped many people!

When we hear from God, we can recognize the paths He wants us to take, the paths He wants us to avoid, and the relationships He wants us to cultivate. When we listen and follow His direction, we are protected spiritually en route to our best life! However, we always have free will, and I love that about God. He never takes captives, only volunteers.

13

THE UNDERGROUND WITCHCRAFT TEMPLE

As I continued down my broken road of New Age and witchcraft, my mind continued to unravel in many ways. Mental problems heightened, money was scarce, I probably had a hundred roommates, and my relationships were addictive and toxic. I also had many jobs and could not stop abusing drugs and alcohol. When I finally did stop, I couldn't stay away from a bar, club, or strip club for more than two weeks, even though I wasn't drinking anymore.

As I approached physical sobriety and recovery, my passion for witchcraft seemed to blaze. I continued my divinations and necromancy. Before finally sobering up, I remember being in my apartment with one of my roommates, Faith. She came into my room, and we casually conversed when we heard a strange noise.

Then, suddenly, all of the lights in the house buzzed loudly, dimmed, and flickered on and off. I figured it was a maintenance problem, and I jokingly stood to my feet and lifted my hands, yelling, "Spirits! If that's you, do it again!"

All the house lights buzzed, dimmed, and flashed on brightly again! I cackled. "Jenny, don't!" Faith laughed uncomfortably. I yelled, "Spirits! If that is you! Do it again!" The same thing occurred. My eyes widened in excitement. Lifting my hands higher this time, Faith motioned for me to stop. I shouted, "Do it again, spirits!" and it happened a third time.

"Oh my gosh, Jenny, stop!" Faith patted my arms down in fear.

"Okay, okay," I laughed. And we both walked out of the room.

This incident is just one example of my infatuation with the demonic, my obsession with the power it brought, and a glimpse into the paranormal in my life. Things like this were not unusual for me. Often, doors in my house would open and close by themselves. Curtains and bead curtains would move, animals would act bizarrely, and apparitions and shadows had become normal. Being physically touched by the demonic was also common, especially in the middle of the night when I would wake up to a presence in my room. These experiences started in childhood and persisted into adulthood.

My mother also had encounters in my childhood home. Horrible and fear-provoking noises and voices would wake me, along with horrific demonic dreams where I was either possessed, dragged from my bed, or trying to escape demons from hurting me or killing me. Sometimes, my bed would shake at night, or I could see my sheets moving. My default mode? Fear.

One of my childhood friends often commented on how things, including electronics, would always drop or break around me. This is common when a person is afflicted with witchcraft spirits. I could not understand why I was experiencing these things but my friends and family didn't. So, like the first psychic told me, I did my best to accept it as a gift and apply it.

When witchcraft became my main "drug of choice" after sobriety, I deepened my knowledge. I began seeing innumerable psychics and mediums, going to crystal shows and psychic fairs. I practiced card and tea-leaf readings regularly, along with herb magic, where I would make sachets with amulets for protection, healing, love, and money.

I somehow got connected to a goddess and witchcraft temple in Southern California and began going there on Sunday mornings before Jesus saved me. This temple was nothing other than a coven led by multiple high priestesses (or high-level witches.) The first time I entered this temple, I was exhilarated. The temple accepted provocative garments and celebrated the divine feminine.

There were even full moon ceremonies where the women danced naked. Surprisingly, I never attended those. I had been dressing quite provocatively for years and was careless about how I affected or distracted people through my attire, or lack thereof. I loved that the temple was so accepting of who I was, even if that was an oversexualized version of me, which honestly wasn't really *me* at all but only a traumatized and demonized version of myself.

I began attending these temple services more often once Greg and I had broken up and when he went to prison. At the time, I felt I needed women's support, and I wanted it beyond 12-step women's meetings. Thankfully, this temple was strictly female, except on special occasions when you could bring a male partner or child, but they had to be invited by a female member. No one who wasn't invited was permitted to enter.

The temple was hidden away in an industrial area. As I approached the front door, I had no clue what I was about to behold inside. Once I opened the front door and stepped into the first room, it was breathtaking. The aroma of herbs, sage, and roses drenched the atmosphere. Everything was captivating and colorful, shining and sparkling. Decks of cards glittered the bookshelves, along with jewelry and enchanted crystals, elixirs, herbal remedies, and teas.

I felt like I had just entered the place I had dreamed of my entire life. I instantly fit in and felt an immediate sense of belonging and wonder. *These people are just like me,* I thought. I craved belonging. I craved connection with people who experienced the spirit realm as I had. The main room had a shop, and a captivating fountain sat in the center as you walked forward. It felt like even the water was magical.

I am unsure if the fountain was made of gold, but I remember it that way. The fountain was trickling and sparkling, my eyes widened, and I couldn't help but say, "Wow!" over and over again. I approached a gorgeous black woman dressed in bright colors with a sash over the front of her. This was indicative of a priestess. She was one of the four high priestesses of the temple at that time.

She had a gorgeous smile with blinding white teeth, and as I approached her before entering the next room, she reached toward me with a bindi (decorative mark worn in the middle of the forehead) in her hand and stuck it to where my third eye was. This was the affirmative practice for each woman as they entered. "You are beautiful," she said, smiling and motioning for me to enter the first doorway into the next room.

The second room was even more captivating than the first, with tables of fruits and loaves of bread sitting abundantly in gorgeous bowls and on beautiful plates, all glimmering and shining. The ceiling was covered with different colored fabrics that hung high and low, creating a tentlike atmosphere. At the same time, couches with beaded and tasseled pillows sat off to the corner under another layer of tapestry. The women gathered around each other speaking of angels, guides, third eyes, and their auras.

As I got some tea for myself, I encountered another high priestess. She wore darker colors and had thick, dark eyeliner. She was older and had long, witch-like gray hair. As we made eye contact, I instantly felt violated by her—dark magic. She was the priestess that the temple members jokingly said summoned serpents, though I did not take that lightly.

I felt nervous and afraid around her, and when I spoke to her, it was like I was stumbling over my words. She was known for doing henna readings; during the appointments she would speak about your future while painting it on your skin in red ink. I talked to her about this once but never made an appointment. Another God cushion, I presumed. When I went through my deliverances, demons and curses were also cast out of me connected to this woman. She wore tribal headdresses and would lead part of the Sunday morning ceremonies.

The third room was dimly lit as we entered. Every wall around the main square was adorned with goddess idols and statues. Egyptian, Greek, Roman, Asian, Islander, Native American, African, and Hindu goddesses filled the space and were seemingly categorized. It was like a museum. As I walked through the doorway, I crossed over a small wooden bridge onto the main square, where I wandered around before taking my seat.

There were altars *everywhere*. Then, they locked the doors when the service started. No one could enter or leave once the magic circle was closed. Nobody could break the energetic barrier because it would instantly weaken it, so it was highly discouraged to go unless there was an emergency. This circle is ritual magic.

Every woman grabbed hands with the one next to her, and we chanted and sang. Then, the four high priestesses would sing to the elements of fire, water, earth, and air. If you knew the chant, you could join in. Each priestess had a different element and performed specific rituals per her element at the altar in the center of the circle. The energy within the room was building, and sometimes, I could even feel physical heat.

Once we recognized every element, we would invoke the spirits. This is the fifth point of the pentagram. Sadly, I have seen rituals similar to this one in modern Disney movies. What we were doing was a magic circle around a pentagram. To the naked eye or the naive, it doesn't look like that right away. Nonetheless, it is an ancient witchcraft practice.

We were encouraged to call forth our spirit guides, angels, deceased loved ones, or pets. The room got extremely loud during this time. Drums pounded, women yelled, sang, and shrieked. Some even began shaking and falling to the floor, touching it, summoning. While others lifted their hands upward as if reaching for something or invoking a new power or energy. It's not the hand-raising you see in a church when people worship, though. They named their spirits and the dead; some claimed even to see them.

Women would also take off jewelry and articles of clothing to place on the altar in the center of the room. On this altar and within the magic circle, these objects would gain supernatural charges that we could carry with us through the week. I often left my favorite moon necklace and rings on the altar. Interestingly enough, once I got baptized in Hawaii, my moon necklace continued to fall off of me. These were cursed objects in my life that I later had to discard because they became portals for the demonic to stay in and around me.

"You are here, you are here, you are here!" we would chant as we followed the lead of our priestesses. What I had witnessed and participated in was an invocation of demons and a group possession. We all felt energized and excited as we found our seats, buzzing. Next was the offering, where we presented our finances to the goddess Sekhmet. Katy, the medium I apprenticed with, originally introduced me to another goddess, Lakshmi (the goddess of prosperity), where I made an altar to her in the corner of my house.

The purpose of the home rituals and altars was to bring in the flow of finances, so offering money and worshiping a goddess was nothing new to me. This act was more of a demonstration of that, where we danced while doing it. After offering time, a priestess, typically the founding high priestess, would speak on a topic, or we would join as a group and participate in different ceremonies.

I remember one time we all gathered together in a very close-knit circle. Each woman's hips touched another's, and we swayed like the ocean's currents. There were many fires in California then, so we began to call forth the element of water. Just then, rain began pouring on our metal roof. Thunder ensued as well. The power in the room grew thick that day as the women hollered for more precipitation. You never knew what to expect. Each Sunday was different.

When the temple service ended, we all linked hands again, chanting and praying, and broke the magic circle. Then, the altars were open for individual worship. My favorite was a

Native American cave that was carved out behind a small curtain. Only one person could fit into this space at a time. It was very interesting and inspired the artist in me. Music played within this cave, and it was darker than the main room.

Small twinkling lights shimmered on the walls with little villages and tiny houses carved out within the cave. Crystals and other objects were along the walls. If I could get to it first after service, I would meditate here for a while. When the women were done at their altars, they funneled back into the second room for food and fellowship. Many of these women, I believe, had good intentions; some clearly did not.

Some people, like me, found their way into this temple due to their brokenness, while others were raised there. Broken people become lost, and lost people are vulnerable to deception. Every single woman in this temple was deceived. My fear of men made this place feel comforting and safe. The parts of me that were rejected or misunderstood by the outside world were accepted and rejoiced here. Again, that deep desire to be seen and understood was being fed, but I was eating from the devil's hand.

When I reflect on this time and think about the women I became friends with, it saddens me. Although some practiced black magic with wicked intentions, I believe the majority just desired peace and community, and they were doing the best they knew to do. This is why it is so important to evangelize as Christians and share the Gospel: the Gospel is true freedom, not counterfeit freedom like witchcraft.

Witches need love, too, and they desperately need the truth. As a Christian, fear should never be an excuse to not share the Gospel. That doesn't mean we don't fall short, because we do, and I have. Multiple times, I passed up an opportunity to share the Gospel or pray for someone because I was "afraid of looking stupid" or "I was too busy." Fear and self-centeredness are barriers that we must break down in ourselves daily.

We are called to die to self. In that, we may be a person's *only* encounter with the true and living God. I would much prefer to look stupid for a few minutes than risk the possibility of somebody going to hell. It's not about us—it's about love.

Surprisingly, even fear can be a legal right for the demonic. The Bible commands us *repeatedly* not to fear. Of course it happens, and there's grace for that. However, living in a perpetual state of fear where phobias are all-consuming, there is likely some demonic activity happening, and fear can be an open door.

Biblically, *fear is a sin.* Many people, including Christians, don't understand or don't know this. I think if they did, their lives would look a lot different. I always go back to the verse in Hosea 4:6 (NIV) that says, *"My people are destroyed from lack of knowledge."* If I had known what I was doing in witchcraft, I would have never done it.

Even the temple I was attending was a facade. Although captivating with its lights, tapestries, fountains, and artistry, the place was evil. Even though I have described its outward beauty, I do not at all glorify this temple or places like it. The

Bible says that satan presents himself as an angel of light, meaning he initially shows you something different from what he truly is: something attractive to *you*. But remember he is the deceiver.

In my relationship with the Lord now, He speaks to me very clearly about these things. We're going to take a detour from the temple to this topic for a moment.

I decided to watch two episodes of a show I had no business watching a little while back. It was oversexualized so I would fast-forward through parts of it. I was interested in the storyline and wanted to see what happened. After watching the first episode, I felt extremely convicted.

I hardly watch any television as it is, due to the sinful nature of most shows. The next day, I decided to watch the show again, by giving episode two a shot. I told myself if it were equally as bad as the first episode, I would not watch it anymore. The second episode was even more disturbing. I felt so guilty that I would even watch something like that.

I did not feel condemned, but I felt wrong about it. I felt almost violated in a way because I was violating my own conscience. When I went to bed that night, I deleted the television app from my phone and canceled my membership, which I had only bought for that show anyway. I laid on my back and looked up at the ceiling.

"I'm sorry, God," I said. "I should not have watched that show. I regret seeing those episodes, and now I feel conflicted and disconnected." The Lord spoke to me, "That's alright,

Jenny. I already knew." I prayed back, "I just really like the main character, and the acting is incredible. Part of me wishes I could watch it." Obviously, I could watch it if I wanted to because, hello, free will. Side note: This is a perfect example of our flesh and our spirit being at war with one another:

> *For the desire of the flesh is against the Spirit, and the Spirit against the flesh, for these are in opposition to one another, in order to keep you from doing whatever you want* (Galatians 5:17 NASB).

My spirit did not want to watch that show, but my flesh was attracted to the glamour and romance of the show. Life is always better for us and those around us when we practice living by His Spirit, not the flesh. The Lord responded to me, asking, "Does this show glorify Me or the devil?" I thought about it for a moment, hoping to find some glorification of God in it, but I could not.

"The devil," I said.

"Is there any good in this show?" God asked.

I wracked my brain, thinking about everything I could pull from episodes one and two. I could not think of one ounce of goodness. "No," I said to the Lord. Tears began to fill my eyes, not due to guilt, but due to the condition of our society. Because shows like the one I had watched are widely accepted and glorified, it saddened me greatly.

Our hearts are very disconnected and hardened when we can regularly watch shows without any remorse or sensitivity.

The types of media we watch reveal how soft or hardhearted we really are. My mind began flickering through other television shows that are popular right now. The majority are really terrible. Tears ran down my cheeks.

The Lord's voice was very soft this entire time. He gently asked me, "Do you know what this show has done?"

I wiped my tears, "No."

God continued, "People watch this show, they become lust-filled, and they masturbate. They watch pornography after this show. In fact, they even go back and search for events this show was based on and exploit the main character all over again. They become vain. They begin to fantasize and look up the main characters and actors and sexualize them in their minds. People become obsessed. You cannot be an advocate for those who are abused and also watch a show like this, Jenny."

I went into a radical time of intercessory prayer. I could not stop crying. I felt the burden of God's heart for a lust-filled and lonely generation. I began interceding for the characters this show was based on. I started praying for the actors and writers of this show as well as the viewers. I prayed over myself and my family, repenting for the episodes I'd watched.

I began praying for the sex industry and all the victims who are subjects in the over-sexualization of our society. I was in an endless well of tears as the presence of God filled my heart and mind. I started praying for those struggling with porn and sex addiction and who struggle with infidelity, loneliness, and fear.

I prayed for the children who have been so severely abused and have wound up in industries that make them sex symbols and glorify their brokenness through degradation. I cried for the two hours I had spent watching the show, contradicting my beliefs. I cried for a blind generation. The Lord held me in that space. I am so grateful today that I am aware of these things and that God spoke to me so kindly and directly about it.

He then asked me, "Do you know why *you* watched this show, Jenny?"

"No," I said, thinking I just liked the actors.

"Because you have been without romance in your marriage for a very long time." I swallowed.

"Do you see how sly the devil can be? Even with you," the Lord said.

I usually have no problem facing the demonic head-on in my own life. This was a lot more sly and came from an unexpected angle that I truly was blind to.

"Yes, Lord," I responded.

"You have been without romance, so the enemy presented a show to you where you could reminisce about the passion of your past and fall into the fantasy of the romance of this show. It even triggered vanity in you."

"That's true," I said.

I prayed some more and fell asleep. The next day I began reflecting on how much in the last 24 hours I obsessively wanted to change my body, skin, and the way I looked. A woman's body goes through many changes after a pregnancy, as mine has since having my son. As a previous model and fitness-obsessed person, I had a hard time with my appearance.

The weight gain and slow weight loss had been difficult for me, even though I had grace with myself. The show heightened my insecurity in this area. It also made me upset toward my husband for not measuring up to the love that exists in my mind, the love he initially presented and promised me. Although I had only watched two hours' worth of this show, it quickly influenced how I thought.

My son and I were staying with my parents in California at this time, and Jay and I had been separated again due to his explosive anger and abuse. I was confused and afraid to leave the marriage fully. I was hopeful to my own detriment, which is not uncommon in abusive relationships. I had prayed about it but kept feeling conflicted about what to do.

We were still in communication during my stay in California, so I called Jay the day after to tell him about the show and what the Lord had spoken to me. I shared how I felt a lack of love between us and what this show was doing to our society. We had a long conversation about positive things we could do for our marriage moving forward, the power of God, and the sex industry. I wanted to believe for something more.

Although I was not fully immersed in the sex industry, I was in it to an extent. And Jay supported it by paying for sexual favors at massage parlors, supporting the porn industry, and more. Most men who don't have a true relationship with

Jesus will fall into the trap of lust in one way or another. Many hidden things in our marriage would be exposed following this separation.

The point is that many television shows, and even more movies, pave the way for men and women to become involved with or supporters of the sex industry. This only launched me further into prayer; I am so privileged to know God today.

14

THE FLAMING EYES OF GOD

As I pursued the world of witchcraft and became more engrossed in it, I found myself occasionally turning to Jesus at times when I was very afraid. When I was attacked by the demonic in the early hours of the morning, being strangled by an invisible force, I would call out to Jesus. And only Jesus. It was deep, deep within me. I knew everything else was a fraud, but my infatuation with the craft and all its features kept me shackled.

One time, I even remember going to an evening church service after being at the witchcraft temple in the morning. I wore my same attire, bindi and all, and ran into an old friend from high school. He was a strong Christian and was very put off by me that day. I recall sensing this from him, but I was so aloof and living in my own glorious little bubble that I didn't pay any mind. It was at this same church where I manifested my first demon.

One evening, while I was there, a prophetic man called on people dealing with specific issues in the building. He said, "We would love to pray for you. Come up to the front and receive." My heart was hurting, and my body was aching. This was before sobriety when I was still on drugs, drinking, occultic practices, and still in an abusive relationship with my ex-satanist boyfriend, Greg.

In desperation, I approached the front of the stage. Dim lighting created a safe space for me to be vulnerable and protected from view. I cried and I cried and I cried. A woman on the prayer team came to my right and placed her hand on my shoulder. "Is it okay if I touch you?" she inquired. "Yes," I said tearfully.

As soon as she began to pray, I started responding in a way I could not control, let alone comprehend. All the muscles in my right arm began contracting and relaxing at great speed, and at different times, a fierce pain moved through me. I began to convulse. "What the **** are you doing? Get out of here! This is so stupid!" a voice started to yell inside me. "This isn't going to do anything for you. What is the point of this? Stop, stop, stop, stop! This is pathetic. You are a loser. *I'm such a loser*. They don't even care about you. They don't care. *Yes, they do*. No. You need to go home!"

Multiple voices shrieked inside of me and began growing louder. *Everything is so awful. It's so sad. I will never get better. I will never get better.* Another voice discouraged me. I was disconnected. The back of my neck was twitching, my entire body shook uncontrollably, and it was difficult to remain standing. The woman leaned over after a short time and whispered, "I am going to ask another woman to pray for us. Is that okay with you?"

I nodded through the convulsions. Tears escaped my eyes, but I felt blank. As soon as the other woman approached me, she placed her hand on my other shoulder, and then the muscles in *that* arm began doing the same thing. I had never felt discomfort like this in my entire life, and I had gone through delirium tremens from alcohol withdrawal multiple times.

The discomfort from this was far worse than any substance withdrawal. It was like I wanted to rip off my skin. The closest thing I can compare it to are those electronic muscle stimulators that chiropractors use to relax tense muscles before an adjustment. It felt like that all over my body and it was anything but relaxing. Today, I know this response to prayer to be a demonic manifestation.

At the time, I had no idea, and nobody told me. I was hunched forward, my entire abdomen seizing. I began folding. I rocked back and forth, holding my abdomen. *Something is happening,* I thought. The woman on my left leaned down, "Sweetheart, do you mind if we take you into the back room and pray for you there?"

I couldn't speak. I nodded again, looking down, shaking and holding my stomach. These women escorted me behind the stage into another dimly lit room with two other women in it. I was still hunched forward. I thought I might faint. They gathered around me, laying hands on me. I recognized that what they were doing was out of love, but the desire to leave became much stronger. They placed a trash can in front of me that I began dry heaving and spitting into.

"Stop this, stop this! What the **** are you even doing? This is ridiculous. They are just making you cry even more! They don't even know what they are doing!" the voice in my head yelled at me. "What the **** is the trash can even for? They are so stupid. You are dramatic. Do they think you're going to vomit? Do you think you're going to vomit? This is insane. This is hilarious. Leave now. Leave right now! Don't you think this is weird? It's time to go home!"

Multiple voices chimed like bells in my mind, "Get out, get out, get out." I couldn't tell you what the women were saying; I could not make out a single word. I was coughing, shaking, crying, and convulsing. I could not bear their hands on me! I finally stood up and said, "Thank you. I have to go." One of the women asked, "Are you sure? Are you sure you're okay?"

I nodded. Wiping the tears from my face and stuffing a couple of tissues into my pockets, I walked out of the room totally and undeniably stupefied. To this day, I cannot remember any of their faces or more of their words. The demonic did not want me free. *Dude, what just happened?* I asked myself. I shared this disorienting experience with a therapist at that time, who said the Holy Spirit could do that, but I had so many other issues going on that we shelved it. I neatly stashed it in a storage unit in my mind on a back shelf in a box that read:

"Things I Won't Talk About." I forgot about this until I walked into that prayer session over six years later, where my first deliverance took place in Irvine, California.

With confusing experiences like this one, paired with all of my supernatural encounters, I still could not stop my psychic pursuit. Part of me thought I was protected because I was baptized at the age of nine. So, I continued in my ways. I joined an underground school for empaths, psychics, mediums, shamans, and the like. I took a few classes there, including a channeling class.

Interestingly enough, despite all I had involved myself in, I was the only one who refused to channel in class openly that day. The teacher initiated the channeling by going first. She warned us ahead of time that she would not blink and that her face might look very strange while she channeled, which it did. I thought she looked possessed (because she was!) and I felt afraid.

She sat in her seat at the head of the room, meditated, and then the spirit entered her. Her eyes instantly widened, and she never blinked. She spoke in a strange voice about things that meant nothing to me, things about the spirit she was channeling. She had even written a book while channeled by this demon that she showed us at the beginning of class.

We then formed a circle, each channeling. As I sat there, hearing and seeing a group of spirits behind me trying to talk to me, I refused access to them. One of the demons grew very angry with me. It was aggressive and at the front of the pack. This spirit appeared as Native American. He had war paint on his face, a feathery headdress over the top of his head, and wearing a loin cloth. He had feathers around his arms and a staff. He began screaming at me.

"Let me speak! Let me speak!" He shook and pounded his staff on the ground. I sat there, tightly wound while continuing to communicate with him and his squad of spirits supernaturally. I continued to tell him no. The teacher looked over at me—it was my turn.

"Are you going to speak?"

"I'm not sure," I said. "I may just absorb this session."

"There is a spirit here who wants to speak through you," she said, looking at me through her glasses.

"I know." Clearly, I already knew.

"He is a Native man with red war paint on him, and he has a staff."

"Yes, I know. I am going to pass," I said firmly. Then, the teacher closed the class with another meditation, and I left. I never went back to that class again and decided channeling in that form was not for me. I did not like aggressive spirits. At least, *known* aggressive spirits. (Note: witchcraft spirits are some of the most violent and stubborn demons; the intention of every demon is to steal, kill, and destroy, period.) If I had let that spirit enter me that day, he wouldn't have entered alone but together with all those other demons standing behind him.

Katy, the medium mentoring me, also took classes at this school. She asked me to be her apprentice, go with her on a call, and help her on calls moving forward. Two women who owned a prestigious antique shop in Long Beach phoned her one day, complaining of excessive paranormal activity in the shop. A little "ghost" boy continued to mess with both owners, among other strange happenings, and they needed our help.

It was like an episode of one of those paranormal shows I loved so much. They called Katy in hopes that she would clear out the space by kindly helping the array of disruptive spirits cross over.

Demons take many forms, but they all have one purpose: the destruction of God's people. They work for satan, the father of lies; therefore, they are liars. John 8:44 (NIV) says, *"You belong to your father, the devil, and you want to carry out your father's desires. He was a murderer from the beginning, not holding to the truth, for there is no truth in him. When he lies, he speaks his native language, for he is a liar and the father of lies."* Demons are deceivers and liars and work through people to do the same things.

On our drive to the shop in Long Beach that morning, I repeatedly heard a demon's name. When I got to the antique shop, Katy and I separated and walked around the store. There were not just one or two demons in this place, but many. The owners jokingly called it "a Disneyland for spirits." Eventually, Katy and I opened and closed two portals in this place: one for what we perceived as darker spirits (and we saw many of them). The other for what we perceived were lighter spirits or what appeared to be a "family."

In reality, all we were doing was making it easier for demons to transfer to another place. We were not helping ourselves or the shop owners; we were only helping the demonic and the kingdom of darkness. Many aspects of witchcraft are done through third-eye and visualization practices. What we did there was entirely through visualization and hand movements.

That day, I felt so proud of myself, like I had finally reached a higher degree of witchcraft—I was fooled.

THE EYES OF GOD

In the next few months, things stayed the same. Until one afternoon, I was in my backyard trying to connect with a friend's deceased fiancé whom I had never met. I began connecting with the spirit realm as I fell deeper into my meditation. A spirit of divination gave me the name and age of this man and then all of a sudden, all I could see was a white veil.

It was rubbery, almost like the texture and thickness of a balloon. Then, I saw what felt like a hundred faces pressing against the veil. Envision a massive white wall made of latex and people on the other side pressing their faces into it. This is what I saw, but up close. And although the veil seemed white, I could see those forces because beyond it was dark.

One face and body stretched so far that it almost looked black when it got close to me. The veil in that area looked as if it were about to snap. I fearfully and quickly opened my eyes, sat up, and stopped the necromancy immediately. My heart was racing inside of my chest. This was starting to feel very wrong, and far more real than anything I had experienced before.

"Man," I said to myself, shaking my head. "I'm done with this." I lifted myself off the warm concrete in my backyard and walked into my house. That was the last time I did necromancy. It seemed something kept trying to stop me from continuing down this road. Before sobriety, my moral compass was seriously off-center. As I came to recovery and worked through my 12 steps, it was as if I was being spiritually reset.

I hardly had a conscience when it came to witchcraft, but the more sober time I acquired, the more of a guilty conscience I seemed to have, which was a good thing. Around that time, I decided to stop directly contacting the "dead." Remember, the dead only go to one of two places: Heaven or hell. If you are communicating with a "dead person" you are actually talking to a shape-shifting demon.

Shortly after my veil experience, I was asked to help a friend who had an insane amount of demonic activity in her home. After I felt and witnessed things as extreme as I did in her life, I called upon Jesus. I put salt around her home (witchcraft), went through her house, and began telling her what objects I knew were cursed. This is an interesting thing for someone active in witchcraft to do. I started pointing out things like specific figurines or paintings of Buddha in her home that felt wicked. Although I was blind myself, there was part of me that did have discernment, and I genuinely wanted to help.

One of the objects she had was tied to a bizarre ceremony and person. It was a cursed coin with Catholic imagery and phrases on it. I took it from her and called the only Christian person I knew at the time: Ashley Anderson. Ashley is a seed sower. I cannot say enough good things about this woman and her role in my life at that time. She always did her best to lead me to Christ without judgment or disappointment.

Ashley met up with me in Newport Beach, and we went to a Catholic church on the peninsula. We asked to see a priest or someone who worked there, told them this was a cursed object, and gave it to them. Now that I am much more equipped in spiritual warfare, I would not recommend doing this, but it was all I knew to do then. Now I know that cursed objects must either be burned or thrown out, never donated, and never given to someone else, lest the curse follow them.

After leaving the cursed coin at the church, we decided to walk across the parking lot to the beach. It was a beautiful afternoon, and I loved to meditate on the beach while listening to the sound of the ocean waves. Growing up in southern California truly is a dream in many ways. Being close to the ocean brought so much peace to my spirit.

On the way out of the sanctuary, I picked a beautifully crafted and symmetrical camellia and brought it with me. It reminded me of a mandala. As we neared the water, we sat down. I stuck the flower in the sand in front of me and told Ashley I just needed to meditate for about ten minutes to cleanse my energy (insert eye roll here).

I had become so skilled in my meditations that I felt I could quickly transport myself somewhere else in my mind. Sometimes, I would leave my body within moments—a lot can happen in ten minutes.

Ashley sat a little behind me, and I set a ten-minute timer on my phone. I would empty out the energy in my body through a funnel I visualized from my root chakra. The energy would leave my body and go into the earth's core, where I would then recycle that energy outward and be left empty and "free." This was just one daily practice I did multiple times a day.

As I quickly entered this spiritual space, I immediately began moving through a breathtaking electric rainbow tunnel. I had never seen anything like this in meditation or in my life! It was vibrant and beautiful, and I began to feel a sense of intensity and nervousness. The colors moved and blended magnificently.

As the tunnel moved somewhat upward to my left, I saw something out of the corner of my vision on the right side; my eyes were still closed in meditation. I could see invisible footprints moving toward me like an invisible person was walking on water and leaving footprints behind. I was so entranced by the rainbow tunnel that I did not want to turn from it.

While the footprints began to appear closer and closer, about to emerge with vibrant colors, the rainbow tunnel disappeared. Suddenly, the tunnel was replaced with a massive blue sky. This color blue isn't even seen on earth. I don't know how to describe it other than being electric.

Suddenly, I was nose-to-nose with God. My eyes stared into His eyes, confronted with His pure holiness and power. Total fear enveloped me, and I was terrified. All I could hear was a resounding, "FEAR OF GOD."

Those words rang as clear as a bell. I jumped out of my meditation, shaking. I had been living my life as if I were my own god, worshiping whatever I wanted with no actual respect for the true and living God, Jesus Christ. I stopped the time on my phone; it was 3:30. This was symbolic, and I knew it immediately. Jesus was crucified on the Cross at Calvary at 3:30 in the afternoon. I had never experienced this form of terror before. It was incomparable to any fear I had ever known.

It was, without a single doubt, the most authoritative power in the entire universe.

"Oh my God, Ashley!" I yelled. I was out of breath.

"What! What is it?" She moved over to me on the sand.

"Feel my heart." I grabbed her hand and put it on my chest.

"Holy moly, it's beating so fast! Are you okay? What happened?"

I took a few breaths. I could hardly collect myself. God's authority radiated through my entire body. It was *so* powerful! "I...I...I just saw the eyes of God," I stammered, rubbing my face repeatedly with both hands.

"What?" she looked at me astonished.

Out of breath, I began explaining the tunnel, the footprints, and the eyes I had just seen as best as I could. I had seen a lot of crazy stuff in my meditations, astral projection in dreams, and witchcraft, but not once had I ever seen God.

The face-to-face encounter lasted less than a millisecond. It was like if I could have stayed in the meditation, I would have died. That is how intense God's power was. The Lord wanted me to fear Him, but I didn't know what that meant. Respecting and reverencing the Lord is radical!

"It was so intense," I said to Ashley. "As the rainbow tunnel disappeared, I saw this color blue like I had never seen before. This color doesn't even exist on earth, I don't think. I've never seen it and don't know how to describe it. And then..."

I took a deep breath, shaking my head, "I saw these eyes and eyebrows. He had white eyebrows, and it was like I could see every single hair of His brow so perfectly. It was insane. I can't even see your eyebrows that clearly right now! And his eyes! They didn't even have a color, Ashley. At least, I don't think so. They looked so intense and didn't just have one color, either. They were like fire and flames. He was nose-to-nose with me, and all I could see were His eyebrows and eyes. Then I just heard a resounding, "FEAR OF GOD" as if He wanted to show me His power or something."

I shook my head in astonishment. "But it wasn't evil, Ashley, not at all. I *know* it was God, but it was scary." I had just been hit with the fear of the Lord for the first time in my life.

Ashley sat there, wide-eyed, jaw unhinged. "Whoa…" she trailed off. "You know, as you were meditating, I was praying and singing worship songs over you, so you telling me this is crazy."

We both looked at the deep blue water beneath the bright blue sky. It was quiet that afternoon, and it was peaceful. The light ocean breeze blew over our bodies and through our hair.

"This is awesome, Jenny!" Ashley's chipper voice broke the momentary stillness. Remember, she was one of the *only* Christians in my life. "Yeah," I breathed out, confused. I couldn't get those eyes out of my mind that night before bed. I didn't know what it all meant. I didn't understand, but I *knew* I had just beheld the eyes and the power of the Creator of the universe, and there is only One.

Ashley texted me as I was going to bed. "Hey, look up this verse. It sounds exactly like what you were talking about." The verse read: *"The hair on his head was white like wool, as white as snow. And his eyes were like blazing fire"* (Revelation 1:14 NIV). John, one of Jesus's 12 disciples, wrote this after being taken up into Heaven and shown many breathtaking, otherworldly, and majestic things—including God.

I was blown away as I clicked the link on my phone to this Scripture. At that point in time, all I had ever read from the Bible was maybe a few psalms. I had no knowledge of the Word of God and most definitely did not know that the Bible ever described God to this degree. This was before I got saved in Hawaii. I lay in bed reading that Bible verse over and over again on my phone.

The Lord had just shown me part of Himself in such an overwhelming way. But why? Back then, I had no clue. Now, I know. Proverbs 9:10 (NIV) states, *"The fear of the Lord is the beginning of wisdom…."* At that point in my life, God was about to release His supernatural and life-changing wisdom upon my life, which would, without a doubt, mark me forever.

15

DELIVERANCE FROM THE GATEKEEPER SPIRIT

Months after this powerful encounter with God at the beach, I landed on the island of Oahu and came to Jesus. As you have previously read, I repented and got rid of what I knew were tools for divination and some other New Age remnants I had. Unfortunately, some objects were overlooked and stayed in my home for many years. Still, a new thing was happening to me. I had reached the shore of wisdom. Now, all I had to do was step out of the boat and claim the land. That was going to be a *big* step for me.

It was not as simple for me for many reasons. As you have read, the lack of deliverance, mentorship, and discipleship when I returned to the mainland was a major pitfall. I also lacked an understanding of my identity in Christ and the Bible. I broke my celibacy stretch, and I eventually got caught up again in crystal healing, pendulum work, chakra imaging, and seeing another psychic—but it was not the same. None of it was.

I was now conscious of sin, and I could not override the emotions that plagued me each time I went back to it. However, I could not stop (that's why deliverance was so significant for me). God convicted me over these things, and I grieved inside when I turned away from Him. I had not experienced this before. Despite a very difficult next few years, I still prayed, read the Bible, and pursued a relationship with Jesus.

In addiction, it is near impossible to be truly close with someone because the drug or alcohol inhibits authentic connection. If we can view sin the same way, it makes it easier to understand. You cannot be genuinely close to a drug addict when they are loaded, just the same as you cannot be close to God when you are under the constant influence of habitual sin. I couldn't put words to it then, but I can now.

The Lord wants us to be as close as possible to Him. It feels so good to be in right standing with God, and although life still has difficulties, there is a deep peace that cannot be expelled. That's because you know you are fully covered by the Lord when you are in His will.

When I went back to see a psychic after I had come to Jesus, she could not get an accurate reading of me. As soon as I stepped into her backroom through a beaded curtain, I knew I was making a mistake. My pride, however, kept me there to see the reading through. As the card shuffling ensued,

I began to pray, and the psychic started to snort periodically and then excessively, like a pig.

The psychic could hardly utter a coherent sentence and kept saying, "Sorry. There are so many roots." Whatever that meant. I knew her demons were manifesting. She asked if I was afraid and then said she couldn't get a clear reading on me. However, she did say there were rows and rows of angels behind me, so many that she couldn't count. I often wonder if what she was seeing were all my demons (fallen angels) as I had not been delivered yet. Or if she truly was seeing the angels of the Lord around me.

Regardless, it was apparent that this was no longer the path I wanted to walk. She was a sought-after psychic in my area and came highly recommended, yet the reading was not good. Now, it was crystal clear to me (as it should have been before but wasn't) that I must stop pursuing witches and psychics to give me hope for my future.

Jeremiah 29:11 (NIV) says that God does that: *"'For I know the plans I have for you,' declares the Lord, 'plans to prosper you and not to harm you, plans to give you hope and a future.'"* I do believe there was a layer of protection present. Still, by being in that place, participating and answering her questions, I was again allowing demons to enter my life by keeping an open door to the occult. I cannot stress enough to all I meet just how dangerous the occult truly is.

My prayers are with those who will read this book and are involved in or are close to somebody engaged in such demonic practices. The Scripture says that we shall know the truth, and the truth shall set us free (John 8:36). Jesus is the truth and the only One who does the true "freeing." When we know Him, we actually get freed.

The trauma work that I was doing at this time began to accelerate. What I mean by that is so many memories were coming up rapidly that I could not avoid them any longer. I began suffering greatly with my sexuality. The wise thing to do then would have been to stay single or pursue celibacy again with a partner while doing the extensive work surrounding the sexual abuse I endured.

Instead, hypersexuality was my response. Out of a crippling fear that my sexuality was being threatened by tormenting memories of abuse and assaults, I invoked sex demons into my body on two occasions. I had a Christian boyfriend at this time and did this in front of him (we weren't walking in Truth); I felt them enter immediately. Now, I was really in for it. Living in willful sin and the lack of deliverance in my life had extreme consequences—and I mean extreme.

Yes, some things I did had a choice factor, while other things I could not stop. These aspects of my spirit were beyond human aid. Many demons overtook me and I did not know my authority in Jesus. Still, I was so unbelievably desperate for change. The Bible talks about sanctification. (That was one of those words that weirded me out, and I didn't care to learn what it meant at first.) Sanctification is the action or process of being freed from sin or purified by God.

Acts 26:18 (NIV) describes this: *"To open their eyes and turn them from darkness to light, and from the power of Satan to God, so that they may receive forgiveness of sins and a place among those who are sanctified by faith in me."* It also says in 2 Timothy 2:21 (NIV) that *"those who cleanse themselves from the latter will be instruments for special purposes, made holy, useful to the Master and prepared to do any good work."*

Sanctification is a *process*. It takes *time*. It took me five years after being saved to step into deliverance. When we keep turning to God, He will keep working on us—but we must give ourselves over to Him if we really want true freedom, as the Bible talks about. Surrender is the only solution. We can have Heaven on earth in our thought lives, our personal lives, and the lives of those around us. This doesn't mean painful things won't happen to us, it just means we are filled with the Holy Spirit, and He supplies provision, favor, and peace that surpasses all understanding.

As Christians, we have the ability to make what many doubt and call a fantasy a reality—heavenly lives! That's because *everything* in the Bible is true. Deliverance, healing, a life sacrificed and full of love, and endless hope—it is all available to us! It took years for me to finally recognize, be aware of, come to terms with, make changes about, and seek deliverance from willful habitual sin. It was a major unraveling! But the Lord has continued to purify me, and now I have been delivered from over a thousand demons! God wants to set His children free!

THE SECOND EXORCISM

Much of what I will talk about in this section may be uncomfortable for some. I want to affirm that I am in no way glorifying evil but shedding light on the reality of demonic power that can consume a person's life. When I share parts of my story, I can sense fear and discomfort in some parts, which is not my intent. That fear, however, can be a magnet to the demonic, so I want to encourage you that if at any moment you sense fear, you can bind that spirit in Jesus's name or set the book down.

Discomfort with this topic can sometimes cause spirits to draw in. However, this spirit world should not be an uncomfortable topic, especially for a born-again, Holy Spirit-filled believer, although I am aware it is for many. The spirit world is much more real than the natural world we live in! Perfect love casts out fear, so remember that!

One of my most intense exorcisms was my second one, just three weeks after my first. When it came to my exorcism, I assumed because of the massive amount of freedom I felt instantly after my first one, I was in the clear and completely free from demons—not so. I was only free from my first layer of them. The demonic, just like the angelic, are reflective of the military. There are ranks of them, from basic qualifications to specialized positions.

There are special ops in the spirit world. Kimberly Daniels, the author of *Give It Back,* describes this perfectly in her book. When someone is afflicted with many spirits, they typically come out in layers. For me, some highly wicked and stubborn ones were cast out in the beginning, but it was toward the end that the larger, more stubborn, and deeply rooted demons were cast from me, and I was passed onto a more qualified exorcist.

A private in the military is highly guarded, correct? This is the same in the spirit realm. I know this through personal experience and personal revelation from God. Many demons tried to hide. If they are overlooked, then they cannot be cast out. Thankfully I had an extremely qualified and equipped group of people whom I consider to be experts in spiritual warfare and deliverance.

I want to encourage you to continue to ask God for wisdom in scenarios that baffle you and confuse you. He has an endless supply of wisdom for His children. All you have to do is ask! *"If any of you lacks wisdom, you should ask God, who gives generously to all without finding fault, and it will be given to you"* (James 1:5 NIV).

So, I had been physically healed from my chronic pain and freed from my multi-mental illness diagnosis and off medication for three weeks when strange and unwelcome supernatural things began to flare up again. Jay was still in treatment then, and we were not married yet, so I shared a condo with my roommate. She was honestly a champ through the hurricane-like warfare that occurred in our home.

Jay had gotten one deliverance and experienced a sense of freedom because of it. Over those three weeks, from one deliverance to the next, I had a heavenly angelic experience in my room. I felt the Lord's peace and knew that He was going to be walking with me on a new road. It felt like I had been on a wide road my entire life; even after accepting Jesus and my wonderful baptism, I was still on this huge road with lots of problems and so many unforeseen pits and traps.

I believed in it, but I didn't have much freedom at all. I was still doing a lot of what I had always done. After my first deliverance and my angelic encounters, it was almost like the Lord pointed out a new road that I couldn't see before, and now it was right in front of me. A narrow path. It gleamed, and it felt intimidating yet so undeniably welcoming.

When I imagine it, it is gold, and a bright light envelops it. I didn't know many on this path, and I wasn't familiar with it, but I was finally committed to it. This new path, where I would fully pursue Jesus, deliverance, and righteousness, would eventually unlock doors to new freedoms. I had a *new* hope—a hope the Lord Himself infused into me.

I hung onto this hope as I moved through a deep spiritual fog for the next year and a half, with the Lord by my side. The fog came over my life, and it was like I could not see either side of me, behind me, or in front of me. All I had (which is everything) was the voice of the Lord to give me direction. Looking back at this time, I envision a large body of water with stepping stones across it, yet covered in fog! My life depended on the steps I was going to take, and if I stepped out of my own will, I would be attacked by unforeseen things.

Picture how camouflaged alligators in a swamp covered in fog would be!

Only an expert would be able to spot the gator. God was the expert in this arena, and the things in the water were the demonic prowling around me. This extremity lasted my whole deliverance, which took almost two years. I had to be attentive to Him and listen very carefully to what steps to take and when. My obedience to Him mattered greatly. When I would test the waters by stepping out according to my own self-will, I experienced a major spiritual attack.

My second deliverance was about to reveal the level of evil I had actually let into my life, and the Lord had to walk me through it so I could testify to everyone the real dangers of witchcraft (and all sin!) and the importance of having the fear of the Lord, which again, is the beginning of wisdom.

THE GATEKEEPER

As I've said before, witchcraft is akin to a gang. You get initiated in, but you cannot leave without a fight. The demonic did not want me free, but because I was now an heir to the throne of Christ (Romans 8:17), my inheritance included freedom. Which, in this case, meant total deliverance. I was about to get jumped out of this gang.

Over these few weeks, some nightmares began to creep in. It was almost the same thing every time. That one woman cursing me in my dream before the first deliverance showed up again doing something similar, yet more aggressively. This time, she would stare directly at me. She had now stopped hiding and was in the business of intimidation. She knew I could see her, and she would put up a fight.

I began to feel that all-too-familiar fear come up again, like an impending doom, and it was strong. I started to struggle greatly to read the Bible and had a horribly difficult time praying. On a night when my roommate wasn't home, and I was by myself, I fell asleep and drifted into a dream. It was the middle of the night. I was in my condo and saw myself sleeping in bed during the dream.

Suddenly, I heard crying, a great wailing. I could hear a tortured soul outside crying and groaning so loudly that it woke me up in the dream. The woman's voice carried down the sidewalk in the courtyard. It was getting closer and louder. If you heard this type of cry in person, it would terrify you. Something was *very* wrong.

In the dream, I woke up and moved over to my blinds, peering through. I saw a woman with black hair approach the front of my condominium. "Let me in!" the woman screamed. Crying louder now and more hysterically, she banged on the front door through the screen. She looked insane. I heard the screen door hit against my wooden front door repeatedly.

"Let me in!" she cried fearfully and angrily. I looked around to see if anyone else in the neighborhood was being woken up by this. I stepped away from the blinds for a moment and peered out again from the second story. She looked up at me. Her hair was black, and her face looked different. This was the same woman that had haunted me in my other dreams, but her complexion had changed, which it seemed to do.

"What are you doing?" she cried. "Let me in! This is my house. This is my house!" She cried and cried in desperation. She was convinced this was her home. Despite her wailing, I did not feel bad for her. I felt terrified. *Should I call the police?* I thought. "Hey, this is not your house," I yelled back. "No! This *is* my house!" She cried and cried, wandering around aimlessly.

Her home had been my body, and the house in my dream represented that.

I woke up with my heart pounding and sweating. This was not just a nightmare that reverberated out of my subconscious; this was something actually occurring in the spirit realm. I looked at the clock. It was three a.m., the witching hour. This was symbolic. I scrambled through my phone and texted multiple friends, who, of course, were not awake to receive my text at that time. I had had chronic nightmares for years and had honestly become so desensitized to them that I didn't bother reaching out to people when I had them. But this was much different.

This was real. The next day, I suffered greatly at work. I kept crying, but I didn't know why. I felt like the woman in my dream with my level of agony. Then I called Sue, the woman who had prayed for me in my first deliverance, and told her about this encounter. We had stayed in contact since the first one, and she became a mentor. Thank God for Sue.

I phoned her from work that Friday afternoon, sitting on the back patio of my boss's deck. I wailed into the phone, tears that seemed to explode from nowhere, and Sue prayed with all her might. "Why don't you come to see us Sunday morning, honey? Does that work for you? Nine a.m.? We can pray this stuff off. I will get a team together. It's going to be okay, honey." Her sweet voice was soothing to my restless spirit. That was God in her.

"Okay," I said. "I will see you then." The next evening, Jay came to stay with me. He got a pass from his rehab, and we spent the weekend together. On Saturday night, I had to drive to a neighboring city to feed some dogs I was caring for. We got in the car and began to drive. We started arguing. The fight seemed to get bigger and bigger. Arguing was a natural part of our relationship, but this was one of those fights that seemed relentless.

"Dude, you have a demon in you or something," Jay cruelly told me. I was offended. I pulled over into the emergency lane on the side of the freeway. We were in a dangerous location.

"Get out," I said, still looking forward with both hands cemented to the steering wheel.

"What? We're on the freeway, Jenny," Jay said.

"Get out!" I repeated.

"What the **** is wrong with you?"

Just then, with no prior thought in my mind, my right arm swung across the car and hammer-punched Jay dead in the nose. I felt absolutely nothing.

"What the ****!" Jay yelled. He wrestled my arms away from him.

"Dude. You are crazy! Get off the side of the road!"

I put my hands back on the steering wheel and, without a word, started the car back up and drove the rest of the way to the house where I was dog-sitting. Jay, cursing the entire time, was totally baffled by what had just happened. An eerie calm fell over me, and I was not my own anymore. Silence. I said not a word. I pulled into the driveway of the home and parked the car as Jay, clearly upset, kept going on and on about what had just happened.

"You need to go get deliverance like now. I'm going to call Sue. You need to go to The Well, dude." he said. The Well Intake was the name of the prayer sessions I had been going to. Both of us were very new to pursuing righteousness. All we had down was no sex before marriage, but our language and behaviors obviously had not changed yet.

The car and the world around us suddenly seemed swallowed up by a dark silence and presence. "I am *not* going to The Well," I said with a guttural voice as I turned my head slowly to face Jay in the passenger seat. Fear. "Oh, my God, Jenny!" Jay screamed. "Jenny! Come back!" I have never seen so much terror on a person's face in my entire life, but it was like I was having an out-of-body experience at the same time.

He instantly put his hands on my right shoulder and shouted, "Jenny, come back! Get out of her in the name of

Jesus, in the name of the Holy Spirit!" A piercing, inhuman shriek escaped my mouth as both of my hands contorted upward and my fingers curled under.

"Uuuaahhh!" the sound trailed off, and a huge pressure within me seemed to come out of my mouth, and all of a sudden, I was back, coughing and crying.

"What the heck just happened?" Tears filled my eyes. "What just happened, Jay?"

"Dude, I don't know what the **** this is, I'm calling Sue! You are going to The Well tomorrow!" he insisted while freaking out.

Jay phoned Sue, swearing and terrified, hardly letting her get a word in. "She needs to come tonight. You guys need to pray over her tonight. I just saw a demon. I am freaking out!" He yelled into the phone. Sue eventually calmed him down. I was now filled with immense fear that radiated through my entire being.

"God. Jesus. Where are you? Where are you?" my spirit cried inside of me. We got out of the car after the phone call, hardly relaxed after something like that. We walked into the home in silence to feed the dogs and let them run around a bit. I turned on the song "Defender" by Jesus Culture. I played it repeatedly as I rocked forward and backward to the song. I probably listened to it over a hundred times that night. Jay was a combination of anger and fear. We were both confused and afraid.

"What happened, Jay?" I asked, desperate. It was like he didn't even want to look at me. His mind, too, was racing.

"Dude, your eyes went completely black," he said. "I've never seen anything like that."

"What?" That caught me off guard.

"Black?" I said.

"Yeah, and you had, like, a goat neck," he said, still not looking directly at me.

It was evident he was afraid.

"A goat neck?" I said. I gulped and touched my neck. My eyes rapidly moved, searching for peace.

"Yeah," he said harshly.

I didn't want to ask any more questions. Jay was not like me. He did not see into the spirit realm. Jay didn't have spiritual encounters apart from when he felt an angel's hand on his shoulder two months prior. God was mainly a distant thing, even though he believed in Him; he thought ghosts, spirits, and demons might exist, too. But that's as far as Jay went with those things. When he had sat in the presence of pure evil and wickedness in the car that night, looking into its face, he was fully convinced that there was a devil and there were most definitely demons.

He knew, without a shadow of a doubt, in the pit of his stomach and deep within his bones, that satan had a plan and that his plan was to destroy and kill us. He also had a revelation that if that level of evil exists, then something much more powerful and good absolutely does, too. He proved to himself that the power of the Holy Spirit was in him when he demanded that the demon leave me in the front seat of the car that night.

This moment marked the beginning of Jay's faith in Jesus Christ. All it took was a mustard seed of faith in God to cast out that devil (Matthew 17:20). But the Bible also says in Luke that if one does not let the Word of God take root in the heart, he or she will turn away or go back to things they once knew—which is what would happen with Jay, even though he was still having encounters with God.

The fear continued to build throughout the evening, and suddenly, a deep hatred toward Jay did, too. We got back to the condo, and Jay insisted we read the Bible. That night, I hated the Bible—I hated it more than anything. I couldn't bear to sit in front of it, let alone read it aloud. It felt like Jay was controlling when he started reading.

He grew frustrated and confused. The Word of God felt like broken glass in my ears. I didn't want to hear it and I didn't want Jay around me. I felt so angry toward him. I wanted to hurt him and didn't know why. I wanted him to leave to drive back to his treatment center in L.A. "I'm not leaving. I'm making sure you get to The Well tomorrow morning," he said. His persistence made my disgust toward him increase. It was not me that hated Jay, but this demon in me that we were both facing.

Although Jay and I remained celibate until we got married, we still would spend nights together and fall asleep with one another. That night, I did not want him anywhere near me. So, he fell asleep on the couch downstairs, and I went to my room. It felt like I was in middle school all over again with the amount of fear that was consuming me. I sometimes slept with my bedroom light on because I was so afraid.

That night, I kept my bedroom and bathroom light on. I couldn't eat anything. I could barely look at myself in the mirror. I felt like I wasn't me at all. I came down with a fever. I had racing thoughts. I had insomnia. I played the same song over and over again and begged God that this would end soon and that all the torment I felt throughout my entire life would end. I couldn't sleep, so I put a movie on my phone that I thought would be heartwarming and comforting: *The Sisterhood of the Traveling Pants*. I eventually fell asleep close to six in the morning with the movie playing on my phone about a foot from my face, propped up on my pillow. I woke less than an hour later with that same feeling I had when I was face to face with a demonic spirit in middle school at the cursed cabin, the same trancelike, dazed feeling.

When I opened my eyes, it was as if my phone had frozen on a bizarre image that instantly terrified me. I quickly took a screenshot in my half-awake, half-asleep state. My heart was racing again in fear. It was the image of a woman, with black hair, wearing a deep blood-red dress. Just like the demon at the cabin, she was propped up on her arms, staring at me. Her eyes were reflective, like cat eyes. They were big, solid black with reflective centers.

At first, I wondered if they had frozen on a character from the movie with dark hair. After the screenshot, I quickly went to use the bathroom and pulled open my photo album on my phone to look at it again, as I was more alert waking up. But the screenshot on my phone was completely black.

An ominous feeling invaded my upstairs bathroom. That was the demon Jay had seen the night before. I ran downstairs and woke him up while my entire body shook uncontrollably. It was hard to speak. I was starting to manifest again, and it was barely seven a.m. My deliverance was not for another two hours. I couldn't wait. I couldn't stay in my house and sit with myself. I needed Jesus. I needed a place that had the presence of God.

Jay got up, confused, irritated, and tired. We quickly got into his car and drove to the church, two hours early. We parked right in front of the small chapel. The campus was large, but the lot was fairly empty so we parked as close as we could get. I wanted to look directly at the cross that stood above the church-house. I sat in his car for almost two hours, shaking, opening the car door to spit regularly because I thought I was going to vomit.

Days before this, I had taken a printed picture I found on Pinterest off of my bulletin board and glued it inside my journal. On the back of that picture, I wrote an angry hateful prayer to God because I was so tormented in the days leading up to my second deliverance. This was my form of expression. I would write prayers like this from time to time because I thought it was just a good way to express my feelings, but no one saw it, and God understood me.

This was actually a demon who hated God. She moved through me and wrote about *her* hatred. How do I know? The random picture that I printed was an abstract painting of a woman in a red dress with black hair and dark black eyes with no irises.

"Oh, my gosh," I said to Jay.

"What?" he replied.

"It's her. I have been painting *her*." My hands began to tremble again.

"What do you mean?" he asked.

I scrambled through my phone and pulled up my website with my artwork. I shuffled through the gallery until I got to the paintings I was talking about.

"Her!" I pointed. "Is this what you saw yesterday?"

Jay's face went pale, and his eyes widened. "Yes."

I swiped through my gallery to another painting.

"Her?" I asked again.

"Whoa. Yeah."

I swiped through more of my paintings.

"Her?" I looked at him, pointing to another one.

We both were stunned. I had painted this demon six times and created one sculpture. Every single one was titled "Self-Portrait." People often asked me why I always painted myself with black hair. "It just feels like that is who I really am," I would say. The evolution of this demon in my artwork became progressively more violent and evil. The paintings got darker, and they never failed to have blood in them, and lots of it.

One painting showed her standing in the center of an ocean of blood. I believe this was the source of my previous fetish with blood. In my last painting of her, the eyes were gone, and she was chained. That was prophetic. I was mortified when I came to this realization of what I had been doing unknowingly. This felt like something out of a horror movie: painting a demon for years and calling it myself?

Jay and I were beyond ourselves at that point. Sue told Jay to walk me to the front of the church. I felt completely out of my mind like I was some feral animal. I was beside myself. I was exhausted. I still had a fever. I had no idea what was happening in my life anymore. *This can't all be real,* I thought to myself. When I entered the conference hall at the top of the stairs, Destiny met me again although she could not pray with me this time. My eyes were wide and vacant, and I didn't want to look at her. I stumbled over my words trying to explain to her what had just happened in the last twenty-four hours. Then Sue came and took me to a room on the third floor.

I sat in a dimly lit room with a big clear glass window and a glass door, cubicles on the other side of us. Helping me this time was Sue, one other girl I wasn't familiar with, and a man from the prayer team. As I quickly explained in detail all that had transpired, I turned my phone to show them the black screenshot and the paintings of this demon. "This is the woman I have been seeing in my dreams, Sue, the one who has been cursing me and cutting herself at me. This is who came to my front door a few nights ago. This is the one Jay saw in me last night, and this is the one I woke up to this morning."

I went through my photos and showed them a few paintings, trembling severely. "I can't even believe this," I said. Sue immediately responded, "Oh. I have seen this spirit in the villages of Africa." Sue regularly visited Tanzania and the Congo, where our friend's nonprofit has safehouses. She had prayed with many people there. I looked at her, shocked. "Are you serious?" I asked. "Yes. She is a gatekeeper spirit."

Africa is known for its witchcraft. You cannot visit these plains, especially the bush, and not expect to witness witchcraft, see a witch doctor, or run into things of that nature. The African people are very spiritual; they are not like Americans in this respect. While many Americans are shut off from the spirit world, the African people are wide awake to it. "What is a gatekeeper spirit?" I asked Sue.

I had never heard of this term before. Gatekeeper, maybe, but not a spirit that does that. She quickly explained that demons have jobs, some of which guard places or people. This gatekeeper spirit had been with me for a very long time. I started painting her in my late teens. Her purpose was to torment me and keep me bound to witchcraft, self-harm, and violence while also guarding my body. She was keeping my demons in and had *tried* to keep the Holy Spirit out.

It is too bad for her; the power of Christ trumps everything, and with the name of Jesus in faith, she would have to leave once and for all. The three of them read to me what the Lord had spoken to them and quickly got to praying. Demons instantly started manifesting and coming out of me. My body shook; it arched like a cat and went stiff. My eyes looked down or were closed a lot of the time. Demons hate Christians and many cannot look into the eyes of a believer for long because they will be exposed.

The power of Christ is too much for them to bear. They have to obey. I wailed as I did in my previous deliverance and in the car with Jay. I growled, hissed loudly like a snake, and snorted. Again, I had no control over what was happening to my body or voice. Sometimes, the demons would talk back and say things to those praying for me in my deliverances, and some of the time I could prevent this. At one point, all the tattoos on my right arm began to burn.

My entire arm was hot, as many of the tattoos were demonically inspired and had occult symbolism. It was mainly Sue doing the heavy lifting, spiritually speaking, in this exorcism. I trusted her and felt she deeply understood what I had been facing. Sue also had years of experience and was spiritually gifted in the prophetic, the discernment of spirits, faith, healing, knowledge, wisdom, and tongues. She was the perfect person for the job. I am so grateful the Lord had used her to set me free and help me maintain my freedom today.

I repented again, like I did almost at every deliverance, as repentance, too, can be a process. Sometimes, we overlook things we have done, or things happen again. Repentance is not just an apology to God but a recognition of the wrongdoing and an effort to completely stop and turn from sin. I knew it wasn't me who punched Jay in the face that night, but the demon. He knew it, too; however, I still repented.

It was in this session that the Gatekeeper spirit was cast from me. Many witchcraft demons, marine spirits, and sexual spirits were exorcised out of me as well; one of which was a spirit of molestation. The Lord had given Sue the knowledge to call this out. This spirit had been transferred to me through one of my abusers growing up. When this demon left my body, I fell forward in my chair, and it escaped through the palms of my hands. It was a strange feeling because there were no holes in my hands, yet it felt like it.

A strange feeling, yes, but one to be celebrated. I felt so much freedom once that demon was cast out! Multiple marine demons were part of this as well. If you have been among deliverance ministries, you know that these types of spirits exist. To many Christians, this sounds bizarre and even made up to some. Those seasoned in spiritual warfare and deliverance ministry know exactly what this is. They are wicked and sensual demons!

I remember seeing a blue crab-like demon that was cast from my body. I felt it as it came up through my esophagus, feeling its claws prod the inside of me before it had to come out from my mouth, that one hurt. This deliverance session went on for almost three whole hours. With hardly one hour of sleep, I was exhausted, and these demons were not leaving easily. The majority were stubborn and tormented my mind, vocal chords, and body on their way out.

There were little pockets of time between the exorcisms, where it felt like I would come up for air, breathe for a moment, maybe cry, and then be pulled back under for the fight. That is the best way I can describe it. One of these moments, I came back, and I was crying. "I don't want to do this," I wept. "I can't do this anymore." It felt like my tears were steaming and evaporating off my hot face. "I am so tired." I looked over at Sue. It was at this moment that I saw Jesus Christ. Sue was to my right and leaned into me, tears in her eyes. "I know you are so tired, honey," she said gently, "But you've got to keep going."

When I looked into Sue's eyes, I did not see Sue; I saw Jesus. I know we can see God in people through their acts of kindness or service, of course, but this was not the case. At this moment, I went into what is known as an "open vision." (Not just a picture in my mind—those are visions.) Suddenly, I was in this heavenly golden circle with Jesus in a gold courtyard and He had His hands on my face, even His eyes looked gold.

It was like He was the one saying, "I know you are so tired, but you've got to keep going." It was deeply tender and full of compassion, but at the same time, it felt like a coach encouraging me and telling me to finish the race. I had a sense of feeling like I had already won. I knew that these demons *knew* I had already won, that Jesus knew I had already won, and that Jesus had, in fact, already won. But I had to believe it and finish what I started fully. I kept going that day and was set free from many wicked demons. Tears still come to my eyes every time I tell this story. The love of God is insurmountable.

After the deliverance, I went into the church service late, where I saw a golden angel at the top of the sanctuary blowing a golden trumpet. I felt at peace. Sue told me I was free that day, but I had an inkling that there was more to come. Still, that did not affect the peace I was blessed with that afternoon. When Jay saw me after the service, he instantly felt the freedom I felt. He was elated to see me back in my body and without torment. He knew that the violent and wicked demon was gone from me.

We went to Long Beach that evening and burned almost every painting I had. We tore the picture from my journal and burned that, too. I gathered clothing, crystals, figurines—anything I had overlooked: books, things from my past, jewelry. We loaded the car and took pile after pile of things to the fire pit. We probably looked like crazy people amongst all the other friends and family partaking in their summer bonfires. We didn't care. We stayed until everything was burnt to ashes. This demon would be bound to Hell for eternity, and she would be blinded by the power of the Holy Ghost (just as she was in my last painting).

She no longer had power over my life. And because of this tormenting reality I existed in for so long, in my heart, I knew it was my duty to expose the dangers and evils of witchcraft. It was now part of my calling as a believer (who had been there!) to deter people from witchcraft's seduction and to help set those in captivity free in the name of Jesus, no matter what (Luke 4:18, Isaiah 61:1).

Naturally, I felt fear of falling asleep by myself for a few nights after going through something that extreme. I had spirits of fear that had not been cast out yet—though they were next. That impending doom, that anxiety I had felt on and off since I was a little girl. I was on the narrow path to freedom now and it felt great! However, not everyone in my life could grasp this. What Jay and I had experienced, and would continue to experience, was supernatural. And the supernatural Spirit of God and the freedom He promises us, unfortunately, can be uncomfortable for many and confusing for some.

Some were even put off and discouraged by it. Even though I had been physically and mentally healed (which was a wonderful thing!), some still could not accept it. This did not snuff out my joy. Actually, it reminds me of all the people who rejected Jesus during His time. Jesus! The Messiah! All biblical prophecy tells in great detail what the Messiah would be like, what He would do, how He would enter the world, and so on. Old Testament experts and religious men who had spent their entire lives studying the scriptures still looked right through Jesus.

Even though He was the Son of God, He was rejected right there in front of their faces! Can you believe that? He loved, He healed, He served, and He performed miracles, yet He was rejected. He threatened the law, He spoke out against religious people and hypocrites, and He sought no honor and recognition for His miracles. He was and is the Son of God, and people still didn't (and don't) believe this despite all of the evidence.

The Lord reminded me of this since I have been writing this book. Still, years later, a handful of people judge my experience, doubt it, and reject it. Some people who had been very close to me began talking poorly about me while others that were closest to me witnessed the transformation firsthand. God was pruning my friendships. I was judged for getting delivered and condemned for believing I was healed, even though I was.

Still, others celebrated it. I was also condemned for stepping away from different 12-step programs because things were no longer the same for me, while others recognized my freedom and celebrated it. Not everyone will understand, and that's okay. When we can't necessarily speak into a person's life, the way we live our lives can be a testimony that eventually points many people to God.

One afternoon, the Lord spoke to me when I felt discouraged while putting things away in my room. "If they couldn't even see Jesus when He was right in front of their faces, how do you expect them to see you?" I paused. "If they rejected the Messiah, they are going to reject you." I didn't say anything back to the Lord, I just stood in silence and reflected. *Consider yourself blessed,* I heard my heart say (Matthew 5:10-12).

A few nights after that second radical deliverance, I was asleep in my condo, and the Lord woke me up. In the Spirit, I saw two angels. I had multiple angelic encounters during this time, but these angels were different. They looked like warrior angels! The Lord showed me one at my bedroom door; he was tall, as tall as the door frame, and large and burly.

He looked as if he was wearing some sort of Roman attire, made of thick leather. But he wore armor, too. He had on a breastplate and had weapons on him, he glowed a bright electric blue. I did not notice angel wings on him. The second one the Lord showed me was on the side of my house. Because I was in a condominium, there was an alleyway and a path to the left side of my home, whereas the neighboring house was on the right.

This angel glowed a bright and vibrant green—he literally glowed! He guarded the entire pathway on the side of my home, from the end of my garage to my front door in length. He hovered above this area, wearing armor and similar attire, but he had wings. His wingspan reached the width of my home from one end of the path to the other. You would *not* want to mess with these guys. The Lord allowed me to see this because He wanted to show me how protected I really was.

That gatekeeper spirit would not be coming back. She had officially been evicted, and security was set up so she could not attempt to come back and squat. Over the next months, I continued to have angelic encounters from time to time, although they were not the same and not nearly as intense as the multiples I had at the start of this journey. After the gatekeeper spirit was cast out of me, I began having deliverances more often and more quickly, and larger amounts of spirits were leaving at a time. They could not be held back. They had to go.

Jay and I got married through all of this. I prayed more about it before making it a reality. Something within me was apprehensive. I didn't want to marry him this quickly, but I wanted to honor God and not be disobedient. I knew I wanted to marry him eventually if things got better. At the same time, I was also trying to prove something to myself and others: that God is *so* powerful that He could even change an abusive, addicted man who hasn't been a father to all the other children he had. My worth depended on it. *Yikes*.

The truth is God *can* change a person like that, or any other person for that matter. The kicker, though? They have to be willing and repentant. The second kicker? Marrying Jay was not God's will for me. I was *wrong*. As the idea of us getting married started to become real, I felt nervous because of our past and the judgment of others.

I thought it was the Lord who had spoken after my first deliverance, which was to marry ninety days from that point. My best friend came out against this, telling me she didn't think it was God, and why would God tell me to marry him in that amount of time? Deception had its grip on me and I refused to listen to her counsel. She told me she didn't support this and would not be coming to the wedding.

When it comes to "hearing" the Lord, many things can be at play. Thoughts can only come from three sources: God, the enemy, and his demons—or oneself. It is important to be able to discern the difference. I had heard and listened to demons my whole life, but while I heard the voice of the Lord, there were many familiar spirits that I would sometimes get confused about whether something was God or not.

If it sounded good, it had to be God, right? Wrong. The Enemy can offer us things that appear good or have the potential to be good, and it could still be entirely outside God's will for our life. I was new to accurately hearing the voice of God, and I didn't know then that whatever I heard had to be taken to the Word of God and compared to His character. If a "word" or "prophecy" doesn't align with God's character, it is *not* God.

However, since this was directly after my deliverance, which I felt peace from, I *considered* it the Lord. There was, however, not a lot of peace in me about marrying Jay. My family felt rushed and upset; other friends supported me but seemed confused, and the enemy used other people's Christian love stories to deceive and distract me from my reality.

If "God" hadn't told me to marry Jay, I would not have married him then. Of course, God will encourage us to do things that make us uncomfortable or die to "self" in some ways to help others, but this wasn't one of those. I was in deep denial. I considered the next few years of abuse as just me enduring what I had to endure and that *this* was "suffering for Christ." Talk about the deception of codependency.

16

GETTING MARRIED AND DIVORCING DEMONS

We were getting closer and closer to our 90-day mark when we would get married before the Lord. We did not have money, so wedding planning went out the window, and the dream ceremony I had always desired would have to be postponed. It was a simple Saturday morning in September when Jay and I married at the same church where we had experienced deliverance.

The church offered us the use of their chapel for free and one of the pastors married us. About 12 friends and family witnessed our ceremony. My hairdresser gifted me a styling that morning, my dress was a $60 rayon gown from Windsor, my ring was a hundred-dollar moissanite replica of what I really wanted, our wedding bands were from Amazon, and my mom bought me a beautiful pink rose bouquet that was probably my most expensive accessory that day.

I was so nervous as my dad (who was equally, if not more, nervous) walked me down the aisle. It wasn't what I had expected. My dad didn't seem happy or at peace, but reluctant. As I walked down the aisle, the wedding song stopped. I was so nervous that I didn't stay stuck on the imperfection for long.

Jay couldn't wait for my father to bring me to him and started walking toward me ahead of time. Our group of friends and family laughed. We looked into each other's eyes that morning and cried as we said the vows given to us—we didn't even write our own. Even though there was chaos in our lives, we were also eager and excited.

Standing before Jay was special. We knew God would continue to change us and direct our footing if we let Him. Our dear friend, Phil, was the wedding photographer. That morning was bright, and the radiance of joy on our faces outshone the sun above us. After the ceremony, we enjoyed a Cuban lunch at a restaurant and then got in our car to head south. Rosarita, Mexico, was our honeymoon destination, at least, our *first* honeymoon destination since we were to have another real wedding and a real honeymoon.

I paid a whopping $400 for our Mexico stay. This was a lot for me since Jay had been in treatment up to that point. However, something began to happen about two hours after we sealed our covenant under God.

After having had three major deliverances, I felt what had become a familiar and recognizable feeling. I was about to manifest again. Something felt very wrong. Looking back now, it was like all the darkness Jay secretly carried was looming over me, too.

I had no idea that the next few years of my life would be me constantly coming up against evil in both the natural and supernatural on account of both me *and* Jay. I used to think it was all because of me. *Oh, no,* I thought. *Not on my honeymoon.* As we pulled out of the gas station to head south, I got a nosebleed and bled on my wedding dress—I knew what was happening. I was quickly overcome with anxiety.

"Are you okay, babe?" Jay asked.

"Yes. I'm okay."

"I feel like something is wrong," he said.

"No, no. It's okay," I assured.

I had gotten nosebleeds before when reading the Bible and spit up blood in a later deliverance (which is not uncommon with witchcraft). I tried not to let my mind become consumed with the fear of yet another demonic attack. The attacks were always the worst before a spirit was cast from me. It was worse if that spirit was deeply bonded to me or had been with me for a long time. This demon about to reveal itself was equally as violent as the gatekeeper, except this one burned with a deeper jealousy and violence over me.

That honeymoon weekend was anything but ordinary. I managed to push back the manifestations the first evening, and we had a decent first night in Mexico. The following two days were unpredictable and challenging. I started to manifest unexpectedly in our hotel room, and Jay, again, was casting devils out of me, sort of. He, too, would manifest, but the focus was always on me and what I needed to change.

I coughed, shook, and wailed as we both experienced the demonic and the power of God as well, but we were tired, and it felt like our inner lights were dimming. I personally didn't feel that Jay was equipped for this, but we did our best to get through it. These were smaller demons that were leaving before the finale of the "husbandry spirit." (Yes, it's a real thing.)

We had been through so much already; we didn't want this to be a lengthy part of our journey, but it was. This was obviously not part of our plan. Jay said he kept seeing a demon the second night. He again described what I had seen as well. Aggression arose between us, and our drive back home to California was difficult and frustrating. Jay hadn't been abusive toward me for months, but sadly, the weekend of our honeymoon, it all began again. This time, my denial grew roots, and I gaslit myself over and over again.

Despite the flaws, we were glad we got married. I thought God was proud of me. That's all I wanted. That following week, I was in that same church on five different occasions, having more devils cast from me. Demons of shame, anger, and more witchcraft were expelled, including more spirits associated with sexuality, like fetishes, homosexuality, perversions, and sexual abuse.

Additionally, there were spirits of unforgiveness, kundalini, guilt, and bitterness, as well as demons that had entered in through curses put on me by occult people. They were all being eradicated in the name of Jesus. I didn't even know some demons existed behind what I just thought were severely unmanageable emotions like resentment and self-pity. However, some demons operate behind those things in people, as they did in me.

One of the spirits that manifested from the warlock (the psychic man I mentioned in previous chapters) felt like a garden snake that moved from my right forearm up through where my collarbone was. Some of the demons would speak out of my mouth or swear, and some choked me or would keep me from speaking when those delivering me would tell me to order the demon to go in Jesus's name. Sometimes, it took everything inside me to say "Jesus."

Demons don't freak out, shake, and tremble at the name of any other "god;" they only have an adverse reaction to Jesus. Mark 3:11 (NASB) states, *"Whenever the unclean spirits saw Him* [Jesus], *they would fall down before Him and shout, 'You are the Son of God!'"* That should speak for itself! They tremble at His name and in the presence of someone who truly walks in the authority of Christ.

Once the demons were called out, and I had broken agreements with them and the *desire* to keep them in my life, the demonic had to leave. Breaking agreement with anger felt hard. It felt like it had "protected" me for so long. I didn't want demons in my life, but for some, it felt like there was a tradeoff. "Keep my anger, gain my safety." This feeling was anything but the truth. Some of them even felt like friends. It was this week that the Lord revealed something to me that I had never heard. The Lord led me to learn about marine demons. I had seen some marine demons in my deliverances. I also recall reading about them in the book, *The Witch Doctor and the Man* years earlier.

I began researching and found Scripture on marine spirits (such as Leviathan in the book of Job). I had to be careful not to spend *too* much time researching these things because of my past. I did not want to obsess over evil or glorify it in any way, but the Holy Spirit guided me on *this* particular search for good reason. I found a Christian video about something called a "spirit-spouse" and how to divorce it.

It was a marine demon, and the most common ways this spirit would enter was through witchcraft and sometimes sexual sin or generationally. Spirit husbands or wives are a widespread element of shamanism, and in some cultures, your shamanic powers are only proven if you are married to one. Had I kept descending into witchcraft, I would have pursued shamanism. My "psychic" ability was just one notch below the shamans, and it was something I had considered pursuing just months before Jesus intercepted.

I began my search on Christian evangelism and deliverance websites about the symptoms of a spirit spouse (or husbandry spirit) and how to get free. Repentance, walking in righteousness, the Word of God, fasting, prayer, and deliverance were all equally important. I began to say the prayers listed on one of the websites and intensely manifested as I tried to read them. This demon did not want me free, but now it was exposed, and there was no way I would leave any stone unturned.

I would get free no matter how long it took or how difficult, exhausting, and scary it was. If you are currently in the thick of deliverance or warfare, keep going. God has a plan for your life, and staying demonized and oppressed isn't it. Freedom, in my experience, often begins with awareness. *Now,* I was aware of this particular demon's hold on my life.

During this year and a half, when I was between deliverances, my prayer team taught me to do self-deliverance. I knew what manifestations looked like and quickly began to learn what they revealed. A manifestation is a clue there is a demon there. Know your enemy, and then eradicate it! I was convinced that this had been another demon that had been with me for a very long time. This thing did not want me close to any men.

Its spiritual influence made me avoidant, abrasive, and abusive. From a psychological perspective, the amount of trauma I had been through also explained this behavior. A lot of my behaviors and issues were spiritual, while some things were psychological and emotional, and God had to train me. God's Word would be key in transforming my emotions and behaviors.

So, what is a spirit spouse, and what does it do? Well, it is a demon, for starters. A spirit spouse or husbandry/wife spirit (these names can be used interchangeably) keeps you in deep bondage, where intimate relationships suffer greatly or don't exist at all. It sexually assaults the individual while they are sleeping, sometimes even while awake. They break down love in the home as well as produce extreme lust.

Many who have been married multiple times and suffer the same issues in their marriages can be bound by this demon. Of course, this is not the *only* reason. My relationships have suffered because of this, but not only this, and I would be foolish to think so. Many encounters with this demon happened in the dream world or at night. Imagine an extremely violent and jealous boyfriend that you broke up with, and what would happen if he heard you were dating somebody else?

He would act out in his possessive and jealous ways toward you and probably your new partner—this is the spirit spouse. Only days after our marriage covenant was made before God, this demon exposed itself, and abuse came back into our relationship, sadly. This spirit first revealed his marine-like appearance with his scaly blue skin and beady eyes and then his human appearance with his dark skin and hair. Some spirits can shape-shift, and this was one of them.

Some symptoms of this spirit include the inability to get married (late marriage) or marriages ending in divorce; regular wet dreams; disinterest in a human spouse and zero attraction or desire for them; being consumed by lust; pornography (or other perversions); constant dreams of a man or woman coming to have sex with you; dream marriages, not involving yourself in relationships; bed shaking; sheets moving in the night and other strange phenomena; sleep paralysis; never having good relationships with partners; constantly feeling as if there's a ring on your finger when there is not; hatred for the opposite sex, etc.

There are many more symptoms if you so choose to research it yourself. Evangelist Joshua Orekhie has great information on this demon, and how to divorce it. Many Christian YouTube videos are helpful as well. Do not fear! Deliverance is your portion and if you are under the oppression of this demon, freedom is coming for you and His name is Jesus! Repent of your witchcraft, turn away from it or sexual sin, walk in righteousness (honor God in the way you live), fast, and seek deliverance.

When I began submerging myself into witchcraft practices at 17, my demonic dreams increased. A presence would accompany these dreams and enter my room often at night. Although I had never physically seen the spirit then, I would feel him enter my room and stand by my bedroom door. When I would fall back asleep, I'd have demonic and terrible sexual dreams that I had no control over.

I would wake up to something physically caressing my legs and what felt like a mild shaking or vibrating of my bed. Although these encounters were common, they were never, ever comfortable. I often felt violated because I was. I remember a time after unintentionally doing astral projecting in my sleep (which seemed to happen often) and trying to come back into my body (I was in rehab at this time). As I stood next to myself on my bed and tried to crawl back into my body, something would not let me enter. I could feel my teeth gnashing, my jaw clenching, and my fists squeezing tighter and tighter as my toes curled under. I began to panic.

Pounding ensued all over my bed, specifically around my body. It was a terrifying and eerie feeling like a hundred unseen people were jumping on my bed. Then, I saw a light down the hall and heard a voice at my doorway. A woman's voice told me to wiggle my fingers and toes and to breathe. As I did this, I found myself able to enter back into my body and I woke up to cold sweats and a panic. I walked out into the lobby that night, afraid.

One of the support staff members knew what I was facing and printed out a sheet on what astral projection was. Having the "natural" ability to do this made me feel special and only endorsed more witchcraft in my life back then. It's funny how few Christians spoke into my life versus all the New Age direction I received! As I pursued Jesus, the uncontrollable astral projections at night stopped for the most part but none of this entirely went away for years. Deliverance put a stop to it.

Demonic sexual assaults were, unfortunately, also part of being bound to a spirit spouse. Once I started going through deliverance, these encounters increased. And each time, I would wake up very upset, of course. I was given so many prayers and scriptures from Christians around me for protection, healing, deliverance, peace, and freedom. Through trial and error, revelation, and the Holy Spirit, I have learned how certain prayers work differently depending on the situation, and how my heart, faith, and pursuit of righteousness make a massive difference. James 5:16 (NIV) says, *"The prayer of a righteous person is powerful and effective."*

The "God, please help me" prayers still existed in my life. However, my prayer life became much more intentional, powerful, and direct. I learned how to declare things over my life and home and grew in confidence and authority in Christ. As I started to step into my God-given authority in Jesus, I began experiencing the demonic becoming afraid of me. *Me!* I *actually* had power over them!

When I went into the church one morning for a deliverance that week, I told Sue about this husbandry spirit. She had never heard of this type of demon before, but that didn't worry her. She began to call it out of me, declaring that I now had an earthly husband, and this demon was not married to me in the spirit realm anymore, and that I was divorcing it that day! This was a vicious and stubborn exorcism. The demon felt like it was the size of a skyscraper honestly and would snort and spit as it refused to leave my body. That morning, it took a long time to get delivered from just this one. I began spitting up mucus, snorting and coughing on the floor as it exited my body, and crying afterward.

Sue and Destiny worked hard that morning. Those women truly were warriors against the demonic in my life. Destiny always made it a point to meet me for deliverance no matter what it took. She would find a babysitter for her daughter, get keys to a church room, pray with me over the phone, and text me in the mornings or late at night to encourage me. She would prophesy over my life and support me. She and Sue were both very gifted, but what they were more than anything was willing. My life has completely changed because of their willingness to help me see this through.

Just as Jay witnessed freedom in me after the gatekeeper demon was evicted, he also saw the same thing when this husbandry spirit was cast out. However, because this demon had been so bonded to me, it tried to come back multiple times. Freedom from it was a marker for major sexual healing in my journey! Sexual perversions and masturbation halted when this demon left me! But because Jay snored often, I would wake up and sleep in our spare room in the condo to get a good night's sleep. What I found interesting was that more demonic attacks would happen when I would sleep apart from Jay.

One night, as I fell back asleep in the spare room, I had a dream. A man was approaching me from far away, and at first, it looked like Jay, my actual husband. Although he looked like Jay in the dream, I knew it was not him. He walked down a winding path that looked charred and dead like the grass had been burned.

When he approached me, I felt this crazy jealous anger emit from him. "You are not my husband," I said in the dream, confused but bold. Just then Jay's face disappeared and the husbandry spirit appeared in its human form (not the marine form). It had wild yellowish eyes that were angry and jealous. Its whole body shook in anger as it tried to move toward me to hurt me. Something was keeping it contained.

"You cannot touch me!" I yelled at it. "In Jesus's name, you have to leave me now. You are not my husband!" The demon shook in anger and fear, and it looked like a layer of disappointment and desperation glossed over its face. It became sad, just as the gatekeeper had been. My body (their house) was no longer their home, which was wonderful for me.

Humans were *not* made to house demons! Humans were made to house the Holy Spirit only and glorify God. An invisible force field remained between me and the husbandry spirit in that dream. Another night following, I felt its presence enter the spare room *again* when I was in there. I felt a heaviness wash over my body as if I was beneath a wave, starting at my feet. I was paralyzed, and because I had been through demonic sleep paralysis and assaulted many times before, I anticipated that I would be strangled next—but something different happened this time.

As it tried to lay on top of me, I heard a "CLINK," like the sound of something hitting metal. I was not being choked. Instead, the heaviness stopped at my chest, and could not go deeper. This demon could not enter me! "CLINK," I heard again as I felt something hit somewhere else on my chest. Then I realized what it was. I had armor on! "I command you to leave in the name of Jesus!" I said as I lay there paralyzed. "CLINK," I felt something hit my chest again, and then it fled.

Peace filled the room, and I got up out of bed. Because I had now pursued a lifestyle of righteousness and was not habitually sinning toward God or myself with sexual sin, I had on a breastplate! It was the breastplate of righteousness that the book of Ephesians talks about (Ephesians 6). This demon tried to enter me but could not, so it hit my armor.

After multiple attempts and no success, the demon left. I was now stronger and more confident than ever! I had another supernatural experience around this time that has marked me since. One night in a dream I saw three bats flying frantically together around my upstairs. They separated and one went into Jay's room, one went into my roommate Sarah's room, and another went into mine. I was confused and afraid as I saw it lurking in the room's shadows and flying about. In the dream, I stepped into my authority in Christ and started speaking the Word of God loudly.

The only Scripture I knew at the time was Psalm 23. As soon as I started speaking this word out loud, the bat stopped and froze in the fold where the ceiling meets the wall, its body black and eyes bright red. It looked petrified as I continued with the psalm, almost as if it had just been zapped with a taser. The bat was stunned and immobile, and then I woke up. The next morning, I learned everyone in the house had nightmares caused by a nightmare demon.

One thing I learned, though, through this dream and others similar to it, is that the Word of God literally paralyzes demons. Demons flee when you know your authority over the kingdom of darkness and the Word of God. They *are* scared of *us*.

17

THE EXORCIST AND THE MERRY-GO-ROUND OF ABUSE

As multiple deliverances and substantial amounts of freedom continued, I grew weary that I had so many demons. When the Lord's Prayer says, *"Deliver us from evil,"* this was not what I had in mind. I wanted a one-and-done deliverance. Hadn't I done enough "work"? At this point, I believe I had undergone 15 to 20 deliverances before I was led to Stuart Greer, a high-level exorcist.

After my third deliverance, I remember feeling more freedom, yet more confusion. *Will this ever actually end?* I wondered. The intensity of the exorcisms and the length of exhaustion following each one (typically about a week of recovery in the beginning) was extreme. I desperately cried out to the Lord, asking, "How long will this take?" It had been four months at that time.

Part of the reason I believe my deliverance was as lengthy as it was is because I had opened a lot of spiritual doors, and

I mean a lot, and I was in an abusive relationship, which is an open door in general. Even though my abuse and fighting back had stopped, I was still on the receiving end, and that was not good. I would pray to God and beg for total freedom—and I mean *beg*. I would ask God to tell me at least how many demons there were and how long I would be in this deliverance process.

I remember reading in *The Witch Doctor and the Man* that it took author Bishop Vagalos Kanco over two years of deliverance and additional time before he could step into God's call on his life. I wondered how long it would take me; surely, I wasn't as demonized as him. For Vagalos, it was very intense. It's hard even to fathom what his deliverances looked like, considering the level of witchcraft he was operating in. The man had directly spoken to satan on multiple occasions. His untangling took *time*, but I clung to his testimony of freedom.

Regardless of the difficulty, Vagalos didn't quit, the Christians in his village didn't quit on him, and, of course, neither did Jesus. His story was one of the very few that got me through what felt like such a lonely and strange part of my life. Many do not know much about deliverance (even Christians) and many more have never even experienced it. During my freedom process, I became awake to the fact that much of the Western Church was asleep.

How is deliverance not happening in every church on every corner in Orange County? I thought to myself. So many people have demons. The majority of people are either afflicted in mind or body. How is the church and its people in such bondage? We should be the example! Where the Spirit of the Lord is, there is freedom. *If there's no freedom in a place of worship, does that mean there's no Spirit of the Lord there?* I had a lot of questions.

The Bible says of all Christians: *"In my [Jesus's] name they will drive out demons..."* (Mark 16:17 NIV). If everyone sought true repentance, a willingness to turn away from their sin, and follow that up with deliverance, they could be fully free and truly operate in the Holy Spirit, which sets others free! Why isn't this happening every time God's children gather? Why isn't this talked about openly in the church? Jesus came to free the captives, giving us the same command.

I felt confused and frustrated, yet at peace and passionate regarding the ins and outs of deliverance, especially my own. With new questions surfacing regularly about deliverance in the church, I kept going to the Lord in prayer, begging for specifics from God on how long this would take for me and how many demons there were. I was desperate to know how much longer I had to fight. I had been on a mental health healing journey for more than ten years at this point and had worked very hard on myself. God knew I would continue to fight regardless how long it might take. He was kind enough to tell me, though.

In my heart I was impressed it would end before December of the following year. That would make it about a year and a half's time—a long way away. *Maybe I heard wrong,* I would tell myself. It wouldn't be the first time. Yet whenever I asked God, I heard the same thing. Since I could not count how many spirits left or how many demons were still in me, I continued to ask God how many there were. He was kind enough to answer that prayer, also!

Sometimes, all we have to do is ask and be quiet and willing enough to hear the answer. My dreams have always been one of the main ways God speaks and reveals things to me. This has only amplified and become clearer the closer I get to Him. So, one night shortly after this prayer, I had a dream. In the dream, I saw the number 1,500 carved in gold. It was carved into what looked like a stone, but the numbers were bold and almost three-dimensional, standing out from the rock. When I woke up, I knew exactly what that meant. There were a total of 1,500 demons that had been inhabiting me.

This revelation didn't scare me or aggravate me, no. It catapulted me into a deeper desperation to get rid of them and an insatiable hunger for God. I had journeyed through the wilderness for years, and it had only prepared me for such a time as this. Jesus was on my side, and none of my enemies could stop me. Slow me down a bit at times? Sure. But I never left the boxing ring, and the Lord coached me through every blow, every knock-out, and every burst of endurance I had in me.

A person without God runs out of energy repeatedly. A person *with* God fights and endures, stands up to the challenge, and rests in the Lord. With God, *nothing* is impossible

(Mattew 17:20). I originally learned of Stuart Greer through a woman who prayed for me at my church, and that he was teaching a seminar. I figured going through a deliverance seminar would be great. I felt like I had a lot of knowledge from my own personal experience, but I knew I needed more, and I wanted to help others. I knew God had not given me the spiritual gifts, like the discernment of spirits and the prophetic call if He didn't want me to use them to help others get free inside and outside of the church.

I was all in.

I showed up nervous. I sometimes would have anxiety around large groups and felt like I stood out too much, even when I didn't. It always felt like part of me wanted to hide, especially in Holy Spirit-filled atmospheres. What was that all about? I had stopped operating in direct and willful sin, although my husband and I struggled greatly. We were hopeful, especially me, that the chaos in our marriage would eventually stop. I had a lot of shame surrounding my marriage. I wanted to "speak life," which kept me in a place of secrecy and denial for a long time.

Maybe I needed more therapy or more deliverance. I was always open to it, desperately wanting to change and walk peacefully. Peace is a by-product of the Holy Spirit, and I believed I could walk in that one day, but it was very hard. And much harder in an abusive marriage—still, I persevered.

I hadn't had a deliverance for over a month at this time, and no significant demonic activity anymore apart from the abuse. I wondered if this was true freedom. I thought it would feel different, more free. I don't know. I felt more peace for sure, but I didn't feel *total* freedom. I was desperate for it. I was so hungry for God and what the Gospel offered. I just wanted to die to myself already.

As I entered the facility, I walked in through the front and made eye contact with whom I assumed was Stuart. I instantly looked down. *Gosh! Why do I do that?* I remember thinking. *I have nothing to hide; I've been delivered from a lot. Stop feeling nervous.* I should have known that, again, it was not me who felt nervous but the demons inside of me that were trembling at the presence of someone who carried the authority of Christ in them.

Demons sense Spirit-filled Christians. They will shake and tremble at the presence of the Lord! They *will* manifest! As the seminar began, I sat toward the front. I felt shaky the majority of the time, and this was a six-hour seminar. That's a lot of information about demons, deliverance, and freedom! And when you have demons inside you that do not want to be exposed, just imagine what that feels like!

After we broke for lunch and came back, I met up with my friend Daniella, who came late, and we sat by each other. She and I had become closer since my deliverances, and she fearlessly prayed for me many times. I felt comfortable with her.

When we approached the doors after lunch, they were locked. The seminar took place upstairs, and there were a few staircases and doors between us and the teaching. Our banging on the door was useless. We eventually found a group of women who located a janitor who opened the doors for us. I wasn't paranoid, yet at the same time, I sensed something was trying to keep me out of there. Things like this happened often for me and would continue to occur beyond this point for a while. We shuffled into the classroom and listened. I took as many notes as I could and bought the handbook they were selling.

Cathy, Stuart's wife, also taught a little—although it was mostly Stuart. I didn't want to look at Stuart, but something in me did not want to back down from staring right at Cathy. *Why am I doing that?* I thought. I kept trying to *show* that I could hold eye contact with her. Why was that? I had demons, that's why. Though demons hate looking Christians in the eyes, they also hate to expose themselves. It felt like something in me was trying to show that it wasn't there by maintaining such prolonged eye contact since demons typically don't hold eye contact in settings like that.

I remember it being so weird but also something I could not control. Cathy and Stuart were experts, after over 40 years in deliverance ministry, nothing could shake them. As the teaching ended and we entered the sixth hour of the seminar, we were about to participate in a group deliverance.

I had never heard of something so strange in my life. Exorcisms were private and vulnerable; why would a group be encouraged? It was explained that demons seem to manifest much more easily in Holy Spirit-filled atmospheres like this one (especially on the topic of deliverance). If a person manifests a demon, it creates a domino effect. This was an equipping of the saints, a hands-on exercise on exorcising demons from our peers or getting them cast out of ourselves!

The Greers went through a list of things, asking people if they were experiencing any physical or emotional sensations as they called out things like rejection, fear, Freemasonry, and so on. As they neared the topic of witchcraft, I lost total control of my voice. At the top of my lungs, I screamed as loud as humanly possible, "No!" My eyes were glued shut and it felt like the scream would never end. My hands squeezed the side of my chair as if I was going to fly from it at any moment.

"Everyone!" Cathy addressed the group. *"This* is witchcraft," I heard her say. She encouraged the group to not be afraid as I continued to manifest. She quickly came over to me and cast out this spirit of generational witchcraft. Stuart continued leading the group through more things on his list. A woman behind me manifested and was delivered from a spirit of codependency. I had no idea that a spirit operating in that existed.

Many, myself included for some time, believe that negative emotions or behaviors are just that. Sometimes they can be, sure. But if a demon manifests when something like "doubt" is being called out, there is a demon in that person causing and perpetuating that doubt. I continued to manifest intensely on and off through the rest of the group deliverance, so much so that I couldn't even pray for anyone else.

When Cathy originally approached me, she asked me about unforgiveness in my life, which I walked through again. She also told me I needed to immediately get rid of the ring I always wore on my left hand. This ring was very sentimental to me. A friend had bought it for me on my one-year sobriety birthday. It was a beautiful opaline ring pressed into a silver band. I always wore it.

However, I regularly placed this ring on the altar at the witchcraft temple to be "charged" when we invited the dead and other spirits in. It had become a cursed object. Of course, my desire to get rid of anything demonic in my life overrode sentiment, so I chucked it in the trash on my way out of the seminar. I also was greatly convicted about the job I had just been hired for at a yoga studio. I hadn't started yet, but Cathy firmly warned me that it was not the place for me.

I felt it in my bones when she directed me to reconsider this. Deep down, I knew the Lord did not want me there, and this confirmed that. Because of my intense manifestations, she also encouraged me to book an appointment with her or Stuart immediately, which I did. *There can't be that much left, right?* I thought. At this point, I honestly didn't know. Something about the demonic is that they hide. So many people go through life with demons inhabiting their mind and body and they don't even know it!

Because many are so convinced that a chemical imbalance is the only possibility when it comes to mental illness, they short-change themselves from actually getting free. Sure, in some cases it is something within the body (not a spiritual problem) that needs to be addressed. A person deficient in magnesium might be experiencing anxiety. Or, it could be a spirit of fear that must be cast out. The same goes for sleep issues.

Insomnia could be a result of a hormonal imbalance. Or there could be an actual demon of insomnia. About two weeks after the seminar, I got into a one-on-one with Stuart at a church in San Clemente. I punched the address into my maps. Strangely, my phone kept routing me to an empty field, saying, "You've arrived." Thinking aloud, I said, "No, I haven't." This happened multiple times, and now I was 30 minutes late for my session. The Greers do not leave their phone numbers on their website, understandably so—as many who are demonized would likely be calling them all hours of the day—so I had no way of contacting them.

Finally, at 9:30 a.m., I got a call. It was Stuart. "Hey, Jenny, are you still planning to come?" he asked.

"Yes. Your church isn't in or by a field, right? My phone keeps routing me to this field."

He laughed, "Definitely not." I confirmed the address was correct, but my phone was still malfunctioning.

"We're dealing with some spiritual warfare here. It's okay. I'll direct you."

Thankfully, I arrived at the church in less than ten minutes and met Stuart at the door. Stuart was a large man who towered over most. He had white hair and glasses, and I figured he was in his sixties. He looked like a "normal guy." But the call of God on his life was anything but that. Contrary to what I expected, his personality wasn't that animated. He walked in a silent authority, like Sue, and was laid-back.

"Hey," he laughed. "I'm glad you made it."

"Me too. That was so weird."

"Yeah, that can happen," he said. "You know, I almost didn't come this morning...."

"Really?" I inquired, confused.

"I woke up and was going about my normal morning routine. When I checked the calendar last night your name had been removed from the schedule. I figured you canceled. This morning, my wife asked if I was still planning to meet you because I was taking my sweet time getting ready. I told her you had canceled and were taken off the schedule. Cathy responded, 'No, she's not,' and showed me the schedule on her phone. It's strange you had been removed from the deliverance calendar on my phone but not Cathy's. Something doesn't want you here." He kind of chuckled and began to open the church doors.

Stuff like this happened often: the enemy was always trying so hard to stop me or slow me down. He wants to disrupt every child of God's life and purpose. So, while sometimes it was really tiring, other times it seemed as if I had endless endurance and faith. The truth is the enemy knows the call of God on every single person's life, and because he can see what they can do for God's Kingdom, he will do anything to prevent it, slow it down, distract the person, and if he's lucky; destroy and kill them. Thankfully, I serve the good and faithful God who continues to make a way for me.

We stepped into a large conference room, and as I entered I began to feel nervous, just like I did in my first deliverance. Stuart sat down on one side of the table, and I sat at the head of it. We discussed my paperwork. Stuart had developed a thorough questionnaire for people seeking deliverance. It is extensive and strategic. With all this information, Stuart searches for patterns (which is also one of my favorite things to do) to see where the demonic could be at play in a person's life.

Because I had been through so much, there was much to unpack. I explained how I had been through many deliverances and that Cathy told me I should book an appointment with him. After looking through my paperwork, he laughed and said, "Boy, you have opened up *a lot* of spiritual doors. So how we're going to do this is I am going to call out some things and the demons will manifest. You let me know if you feel anything, hear anything, etc., okay?"

"Sure."

"Spirit of witchcraft..." He trailed off in a stern and authoritative voice.

I began to manifest instantly. The majority of my first session was a blur. I practically lost my voice after those three hours because I was screaming the entire time, and I mean long screams and coarse yelling that felt like it had no end.

After each scream, I could feel the entity leave me, and I would collapse forward, catch my breath, or start crying. There was a lot of wailing, shaking, screaming, yelling, hissing, growling, snorting, coughing, spitting, speaking, and singing in a demonic tongue (that scared me). There was also convulsing, banging of my fists and feet, being thrown on the ground, contorting, pushing my chair backward with my feet until I hit the wall, and the list goes on.

It seemed endless. Of course, I couldn't count them; I just knew the Lord had said 1,500, and after each session I hoped I was getting closer and closer to the end of it. Stuart said I would know when I was truly free by the fruit of my life and the peace (or quietness) in my mind. I clung to this with all my heart and looked forward to the day my torment would end.

After three hours, I left feeling hopeful, encouraged, and exhausted. I saw Stuart multiple times, with equally as intense deliverances. Almost a year later, the Lord had me return to Stuart. I didn't know why, but I was obedient. In this session, Stuart commented on how free I looked and inquired why I returned.

"What's been going on?" He asked while sitting in an armchair across from me.

"Well, nothing really. Just some arguing with my husband. I just wanted to listen to the Lord because He told me to come back, then confirmed two more times, so here I am," I said.

"Okay. Is anyone praying against you guys?"

"Ha, I don't know. How would I know?" I asked.

"Not sure, just checking." Stuart shifted in his seat and leaned forward.

"Let's just start with what we know. If there's any spirit of witchcraft..."

Immediately, laughter within me bubbled up and cackled out of my mouth, and I began to manifest again. *Oh no.* I thought. *How could this happen again?* My body began contorting, although not as severely as before. I now knew my authority in Christ and didn't give myself over to what the demons were trying to do. It was a literal fight.

Eventually, the demon was cast out, and I was left holding my ears and neck. "God! Ow!" I said, slumping into my chair, rubbing and holding my neck and ears. "What the heck, Stuart! That hurt!" I said.

"You okay?" he asked. Stuart was always so calm and nonchalant. Nothing surprised him; he had seen it all.

"Yeah. Man that burned! It felt like a sheet of metal flew out of my body." That was the best way I could describe it. You could take a pen and draw a line from my ear lobes, down my neck, down my shoulders, all the way down my arms, and to my thumbs on each side; that was where the pain was. It literally burned—hands down, my most painful deliverance.

"I am so confused," I said. "I won't even watch witchcraft commercials. I am very serious about not subjecting myself to it."

"Well, did anything happen recently?" He asked.

"Actually, yeah. I went to this yoga class a few weeks ago. I was in so much pain and had so much tension (this was after I had my son). I went to a class where the teacher was reiking the room, and the entire practice was about chakra centering. I should have left but I got a babysitter and everything so I just prayed in tongues the whole time."

"Oh." He said. "That doesn't matter. You still participated. Some of the most extreme deliverances I have seen are from reiki and yoga masters." Note that Stuart has been doing deliverances worldwide for more than 40 years. His first exorcism was with a bride of satan when he was 18. He has delivered people who have done and been part of some of the most extreme things that you couldn't even imagine if you tried. For him to state this was eye-opening for me.

"So, what do you think?" I asked, still holding my ears.

"I think we should check if there are any demons connected to yoga for you."

"Really? Is that a thing?"

"Sometimes," he said.

Stuart then began to call out demons connected to yoga, and lo and behold, I manifested. For over an hour, Stuart was casting out demons connected to yoga. I already had a spirit of kundalini driven out of me, but there was more. My hands began to go into mudras, and my body unwillingly began contorting into yoga postures. Again, I resisted the manifestations as well as I could. I started getting visions of idols and stone statues on top of mountains that were holding yoga poses, like warrior one and warrior two (very common yoga poses in standard vinyasa flows).

Once all the demons had been cleared out and I came back to the surface, I was shocked. "Does this mean I can't do yoga? I do yoga every day. Christians always ask me how I feel about yoga, and I say it's fine. I'm so confused now! Are there always demons in yoga? What does this mean?" Part of me felt beside myself because this "grounded" me for so many years and was part of my life.

"Well, just like you are in recovery for drugs and alcohol, consider yourself in recovery for yoga," he said bluntly.

"So, I can't do yoga anymore?"

"You can if you want demons. But if you don't want demons, I would advise against it."

"Okay, so does everyone get demons from yoga?"

"No, not everyone. I have done deliverances with people who do not manifest or have demons as a result, but what I have noticed is that with people who had a witchcraft background, they do. Those witchcraft spirits are looking for ways to get back in."

My mind was blown.

"Everyone has their cross to bear, Jenny, and this is yours," he said.

"*One* of mine," I laughed.

We ended with some small talk and I left for home. Since then, I have regularly stretched my body but have never done yoga again. As I pursued the Lord, I struggled in my relationship with Jay, which seemed to distract me from God even though we would go to church together and sometimes try to pray together. It felt like there was always friction and some form of abuse.

I began to enter a place of denial, ignoring the issues or thinking if I just got closer and closer to perfection, sought more deliverance, or did more self-work and personal reflection, that the anger, intimidation, abuse, and argumentativeness would subside.

I hoped the closer I got to God, the closer he would get to God, and we could both walk in freedom. It always seemed like everything was my fault, and in the past (before deliverance) I was violent and chaotic, but a lot of it was what I know now to be called "reactive abuse." It is a reaction to perpetual verbal or physical aggression and often happens with victims of narcissism. That's not a cop-out either; I take full responsibility for my behavior. However, it did help to explain things. I am naturally a squishy, hopeless romantic, so constantly being on the defense was hard.

We had multiple physical fights during my deliverance process, and as Jay learned he could cast devils out as a believer, he started abusing this. For a time, whenever I was acting a certain way that he did not like, he would accuse me of being a demon, corner me, grab the collar of my jacket or shirt, throw me on the bed, and command demons out of me. A few times he had his hands wrapped around my throat and sat on top of me. It never worked.

His behavior was abusive. He was using aggression, intimidation, and control to try and change something he didn't like, which wasn't a demon. This kind of behavior is called spiritual abuse, and it is entirely ungodly and demonic. The Spirit of the Lord is never intimidating, manipulative, controlling, threatening, fear-inducing, or agitated and angry. If someone is operating in any of these things during your deliverance, it is not the Spirit of God but a demon in that person influencing them. Yes, someone may violently manifest while being delivered, but one should never, and I repeat, *never* force a deliverance on any man, woman, or child through intimidation.

When this happened, I often prayed to God in my heart to help me and make it stop. I was afraid, and I knew this was wrong, but through my long on-and-off, abusive relationship with Jay, I learned that fighting back only made things worse. The longer I stayed with him, the more fear could take root in my life. I eventually adapted from fight mode to flight mode to freeze mode and then into a deep state of denial. These led me into a fawn mode, where I ultimately began placating him often to prevent potential outbursts.

I want to take a moment to pause my story and pray for anyone who has experienced spiritual abuse in any form, including church hurt:

> Heavenly Father, our good and gracious God, we love You with everything inside us. Lord, I pray for every person

reading this book who has been dominated in certain situations by the power of darkness through "godly people" to be fully set free from the pain, offense, anger, or fear that has resulted from the spiritual abuse or hurt, including PTSD that came from it. We know You are love, and Your heart is to operate through Christians in full love and humility, Lord. And we know that those not operating from this place have their own struggles, and we pray You correct them in love and set them free from whatever has tormented them.

If there is unforgiveness and resentment in your life, now is the time to let that bag of rocks go! If you frequently think about how someone has harmed you or wronged you, no matter what it is, it is in *your* best interest to forgive this person or people for *you*. It does not always mean reconciliation, but it does always mean personal freedom in heart and mind. If you keep replaying what this person or people have done, I encourage you to say, "I forgive [person's name] for [wrongful act] right now." It could be a million and one things or a bunch of people.

Take your time and say each name out loud. When we choose to forgive, it is an act of God's will. The Holy Spirit will come in and heal your emotions tied to the hurts after this. Each time you feel offended or find yourself in this place, pause and say aloud whatever it is. Maybe someone cut you off on the freeway three days ago, and you're *still* thinking about it—forgive that person! There have been periods when it seemed like I had to forgive multiple times a day, every day, because I continued to be harmed and sometimes offended.

That is not to say that boundaries are not necessary. Even Jesus Christ had boundaries, which were kind and loving to all parties involved. As someone who has faced many forms of abuse and developed a high tolerance for significant distress, I deeply understand that resentment can come with that. I also understand that abusive cycles, especially if they were initially modeled in childhood, can be difficult to break. I want to remind you that if you have Christ in you, you have the ability and authority to break any toxic, abusive, or generational cycle or curse in Jesus's name.

Footwork is important. Often, you need to take action for yourself if any form of abuse has victimized you. God is faithful in fully healing you, so I encourage you to hang in there and seek God if this applies to you.

Through my abusive cycle with Jay, I pressed deeper into God than I ever had before and was always willing to do the work and put in the effort to change. We had worked with multiple counselors and therapists (I think a total of eight), yet things weren't changing, and if they did, it wasn't for long. Often, he would shift focus, lie, or not do the work. I felt like I was carrying a lot of the weight and it made me weary.

Just six months after being married, I called the police about my husband. Though the physical abuse had become less, there was still abuse, ongoing harassment, verbal and psychological abuse, manipulation, intimidation, and degradation. When someone's self-esteem is low, they are much easier to control. Abusive people will always attack someone's self-esteem which becomes a slow and degrading process over a period of time.

I ran down the stairs and outside. Neighbors peered through their blinds at the scene as Jay came after me, pressing his nose to mine while I was on the phone with our relationship coach. This happened in the center of our complex where a circle of homes faced us. The waves of intimidation were intense and scary, and I typically had to self-deliver myself from a spirit of fear as it often came back in these situations.

Old feelings of humiliation rose within me as I waited for the police outside our house. Things like this weren't new to our relationship. This was the second police report I had filed against Jay. My friend filed the first one because of how afraid she was for me. An anonymous person or people had contacted security at a 12-step convention years prior, where four security guards approached me and asked me if I was okay. This cycle just wouldn't let up, but now I was married to the cycle.

"Are you being abused, ma'am?" the security guard had asked me at the 12-step convention.

"No, it's fine," I had said. Jay had not physically touched me at that conference, although he had chased me around, humiliated me with his anger, and intimidated and harassed me openly. I didn't think that qualified as abuse at the time, so I denied it.

"Are you sure he isn't abusing you?" the guard had asked sternly, concerned and frustrated.

"No, he is not," I had said as tears rolled down my cheeks.

"Really? Because your words are saying no, but everything else about you implies that he is."

I looked away in shame, saying, "I am fine."

At the condo, the police came to my door, and I was now filing this second police report. I had thought that the abuse would end since Jay had come to Jesus but it didn't, and I couldn't understand why.

I went inward, thinking I needed to be more communicative, gentler, more affirming. I always needed to be *more*, leaving me feeling *less*. I was confused and conflicted, which is the typical "victim" mentality of fixing and self-blame. The officer filed the report and looked me in the eye.

"You know, when things happen like this, and especially if they've happened more than once, they never get better. Only worse." He tilted his head, as if implying I better be careful.

The officer looked back down at his notepad and jotted down more information. "I would encourage a restraining order."

"Yeah, I don't know..."

I thought, *This officer is probably not a Christian. He probably doesn't believe abusive people can change. I used to be abusive, and I changed. Anyone could change.* I went into a whole internal monologue, convincing myself that this officer was wrong and that, although Jay acted out, he would eventually be redeemed. I mean, God had told me to marry him. Right?

18

FREEING THE SONGBIRD FROM ITS CAGE

A week after the abuse, we had little to no communication. One day I was skating with my friends on the boardwalk in Newport Beach, and I passed someone who looked freakishly like my childhood abuser.

The man even waved at me. Older men waving at young girls at the beach was nothing new, so I decided to skate past him again to see if it was who I thought it was. I began to panic in my mind, and I immediately wanted to be around Jay as he was one of the few people who knew more about my abuse than most, but still didn't know a whole lot. We had texted, and he was planning to come over.

"Spend an hour with me before he comes over," I heard the Holy Spirit speak to my heart.

"What? It's fine. I spent two hours with You this morning, God."

I overrode God's direction and didn't listen to the conviction. When Jay came over, God spoke to me again.

"Do not be intimate with him."

"What? He's my husband," I said back to God, again, ignoring what He told me and doing what I wanted instead.

As the evening progressed, the Lord spoke to me for *a third time*.

"Tonight is going to be a rough night for you," God said. I figured this was because Jay and I got into an argument and there was some tension, but it wasn't a big deal. Jay went home that night, and I got ready for bed, then curled up with all my pillows nested around my head, my dogs in my room, and the audio Bible playing. I fell right to sleep.

That night, I had a terrifying dream. It was another demonic attack. I knew what was happening in this dream was actually happening in the spirit realm, as this was a common thing I experienced. God often speaks to me through visions when awake and dreams when asleep that reveal what supernatural things are occurring—typically what demons are around, what their functions are, what they are doing, and how to get rid of them. I can always tell how strong I am in the Spirit by how I respond to the demonic in my dream life.

On this particular night in my dream, I was standing next to my bed, looking at myself sleeping.

(Side note: I understand this sounds like astral projection, but through deliverance, that stopped, and the Lord allowed me to have these dreams in order to provide me with information, like what demons were oppressing me. He gave me views like this so I could see them as well as myself. It was in my dream life during my deliverance process that I truly began to step into my authority and learn how much I had in Christ.)

As I stood next to my bed staring at what was supposed to be me, it looked like half of me was Jay. It was very bizarre and almost perverse. I felt the presence of the demonic around me. The pressure, the gnashing of teeth, and the undeniable fear that always accompany demons were in full effect. I began to call out things like a spirit husband or spirit spouse to leave in Jesus's name. I began calling out different demons, commanding them to go. Nothing was changing. What spirit was this, and why wasn't it obeying me? It felt like I was in this loop forever.

Typically, with demonic encounters, they will stay for a short time, but when I step into my authority, they leave. This wasn't the case this time. I became flustered but still authoritative. Suddenly, it dawned on me that I could call on the Lord's angels for help. I knew there were warrior angels because I had seen them, and I knew God wanted to help and protect me.

Stuart told me that when dealing with the demonic, to remember I was on the winning side. He said, "Many just rebuke demons. That's fine. But we can also fight on the offense. We can command God's warring angels to come against demons to set ourselves or others free." (Note: this is not praying to angels, this is praying to God to call for help.) Scripture says, *"He will command his angels concerning you to guard you in all your ways"* (Psalm 91:11 NIV).

I recalled this as I stood next to my bed. I said, "Lord, if it's in Your will, I command Your warring ang...." Before I could finish the sentence, I felt a firm physical hand touch my head, and I woke up to a demon being cast out of me. My mouth opened and I yelled, letting out an eerie wailing sound that felt like it went on for a long time! It woke both of my dogs! I knew something had just left my body! I have experienced the demonic being cast out of my mouth before in the form of screaming, so I knew exactly what it felt like.

"What the heck!" I said out loud, rushing over to turn on my light, almost tripping over my dog.

Norman, my blind rescue, was anxiously pacing, while my other dog, Gary, sat up on the bed, wide-eyed. I reached for both of them to comfort myself, shaking.

"What is going on? What is that? Lord! What just happened!?" I immediately put on worship music and read my Bible in bed for the next two hours. I was honestly afraid. I had been pursuing righteousness diligently, so this was confusing. I recalled a time after my first or second exorcism when the Lord's angels came to me in the night, and I received a deliverance. It had felt like water was coming out of my ears that time, but it wasn't a shock like this one was.

If you are not affiliated with deliverance or deliverance ministries, this can sound very strange. When I look back, it is *strange*, and I don't always understand it all. However, it is very real, and anyone who serves or works in this ministry knows exactly what I'm talking about. When you have encountered the supernatural like I have, you begin to expect the bizarre and not become so shocked by it. Demons are wicked and weird, and we don't know all of their ways, and angels, although of the Lord, are a mystery too.

After two hours of listening to Tasha Cobbs' Gospel music on repeat, I finally fell asleep. That morning, the Lord woke me at about 5 a.m. The Holy Spirit spoke to me, repeating three times, "Your house is clean so that the spirit couldn't stay." Often when God repeats a word to me, He wants me to understand the importance and power of what He is saying. Our bodies are temples, a house for the Holy Spirit (1 Corinthians 6:19-20). God was telling me my house (my spirit) had been made clean.

I felt the peace of God physically wash over me like a warm, smooth wave. Then the Lord continued, "That was a spirit of masturbation that came in through being intimate with Jay. He has a spirit of masturbation, perversion, and addiction, and he needs to be delivered." I was shocked at how God was revealing this to me, yet I wasn't surprised.

The Lord allowed me to experience the demonic firsthand when it came to soul ties. I believe that is so I could know and explain soul ties not just from a biblical standpoint, but from personal experience with it *and* deliverance by God. Sometimes soul ties can be a controversial topic in churches;

however, it is entirely biblical. The Bible suggests both godly and ungodly or holy and unholy soul ties. So, what is it?

A soul tie is a spiritual bond between two people. A holy marriage is a perfect example of that. Two become one flesh. On my social media platforms, I go in-depth on the legal rights of demons. Soul ties are one of them. One of the many ways people can become severely afflicted by the demonic is by living in direct and willful sin, such as having sex outside of marriage. If you are operating in this sin, there is demonic influence behind it.

If you sleep with a person who has multiple demons, they can transfer to you through having sex with them, as this sin of premarital sex *is* an open door. Maybe you've never dealt with anger before, or never had a desire to watch porn before, but after you sleep with a certain person, you feel like your temper has changed, or maybe you have a lust for porn that you didn't have before. This was likely a spiritual transfer.

Pause and think about this for a moment, reflecting on your life after sinning with sexual partners. Was there some sort of shift? Some might be more obvious than others.

I have a friend who is currently an atheist (not for long though, mark my words!). He has never been what I would consider an aggressive person. After his last relationship, he mentioned that he had never acted in the way he did before being with a certain woman. She had major anger issues and drank all the time. It was toxic. He soon became verbally abusive like she was and started to drink more than he ever had before.

We could call this being influenced by a person, and sure, that is possible. But he had been having sex outside of marriage with a person who was operating in so much dysfunction that he found himself operating in the same things, even after their relationship came to an end. There was an open door, a soul-tie, and likely a spiritual transfer.

Another example that I mentioned early on in this book was when I had demons cast out of me from things I had never participated in, like satanism. It was because I had slept with a former satanist that those spirits came through and inhabited me. This can also happen in marriage. For me, it obviously did, but because of my pursuit of righteousness, those spirits could not stay. Jesus had me covered. Had I been living in direct sin, I believe they could have. There is a hedge of protection we have as Christians that shields us from the demonic.

However, when we are in sin, there are holes in the hedge, aka entry points or "legal rights." Everything the Lord commands us to do is because He loves us. Sex outside of marriage damages us on multiple levels, and soul ties are just one of those.

Soul ties don't always come through sex, though. They can occur from any form of abuse (think of trauma bonds or Stockholm syndrome). They can develop through unhealthy relationships with friends, family, or others, and this can sometimes happen if you are regularly praying with a person. Warfare can come at you. This does not mean to stop praying with or for them; it simply means ensuring you are wearing the full armor of God and, if necessary, breaking the soul tie by commanding all sin and warfare to return to the throne of Christ in their own life.

When you feel like there is a relationship of any kind that you can't let go of, can't set boundaries with, or that you obsessively think about or dream about (maybe even years after the person has exited your life), there is likely a soul tie. I was in a sex and love addiction program, and this was a common issue for me and people there. It was something many people in the meeting had to fight often (the obsession or addiction), but it really can be as simple as saying and believing a soul-tie-breaking prayer, taking thoughts captive, and resisting the devil—when you resist him, he will flee!

A holy soul tie, however, can be an incredible thing. A marriage that is operating in the Holy Spirit will have a holy soul tie between the two partners, and it will be blessed! Some friendships and family relationships can also have holy soul ties. That being said, just because a person is a close friend or family member does not necessarily mean the soul tie is holy or healthy!

First Samuel 18:1 (NIV) says, *"After David had finished talking with Saul, Jonathan became one in spirit with David, and he loved him as himself."* This is a positive benefit of a soul tie in which the level of love can greatly increase toward the other person. The following is an example of an unholy soul tie:

> *Do you not know that your bodies are members of Christ himself? Shall I then take the members of Christ and unite them with a prostitute? Never! Do you not know that he who unites himself with a prostitute is one with her in body? For it is said, "The two will become one flesh"* (1 Corinthians 6:15-16 NIV).

In this second example, sleeping with a person creates a spiritual bond, where two people essentially become one, thus opening either person up to the demonic in the other person's life if they are living in sin or have not received some sort of deliverance or don't know who they are in Christ. The prostitute is just an example—this can be applied to any person. If you are reading this and are questioning whether or not there may be some unholy bonds in your life, I encourage you to seek the Lord's wisdom and break all soul ties.

After this demonic soul-tie encounter in my room that night and the Lord's freedom, I shared it with Jay. He responded hesitantly and then said, "That is probably true," recognizing that he felt he was afflicted with those things. For the next month, I continued to get demonically attacked, specifically, sexually. I would get up early and go to God in prayer, in tears, begging Him to show me if there were any other open doors in my life, or if there was anything I hadn't repented from, or if there was anything in my house that was allowing spirits to afflict me. My heart was desperate for answers. One week, I had multiple prophetic dreams, words, and visions for people at random.

Prophetic words weren't new to me, but having so many in a week was. Some of the people I had words for, I knew well; others I didn't. One dream I had regarding my old roommate was spot on, down to a person, how they looked, and their name. That man is her husband today. That morning, while I was on the phone with her, she said to me, "Never doubt yourself. This is a gift from God."

Although not a Christian, her words landed on my heart, and I knew it was the Lord speaking through her to me. The Bible says we are each given gifts from God. Yes, we are to seek after the spiritual gifts earnestly, but some are given to us at birth and can come more naturally. The next night, I had *another* prophetic dream. This one was not good. In the dream, multiple people, all holding gadgets like phones or laptops, were trying to get into my house.

This was similar to the gatekeeper spirit knocking at my door, yet there were multiples, and they all were trying to get inside but could not. They were all looking down, distracted, and bumping into each other. In my dream, I closed the drapes and then had another terrible pornographic dream where I was sexually attacked.

After this dream, the Lord spoke to me and showed me Jay had been watching porn again (hence the gadgets). When I woke up, I knew this was why I was continuing to get demonically attacked. I didn't have an open door, but he did. My husband was under major perversion. I confronted him and let him know that when he was ready to talk about what he had been hiding, I was here. Granted, at this moment in time, I was not made aware of the level of awful and perverse things he was hiding; I just knew of one, and that was porn.

He denied everything, became angry and defensive, and after a few days finally admitted to it. He sought deliverance again. I was not sure the deliverances would work, though, and I became skeptical of his actual desire to be free. He would do whatever I needed to trust him again for about a month or two, and then go right back. The change never lasted. An apology without true and lasting change is just manipulation. It felt exhausting and sinister.

Others were also under his spell, and I felt conflicted when I tried to expose him or defend myself to people, especially religious leaders. The manipulation became so extreme that I soon joined him in his delusional world, where everything he said was the truth, and my perspectives, feelings, opinions, thoughts, and actions were all wrong.

Even when I knew I wasn't wrong, I gave up defending myself because of how exhausting it was. I was not allowed to be a person. This was narcissistic, sociopathic psychological abuse. For the next few years, I moved deeper into denial of who he actually was and what he had been doing.

Granted, I did learn to seek the Lord for every single thing I did in that marriage post-deliverance. God led me, like a ship in a storm through rocky coves. God would tell me when to leave and would share with me what demonic stuff was taking place. Having spiritual eyes can be intense, but at the same time, very helpful. My desire to honor God far surpassed my own feelings, the opinions of others, and my fear of Jay.

Being in this relationship was scary, but being outside of God's will was scarier to me, so I hung in there, *thinking* I was doing the right thing by staying. Part of me wonders if not for my son, Reign, I would have left as promptly. Reign and I left Jay three times before finally going through with a protective order that protected my son and me. I call Reign my rescue mission baby.

When it comes to abuse and abusive cycles, people always ask why the abused person doesn't just leave. Typically, the victim doesn't even fully understand why. On average, a person will try to leave an abusive relationship seven times before finally getting out, according to the National Domestic Violence Hotline. If there's extreme control, like there was in my marriage, you aren't allowed to leave and must find a means of escape. I believe God always provides a way out; we just need to listen to Him.

The day we left Jay, I had about an hour to myself and went for a drive. This was rare. Days leading up to this, I had felt increasingly hopeless and trapped. Moving out of state, where I hardly had any friends and no family around, made the isolation of my situation more challenging. This couldn't be God's plan for my life, could it? To endure constant abuse and intimidation, remain loving and warm toward my husband, pretend to the outside world everything was fine, all the while raising a child in this environment?

I just kept waiting, and now five years had been lost. How was I to pursue my ministry, write my books, create my art, teach on my social media platforms, build what God was asking me to—all the while feeling like my home was a jail and I was just a songbird in a cage singing worship songs in the morning? Something wasn't adding up and hadn't been for quite some time. What was I missing? The tension had become so thick, and I had become so conflicted in all of this—trying to find God's will for me and my son.

Surely, the heart of God was not for me to remain in this broken relationship. In September of the year prior, I told the Lord I would endure one more year, but after that, I would leave. I was now in September of the following year, and nothing had changed. In fact, it was exactly the same, if not worse.

As I drove down the road in my car by myself, I began to weep. Lonely tears I had bottled up exploded from my eyes as I began to cry out the most desperate prayer of my entire life: "Help me, God. I love You. I want to do what is right. But help me, help me!" I began to scream out to the Lord like He was my only lifeline, because He was. I had been in this sea of denial and was finally coming out of it. I felt like Tom Hanks in *Castaway*, slowly dying at sea. My skin was burnt, my lips were parched, and I was starving. I didn't just need a drink of water; I needed to be rescued.

"God! Please help me! You have angels on Your side! Do something! Send them to help me!" I screamed out in my car, begging for my life. For my son's life. "Either You perform a miracle, or get me out *now!*" I wasn't mad at God, not at all. I was desperate. I wept on my drive home and walked back into my house as if things were the same.

Three hours later, the police were called, and God helped me escape my husband. Our son had been endangered, and after telling Jay I was just running to the park with Reign, I finally escaped from under what felt like satan's thumb.

The lead officer with the Keller Police Department in Texas was called to the scene. His kindness and heart for safety are something I will never forget. I was in a state of trauma, and he was patient enough to repeat to me three times just how to get a protective order the next morning. It was because of his patience and prompting that I *finally* went through with the order, after years of accepting the abuse.

The next morning, I wanted to make sure this was God's will. I was exhausted and emotional. I could hardly enter into the presence of God. But I sat at my friend's table, with a strong cup of coffee and asked, desperately again, "God, what do I do?" The Lord instantly responded, "Get the protective order, Jenny."

Then He immediately gave me a vision: I saw a bunch of burrows in the ground, as if a huge slab of land was cut in half, and I could see all the little burrows different creatures had made. I saw myself in one of them. And then I saw the hand of God cover the top of it. He was showing me I was safe, hidden, and protected, not just by a document and the court system but by His very hand. *Snakes can enter into rabbits' burrows and eat their young,* I thought. No snakes were coming for me or my son, though, because the hand of God was over us. I would be so hidden that nothing could harm or get to me anymore. The Lord had sent His angels, and He answered my prayer.

For many victims of abuse, especially by a narcissist, it can feel like you've been put under a spell. To a degree, you have. If you've seen a cartoon where a character has a spell put on them, they are in a trance-like state and easily controlled. This is what happens in narcissistic relationships. An abuser will strip a person of their self-esteem, and the lower it gets, the easier the person is to control.

There are, however, moments of clarity in abuse when it feels like the spell has been lifted momentarily. I personally can parallel this to getting sober. I experienced moments in my addiction of being completely sober and aware of everything going on around me, my thoughts, my feelings, and the true reality and nature of my situation. The term "moment of clarity" is often used to describe these pockets of clear-headedness that eventually lead a person into recovery and breakthrough.

This also happened to me in my abusive relationship. For almost a year, I prayed for God to remove any manipulation from me and allow me to see things clearly. I'm not kidding you, once I was awake to it, there was no going back to sleep. Witchcraft at its basic level *is* control and manipulation. If someone is regularly operating in these things, they are usually under witchcraft demons, many times including the spirit of Jezebel (which is often a narcissistic person). Jezebel hates prophets and uses sexual perversion, manipulation, complacency, lies, control, and abuse to dominate people in any and all settings. If a person has given themselves over to extreme pride and sexual perversion, this spirit can attempt to move in.

I am grieved to say that, as I write this, Jay did not pursue the path of freedom but went back to the same behaviors he was used to, which unfortunately led to the protective order. Some people become so accustomed to hiding their hearts that pride and shame can become paramount to the point that they refuse to let God into their secrets, let alone other people. Isolation like this is devastating.

Even though the Lord already knows everyone's secrets, He will not step into a person's life or issue uninvited. However, that doesn't mean He won't display His power to a person. It broke my heart to watch Jay refuse God again and again, but this time was different, for me at least. This time, my hands were completely off. Some of us will help people to the demise of ourselves. This is called self-abandonment, and there is typically a deep absence of *true* self-love and self-worth that needs to be addressed.

The Bible mentions having demons cast from you and what the process looks like afterward if you don't turn away from old behaviors. Matthew 12:43-45 (NIV) tells us:

> *When an impure spirit comes out of a person, it goes through arid places seeking rest and does not find it. Then it says, "I will return to the house I left." When it arrives, it finds the house unoccupied, swept clean and put in order. Then it goes and takes with it seven other spirits more wicked than itself, and they go in and live there. And the final condition of that person is worse than the first. That is how it will be with this wicked generation.*

This passage out of Matthew describes the dangers of getting delivered and going back to sin or living in a state of unrepentance. It is extremely dangerous. A demon's goal is to destroy and kill, right? If you've had one cast out of you, and that one wanted to destroy and kill you, imagine seven of them coming back with the same intention. Imagine doing this over and over again!

A person can completely go off the deep end in cases like this! This is why when I do deliverance personally for people, I make sure they *fully* understand repentance and forgiveness. It doesn't mean we won't make mistakes in the process, but it is the most sincere and repentant people who get free and stay that way.

It was interesting to witness this firsthand with Jay, because at first I didn't know what was happening. When a person receives a deliverance, and they don't repent, it gives the demons in them the legal right to manifest. This was explained to me after Jay's last deliverance, where nothing happened in the session, but it led to a three-day manifestation.

This was continuing to happen, but I didn't understand why until the end. I am currently in the middle of a divorce with my husband. If it wasn't already made clear, the Lord led me out of this marriage. We had our son moved to Texas, bought a house, and his anger, control, and manipulation amplified, and I felt isolated. Half the time after Jay would receive a deliverance or get prayer from an anointed person, he would get home or get in the car and become angry or violent.

The Bible discusses people like this in 2 Timothy 3:1-5 (NIV), which practically outlines narcissistic abuse. It talks about the nature of people in the end times, which I personally believe we are in, or at least nearing. It reads:

> *But mark this: There will be terrible times in the last days. People will be lovers of themselves, lovers of money, boastful, proud, abusive, disobedient to their parents, ungrateful, unholy, without love, unforgiving, slanderous, without self-control, brutal, not lovers of the good, treacherous, rash, conceited, lovers of pleasure rather than lovers of God—having a form of godliness but denying its power. Have nothing to do with such people.*

God clearly does not avoid abuse in the Bible. In fact, He has Paul call it out and then end with *"Have nothing to do with these people."* If I had known God's Word sooner and understood the character of God, I wouldn't have entered into this marriage. However, now I do know the character of God, and I am blessed to have such an incredible son born from this relationship. My time spent in abuse was not wasted. I was learning about God and growing closer to Him. As I grew closer, my discernment that more evil was present was spot on.

It's interesting how the farther you get away from someone or something toxic, the more is often revealed. In my case, there was not just all forms of abuse, but a vault of secrets that came out that devastated and scared me. For a long time, I made excuses, pardoned bad behavior, and gave Jay the benefit of the doubt. My heart was hopeful for change.

I will spare you the multiple abuses and incidents that led up to the current circumstance. However, despite everything Jay has done, I know that God will be right there with open arms if Jay ever decides to come to Him. The Lord told me at the start of all of this to take my hands completely off Jay's healing, as it's not my fight anymore, and honestly wasn't to begin with.

Despite the wickedness in people, God still created them and wants to bring them back to a place of wholeness with Him, but only if they want it. The Lord does not see people the way the world sees them. I grieve for the people whose consciousness is so deeply seared by sin and evil that they neither feel guilt nor empathy for the pain they have caused. That is a lonely and dark existence.

I believe God is the just God and He brings righteousness, justice, and order—evil doesn't just continue to get away with evil. Psalm 9:16 (NIV) says, *"The Lord is known by his acts of justice."* This is undeniably true—but He is also a gracious Father. It's the kindness of the Lord that brings a person to true repentance.

The pain of my relationship was very real, and I walked through many different emotions before I returned to a place of peace. It wasn't easy. There was a lot of evil. Maybe you are wondering how I could not hate Jay with everything in me? How could I not want revenge? The old me definitely would have. How could I not wish he would just die so he could go to hell and get what he deserves? The truth is, I did. There were a couple of days when I wanted him just to die, because it felt like my peace and life depended on it. I was in so much fear and pain.

Yet, every time that crossed my mind, I couldn't bear to think where his soul would be in eternity. God even showed me what it would look like if Jay did go to hell. I don't believe this vision was prophetic—it was meant to convict me of the state of my heart. (Trigger warning.) In the vision, I saw Jay in a black cell with his skin melting off and crying out for someone to help him. He was looking up, desperate and screaming, but no one was there. It reminded me of a child. I wouldn't want that for anyone, not even my worst enemy.

How awful to be bound in hell forever. Where water doesn't exist, or blood, or community. Just torment, indescribable fear, regret, and physical and emotional pain. You're always thirsty, hot, lonely, and afraid. Demons have every right to attack you and shred your flesh—because there is no God in hell, there is no healing. And because there is no blood, there's never the opportunity to bleed out and die. You are already dead, and you are trapped. Don't believe me? Take some time and research "Hell NDEs." It's real and it's gruesome.

It's not just pedophiles and murderers that send themselves to hell; it is also the prideful and the unforgiving. Those who don't believe just because they don't want to end up there. Those who do good things by the world's standard but reject God end up there. Those who are riddled with unforgiveness and don't want to release resentment end up there. Even "Christians" can wind up in hell. Saying a salvation prayer isn't a ticket to Heaven. The Bible says that unless you are born again, you will not see the Kingdom of God (John 3:3).

God's Word also says that to the extent you forgive is how God will forgive you (Matthew 6:14-15). Hell is God giving the person what they want—total separation from Him. God doesn't send people to hell; people send themselves. Hell is a choice. If someone comes to mind as you are reading this, I encourage you to forgive them.

People perform unthinkable and unbelievable wickedness in this world. The night I learned of some of the things Jay had done, I rushed to the bathroom five times, on the verge of throwing up. My nervous system was rattled. I wondered if I would ever emotionally heal. I have mentioned forgiveness multiple times in this book—it is not by mistake—I believe it is by God's design and divine timing in my own personal life. As I near the end of this book, the significance of forgiveness is amplified.

The heart of Jesus is for us to love and forgive and to express that with honesty and integrity. I am not saying what has happened to you does not require validation, because it does, or that it does not require the need to be heard, because it does. To be fully free in heart and mind, forgiveness is the key to that locked door. If you want to move into the next phase of your life, the one you've always imagined that is filled with peace and joy and your heart's desires, it's through a door called forgiveness, and it starts with forgiving yourself.

19

A CAKE WITH DAISIES

As I sat down to write this chapter, I closed my eyes for a moment and took a breath—not something I usually do when I write. As I shut my eyes, God gave me a vision of me as a little girl. It looked like a scene out of *Alice in Wonderland*—where Alice is playing in a field of daisies just before she quite literally falls into Wonderland. I was dressed in the same attire as Alice, with greenery all around me. And I was holding a birthday cake. A big, white rectangular birthday cake with little frosted and candied daisies adorning the outer edges.

What a random vision, I thought.

"What does it mean, Lord?" I asked out loud.

I immediately felt the joy of the Lord and the pride He has in me. He is very proud of all of us, all His children.

"All that greenery around you."

"Yes?" I questioned.

"That's life. There is so much life around you." I felt Him smiling. "And that cake is celebratory. It's a cake that never gets old, never loses its flavor, and you always want it. This represents the zeal you have for freedom for yourself and others, and it never gets old."

"That is something to be celebrated," I nodded. "And the daisies, God?"

"They represent all the things you have been through, all the difficulties that have actually produced growth and life in you. You create something sweet and beautiful from the things that have been a trainwreck in your life." *Trainwreck is an understatement*, I thought.

"And others see it," He said.

The moment grew heavy with love. I began to cry in gratitude, thinking about all of the daisies on the cake, all of the pain, heartaches, traumas, and fears—so many of which I have shared in this book, and some I have not. I thought of all the times I didn't think I'd survive, I'd never be restored, I'd die, I'd never be good enough, and I'd lose everything.

All the times I came up from the waves, eyes on the shore, thinking I was finally about to reach my destination of "free and healed," just to be yanked under the water again. All the times the devil had my feet, but God had my life. Jesus has continued to rescue me again and again, which in turn has always brought me to another level of freedom, combined with a stronger desire to help people get to know the real Jesus, who truly wants to love us back to wholeness.

The original intention of this book was to bring others to freedom. Little did I know that by the end of it, God was bringing me into total freedom. And freedom from the one thing I was blind to my entire life—my deep feelings of worthlessness from which stemmed all other pains, addictions, and acceptance of abuse.

The Lord has been so kind to me as I have left the abuse, encouraging my self-esteem and confidence with not only basic psychology tools (like boundaries and self-care) but He reminds me, in my mornings, in my little closet with its pink lights, just how much He loves me. He tells me, "Ask Me what I think of you." And when I do, He responds saying, "You are not a diamond in the rough but a diamond on display for all to see. You are a green rose to me, unique and rare." (Something I didn't even know existed until God told me and I researched it.) He tells me, "You're a gem," and "I'm so glad you're here," when I turn my attention to Him.

When I went walking with my son one afternoon, I moved Reign's stroller car around a bug that was crossing our path, something I do without much thought. The Lord spoke to me then, saying, "I love that about you. That you even consider the little things." He tells me that I mean everything to Him and there's no one else like me. He tells me I am good enough and that He loves my heart for people. He tells me He loves how observant I am and that I notice patterns others don't. He reminds me that He has created me, and He loves me just as I am, and that I have always been and always will be good enough for Him.

If I need a self-esteem boost, all I have to do is come to Him. When I have moments of resisting God, I push myself to go upstairs to my worship space, which I made just for Him. As I pace and sing, I am always met with God's presence and His outpouring of love. I cannot hide when I worship God. I know part of my heart is hardened when I struggle to do so. When I push past that invisible barrier and sing, it usually ends with me on the floor in a puddle of tears, asking God to heal whatever part of my heart is exposed during that sacred time. Or, just thanking Him for who He is.

Something I've learned in my long, wayward, detour-involved journey to Jesus is that first of all, it's not perfect, and healing isn't linear. God does not expect perfection; He just wants to love you. And second, when I resist spending time with God, it's usually because there is a pain or multiple pains that I would rather avoid, and pain is unavoidable in God's presence.

I've wondered if that's why so many won't turn to Him. Some people go their entire lives running from their pain. Addictions and poor habits develop as a form of shielding our hearts from the pain we wish to evade, but when we do this, it wears on our minds and physical bodies and makes us sick, tired, and restless. When we stop running from the storm and run into it, God is by our side. When we don't hide from our battles but run full force toward our pain with the shield of faith covering us, God moves radically. I have found that most people don't get free of their demons if they are unwilling to address their pain, shame, or things that keep them from knowing Him truly.

In nature, when there's a storm, cattle will actually run from it until it catches up with them. They grow weary in their means of escape, but eventually find themselves in the midst of the storm, anyway, producing a double suffering. Buffalo, on the other hand, will recognize a storm and run straight for it. The storm quickly passes, and they are not nearly as exhausted as the cattle. As mentioned in previous chapters, God uses everything in nature to show us and teach us. We can always find parallels in nature that reflect our own lives. That is not done by mistake but by design, I believe.

God is patient and kind—*deeply* patient and kind. It is not in His heart that anyone should perish, be tormented, riddled with pain, lack, or fear. The more honest the surrender, the more life-changing the freedom. My former sponsor used to always say to me, "God doesn't call the qualified, He calls the willing," which reminds me now of Isaiah 6:8 (NIV), *"Here I am. Send me!"* Throughout my marriage, I wanted to be used by God, and I was. But not to the degree I knew I was being called.

As a result of escaping the abuse, I lost nearly everything. My car, my home, my finances. Bank accounts were drained immediately after I filed, and the court system took over two years to finalize the divorce. This was painful and scary, but the long game allowed secrets to be brought to the surface and character and lies exposed. In one week, my car got repossessed, my dog died, my grandma died, and my house went into foreclosure for the second time.

On the seventh day, when I was notified that I would actually be losing my home, amidst all of the stress from court, single mommying, finishing ministry school, and working, I sat in my empty dining room and laughed. I had become battle-hardened in the best way. It felt like I was losing everything, but I was actually just surrendering what wasn't mine. I told God if anything we owned was bought with dishonest money, He could take it. Shortly after that prayer, those things vanished.

For years leading up to this, I had been praying for the spiritual gift of faith. I wanted radical faith, and ironically enough, it was born in *this* season. The scorching fire that tried to burn me failed. The wind that stormed past my feet made me tremble, but I did not fall. The rain that whispered "destruction is coming" never turned into a flood. And I stood on my firm foundation in Christ, a little bloodied but not broken or dead.

A new wave of fearlessness was on the horizon. My family helped me financially, and I moved in with a friend on the East Coast where I began to build again on wobbly legs. Brick by brick, and this time with Jesus as my Husband. God showed up as my Defender in court, and at the final trial I didn't even have to testify. I finally got full custody of my son, entered into safety, built a business, and lived in an apartment by the beach. Rebuilding with rubble all around you is hard, but it's not impossible with God. Just more growth and surrender.

The more I surrender, the more I actually see the Spirit of God moving in my life. He has sent me into some of the darkest places carrying His light; and each time, I surrender my will. He's used me to lay my hands on people who were sick or injured and actually see them recover. I want to do His will, and when I don't want to, I pray for the willingness to be willing, and the strength to be obedient despite my self-centeredness, apathy, laziness, pride, or fear.

I lived in earth's hell for so much of my life, and many people reached into the pit I was in to either pull me out or just hold my hand while I sat in my sin. Now I get to do that for other people. And it's all because of *God and unto God.* We truly can do nothing without Him. People get sober, but not without God. People experience blessings, but not without God. People forgive, but not without God. People face their fears, but not without God. People love themselves, others, and the world around them, but not without God—because everyone who has love in them has God in them.

People's bodies get healed through food, medicine, or miracles—all of which is with God. People work through their traumas, but the endurance to do so is only with God. Whether you recognize it or not, you are not sitting there reading this book and breathing without God. The *Big Book of Alcoholics Anonymous* states, "in the spirit of every man, woman, and child is the fundamental idea of God."

People yell out, "Oh God!" when something tragic happens. Why do that if He doesn't exist? Because there is a fundamental *knowing* that there is the Designer of life—and sometimes it takes some of us a while to put the face of Jesus on that idea.

When people are desperate beyond measure, they find themselves in churches or reaching out to someone who "knows God." Why? Because they seek hope and an answer. Something in them *knows.* Even people who reach out to healers or witches are *still* seeking. Cindy McGill says that witches are closer to God than you think, and I would agree; I was.

A prophetic word, a prayer, or a healing touch can radically shift a witch's awareness and either introduce or reintroduce them to Jesus. Cindy also says that some people are in the "process" of getting saved. This is why I say, never underestimate the power of an encouraging word or prayer for someone. These seeds, planted over time, *will* flourish in the right season.

Sometimes it takes a ton of water and seed sowing to make that happen, and sometimes you get to experience the flourishing firsthand in someone's life. Either way, there is beauty in it all. It took decades of seeds being sown into my life before salvation and before the fruit for others appeared, but look what He can do!

I pray that if you've learned anything from my story, it is that *Jesus is alive and real and that every word He's spoken is truth.* No amount of sin, trauma, or pain can separate you from His love.

As I come to a close, I envision a cake with daisies around every edge, and I thank God that *He* is to be celebrated. He is powerful, and beyond that, He is *love*. If you need *anything,* God can give it to you. You just have to be brave enough to ask.

I love you.

ABOUT JENNY JOY

Jenny Joy is a writer, artist, mentor, evangelist, and liberator. Jenny has mentored both women and men for nine years and is motivated to help bring others into wholeness who come from traumatic, addicted, abusive, or dysfunctional backgrounds. With a deep understanding of the hooks that trauma can wedge into hearts, she gently and lovingly helps remove the hooks, brings salve to the wounds, and helps create a safe space for the individual to receive true healing from God. We cannot fully heal if we are not willing to receive the love of Jesus. She helps people get to this place.

After Jenny got radically saved out of witchcraft in 2013 and accepted Jesus as her Lord and Savior, she has been carrying the prophetic gifting into different environments, encouraging people to step fully into what God has called them to do and be. She is bold and fearless and willing to go wherever God asks her.

Jenny Joy is an experienced professional in the field of trauma and mental health, as well as being seasoned in multiple 12-step programs. However, she is not a therapist. She is a mentor and a guide.

Her program is designed to provide clients with the necessary tools for healing, all the while catapulting them into the heart of God so they can achieve the best possible spiritual condition yet!

If you're ready to break down your walls, climb out of the tower of lies and deception that isolate you, and dive into the river of freedom, then this program is for you! Step out of the trauma and into the life God has for you—an abundant life filled with endless hope, peace, and a sense of belonging that never fades.

Website
JennyJoyHappy.com

From

Jessi Green

Where is the Jesus I *thought* I was following?

If your faith feels more like a dying ember than a radiant light, perhaps you haven't met the real Jesus.

At her core, Jessi felt dry and lifeless. Weary of anemic religion, she had almost given up on Christianity, until one day, she came face to face with the real Jesus whose eyes burn like fire! His gaze lit a spark within her, fanning the tinder of her soul into a glowing blaze.

Today, Jessi burns with a vision to see a holy fire sweep across the nation. She and her husband, Parker, lead the Saturate OC revival movement in California, where they introduce thousands of people to the real Jesus, and see lives radically changed!

You are just a few pages away from a similar encounter. In *Wildfires,* Jessi Green invites you to let Jesus breathe upon the embers of your soul, until your whole life burns for Him!

This is the moment where you break free from feeble religion and a decaying culture. Lay your life upon the altar, and let Jesus kindle a wildfire in you!

Purchase your copy wherever books are sold.

From

Jennifer LeClaire

Your Holy Spirit Handbook to Surviving Last Days Deception.

On that day many will say to me, Lord, Lord, did we not prophesy in your name, and cast out demons in your name, and do many mighty works in your name? - Matthew 7:22

Are they prophesying by the Holy Spirit... or ministering under a demonic influence?

Jennifer LeClaire received a startling prophetic word that a showdown was coming to the body of Christwhere both true and false prophets will be exposed. In this book she presents a confrontational yet constructive word of warning to the contemporary Spirit-empowered movement. More than ever, there is a great need in the modern prophetic community to be discerning of what is true and what is false.

When you learn to recognize and resist satans counterfeits, you will build your life upon unshakeable Truth and thrive in victory during days of darkness and compromise.

Purchase your copy wherever books are sold